Understanding the Commercial General Liability Insurance Policy

Dwight M. Kealy
Attorney at Law
MA, JD, CIC

First Edition

Copyright © 2015 Dwight M. Kealy / Dwight Kealy and Associates, LLC.

All rights reserved.

ISBN: 978-0-578-16058-0

This book may be eligible for Continuing Education Credit from the Department of Insurance in your state.

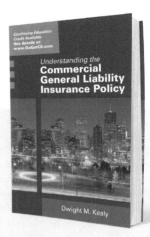

Dwight Kealy is an attorney and a licensed insurance producer who spent more than a decade in the commercial insurance industry where he was Chief Operating Officer/Vice President for one of California's largest insurance agencies for contractors' liability insurance. Dwight is a Certified Insurance Counselor and Faculty Member with the National Alliance for Insurance Education and Research where he teaches commercial casualty classes. Dwight is a member of the American Bar Association's Forum on the Construction Industry and the American Bar Association's Tort Trial and Insurance Practice Section. He lives in Southern California with his wife, two children, and lab/great-dane dog.

Contents

Chapter 1: Introduction

An insurance policy is a series of promises exchanged between the insurance company and the policyholder. For example, an insurance company might say that it will agree to provide up to $1 Million in coverage in the event that you accidently burn someone else's building, as long as you pay the insurance company $1,000 in premium. Your contract with the insurance company is based on two things: 1) The insurance company has promised to pay up to $1 Million in the event that you accidently burn someone else's building, and 2) You promised to pay $1,000. To ensure that the insurance company is only going to have to pay if the fire is an accident, they may add an exclusion for things like "expected or intended injury".

Over time, the CGL insurance policy has taken shape around five basic elements:

1) The Insuring Agreement
2) Exclusions
3) Exceptions to Exclusions
4) Conditions
5) Definitions

As a way to explain the five basic elements in the insurance contract, let us compare it to a contract that a parent enters with a child to encourage good grades in school. The parent offers the following contract:

<u>Contract between Parent and Child to Encourage Good Grades</u>
I will give you $100 for every "A" that you receive on a "Report Card". However, I will not pay for "A's" that you get in a class where you cheated on an assignment. I will not pay for "A's" in your Physical Education class, unless your Physical Education class is an academic class where you aren't just getting "A's" to run around and play. I will also not pay for "A's" in your Music Class, unless your music class is an academic class that includes music theory and you aren't just getting "A's" to play an instrument. You will not get paid for any "A's" if you fail to tell me within one week of receipt of a grade of "C" or lower on any assignment or test in any class.

I know, some readers of the above are probably just thankful that their parent was not an attorney, but the elements of the Parent/Child Grade Contract will help us explain the structure of the CGL Policy.

1. Insuring Agreement

Example: I will give you $100 for every "A" that you receive on a "Report Card."

The first part of an insurance policy is an insuring agreement. This is the part of the agreement where the insurance company (or parent in our example) agrees to pay in certain situations. For the parent, it was an agreement to pay for "A's". In an insurance policy, it could be an agreement to pay for bodily injury or property damage that occurs during the policy period. There needs to be an event that triggers the obligation for the insurance company or parent to pay. If there is no occurrence or no "A's" on the "Report Card", then the insurance company and parent have no obligation to pay.

2. Exclusions

Examples:
- I will not pay for "A's" that you get in a class where you cheated on an assignment.
- I will not pay for "A's" in your Physical Education Class.
- I will also not pay for "A's" in your Music Class.

Exclusions limit the insuring agreement by removing certain things that the paying party thinks are outside the scope of the agreement. In the contract between parent and child, the parent does not want to pay for "A's" unless the child was doing substantial academic work. The parent feels that if the child is cheating or just playing around for fun, then the child did not do the substantial academic work necessary to receive $100 for the "A". In the case of a CGL insurance policy, the insurance company might exclude bodily injury or property damage arising from a policyholder intentionally burning a house or speeding around in a watercraft. These may be exposures outside of what the insurance policy intends to cover. Both the Parent/Child Grade Contract and the insurance company start with a broad agreement to pay. All that the student has to show is an "A" on a "Report Card". All that the CGL Policyholder may have to show is bodily injury or property damage caused by an occurrence during a policy period. The insurance company, like the parent, then uses exclusions to limit the exposure to those specific instances when the paying party intends to pay.

3. Exceptions to Exclusions

Examples:

Exclusion: I will not pay for "A's" in your Physical Education Class,

Exception: unless your Physical Education class is an academic class where you aren't just getting "A's" to run around and play.

Exclusion: I will also not pay for "A's" in your Music Class,

Exception: unless your music class is an academic class that includes music theory and you aren't just getting "A's" to play an instrument.

As you can see from the Parent/Child Grade Contract above, an exception to an exclusion actually means that there is coverage. The exception removes the conduct from the exclusion. Since the conduct has been removed from the exclusion, it is not excluded.

The starting point in the Parent/Child Grade Contract was that there would be no payment for A's in the child's Physical Education Class. A grade of "A" in Physical Education is excluded. There will be no $100 for that "A". However, if the child can prove that the Physical Education class was an academic class, then the "A" in the student's Physical Education class is essentially removed from the Physical Education exclusion, and the child could get paid $100 for the "A" in that class. Similarly, I alluded to the fact that the CGL

Policy contains an exclusion for liability involving watercraft. The CGL Policy starts by saying that anything to do with watercraft is excluded because the CGL Policy does not intend to have anything to do with whatever liability exposures watercraft may experience at dock or out on the water. However, the CGL Policy provides an exception for liability arising out of watercraft that are ashore on the policyholder's premises. When a watercraft is ashore on the policyholder's premises, the CGL Policy realizes that it is an exposure on the premises—which the CGL Policy is willing to cover—and not an exposure at port or out at sea. The exception for watercraft ashore on a policyholder's premises removes the watercraft in these situations from the standard watercraft exclusion. Since it is no longer part of the exclusion, then there should be payment according to the terms of the insuring agreement.

> The Insuring Agreement: Tells us what is covered.
> Exclusions: Tell us what is not covered.
> Exceptions to Exclusions: Tell us specific items that are removed from exclusions, thereby making them covered.

4. Conditions

Example: You will not get paid for any "A's" if you fail to tell me within one week of receipt of a grade of "C" or lower on any assignment or test in any class.

The insurance policy's "conditions" are intended to provide boundaries to the insurance company's obligation to pay. The impact of "conditions" can be severe. For example, in the Parent/Child Grade Contract, the parent insists on knowing about any grades that are "C" or lower. Hopefully the parent's intent is to pay the child and see the child succeed in all subjects. If the parent learns about a problem area early enough, the parent could try to help the child succeed. However, if the child does not communicate with the parent in a timely manner, it may be too late for the parent to help. The parent may not be excited about paying $100 for an "A" in one subject when the child receives F's in all other classes. If the child fails to notify the parent about a grade of "C" or lower on any assignment, the parent in this Parent/Child Contract is free from having to pay for *any* "A's."

Similarly, the insurance company may require notice of an occurrence within a reasonable time after the policyholder learns about the occurrence. The intent of the insurance company is to make sure that they can defend their insured effectively according to the terms of the policy. If the policyholder waits for years before informing the insurance company, the insurance company may be limited in its ability to defend the policyholder. To ensure that the insurance company receives timely notice, they can require timely notice as a condition of coverage. If the insured fails to provide timely notice that prevents the insurance company from being able to provide an adequate defense, the insurance company could deny payment to the policyholder.

5. Definitions

Example: I will give you $100 for every "A" that you receive on a "Report Card".

It may seem odd to include "definitions" as one of the five basic elements of a policy. I include them as a basic element because they are too often ignored, and they can have a huge impact on coverage. For example, you may have read the sentence above and thought that you understood the basic terms of the agreement, but do you? You will notice that "A" and "Report Card" are in quotation marks. A little trick for understanding insurance policies is understanding the role of quotation marks in an insurance policy. Quotation marks are not used for irony or emphasis in an insurance policy. Quotation marks are used in an insurance policy to designate that the word or words within the quotation marks are defined elsewhere in the policy. The definition section is often at the end of the policy and, unless you are someone who enjoys reading the dictionary, it may not seem like an interesting place to read. Plus, you may not think that you need to read the definitions because you think that you understand the meaning of the word or words in quotation marks. However, in our Parent/Child Grade Contract, the child may want to know if an "A" includes an "A-". Does the definition of an "A" include an "A+"? If "A-'s" and "A+'s" are not included in the definition of an "A", then the Child may be surprised to receive $0 for a "Report Card" filled with all "A-'s" and "A+'s"…but no "A's". If there are no A's, then the parent has no obligation to pay. "Report Card" was also in quotation marks. Is a "Report Card" defined as a "Semester Report Card", "Quarterly Report Card", "Weekly Report Card", or an "Annual Report Card"? As you can see, definitions have a huge impact on how much the student might get paid.

> Quotation marks are used in an insurance policy to designate that the word or words within the quotation marks are defined elsewhere in the policy.

Just as definitions made an impact on the Parent/Child Grade Contract, definitions in an insurance policy make a huge impact on coverage. For example, Coverage B provides coverage for "Personal and Advertising Injury". People may read the words "Personal and Advertising Injury" and feel that they have all kinds of coverage for any lawsuits involving personal or advertising injury. This may seem reasonable, but it ignores the realization that "Personal and Advertising Injury" is in quotation marks. This means it is specifically defined in the policy.

If you read the definition, you will find that "Personal and Advertising Injury" is defined as seven specific personal and advertising injury offenses. If it is not an offense that is within one of these seven offenses, then it is not "personal and advertising injury". If it is not "personal and advertising injury", then it will not be covered under Coverage B. Finally, I should warn you that some insurance companies may seem sneaky with their definitions. Too often policyholders read over a policy and are satisfied to see that there is coverage for "bodily injury", or an "occurrence", or "damages", but fail to go to the definitions to see how the insurance policy defines these terms.

Burden of Proof

I hate to jump right into the courtroom, but the above discussion on the Insuring Agreement, Exclusions, and Exceptions are especially important when there is a dispute over coverage between a policyholder and an insurance company. The terms are important because they shift the burden of proof between the parties. The burden of proof is a legal concept that determines which party has the responsibility of proving their point. Success or failure in a case can often pivot on who has the burden of proof, and whether or not the person with the burden of proof has enough evidence to prove whatever they are trying to prove.

For example, let us say that you accuse me of stealing your car. Your car is of sufficient value that stealing it would make the convicted thief guilty of the felony of grand theft auto. If you accuse me of stealing your car, I do not have to run to the police station and argue that I did not steal it. I do not need to provide all of the evidence that could confirm where I was on the day when you say your car was stolen. I do not need to bring in alibis to the police station and have them confirm that they saw me driving around in a car that was not your car on the day that you say I stole your car. I do not have to do anything because I do not have the burden of proving that I am innocent. In our legal system, we are presumed innocent until proven guilty. You can report the theft to the police. The district attorney who prosecutes crimes then has the burden of proving that I am guilty. If I had the burden of proof, I could face jail time if you accuse me of stealing your car on a day when I was at my office writing this book because I would not have any alibis to help prove that I did not steal your car. Since you have the burden of proving every element of your accusations against me, I am not going to jail unless you—or the district attorney representing you—can prove beyond a reasonable doubt that I stole your car.

The Policyholder has the Burden of Proving that there was an Occurrence

When it comes to disputes between an insurance company and its policyholders on whether or not there should be coverage, the first burden of proof rests on the policyholder. The policyholder needs to prove that there was an occurrence. This triggers the insurance company's duty to defend. This duty of the policyholder to show an occurrence is not always as high of a burden as it may sound. For example, in California the mere possibility or potential for coverage is sufficient to trigger the Company's duty to defend and indemnify (*Montrose Chemical Corporation v. Admiral Insurance Company* (1995) 10 Cal. 4th 645). Any doubt as to whether the facts give rise to a duty to defend is to be resolved in the insured's favor. (See, *Horace Mann Insurance Company v. Barbara B.* (1993) 4 Cal. 4th 1076; *Wausau Underwriters Insurance Company v. Unigard Security Insurance Company* (1998) 68 Cal. App. 4th 1030). Even though these cases show that the burden may not be very high, the burden still rests on the insured to prove that there was an occurrence that creates at least the possibility or potential for coverage. If the policyholder does not prove this, the insurance company has no duty to respond.

Reservation of Rights. Sometimes an insurance company will respond to an occurrence with a "Reservation of Rights" letter. This letter is the insurance company's way of saying that they are reserving their right to not pay anything if they can establish that coverage is excluded. They realize that they have the duty to defend since the insured provided proof of an occurrence. The insurance company just wants to make it clear that if they can establish that there are exclusions in place to deny coverage, there will be no coverage.

The Insurance Company has the Burden of Proving Exclusions

Once the insured satisfies the burden of proving there was an occurrence sufficient to trigger coverage, the burden then shifts to the insurance company. The insurance company may defend or indemnify according to the terms of the policy, or the insurance company may argue that the occurrence in question is excluded from the policy. If the insurance company wants to argue that coverage should be excluded, the insurance company has the burden of proving that their policy exclusion removed coverage for the occurrence. This is significant because sometimes an insurance company will argue that the insurance company will not pay unless the policyholder proves that the occurrence was not excluded. This misstates the burden of proof. The policyholder does not need to prove that there was an occurrence that was not excluded. The policyholder only needs to prove that there was an occurrence. If the insurance company thinks there is an exclusion that would prevent coverage, the insurance company has the burden of proving that there is an exclusion that prevents coverage.

The Policyholder has the Burden of Proving Exceptions to Exclusions.

If the insurance company proves that coverage is excluded, the burden then shifts to the policyholder to prove that there is an applicable exception to the exclusion. If there is an exception to the exclusion, then there would be coverage.

Illustration of the Alternating Burden of Proof in Insurance Litigation

Parent/Child Grade Contract	CGL Policy: Bodily Injury Involving Watercraft Ashore on Premises

1) Insuring Agreement: The burden is on the child and policyholder to prove that the event that triggers payment has been satisfied.

Child tells parent, "I got an 'A'."	Policyholder tells insurance company, "There was bodily injury."

2) Exclusion: The burden is on the parent or insurance company to prove there is an exclusion that prevents payment.

Parent says, "I am not paying because your 'A' was in Physical Education, and that is excluded."	Insurance Company says, "We are not paying because the bodily injury involved watercraft, and watercraft are excluded."

3) Exception to Exclusion: The burden is on the child or policyholder to prove that there is an exception to the exclusion.

Child says, "You need to pay because my PE class fell within the exception that allowed payment for PE classes so long as they were academic in nature and here is the syllabus that proves that the class was academic in nature."	Policyholder says, "You need to pay because the bodily injury with the watercraft fell under the exception to the watercraft exclusion that provides coverage for bodily injury caused by watercraft ashore on my premises and here are the facts that prove that bodily injury was caused by a watercraft ashore at my premises."

What does the person with the burden of proof have to prove?

The above examples on the shifting burden of proof are pretty straightforward as to whether something is covered, excluded, or subject to an exception to an exclusion. What happens if the policy contains an exclusion or definition that prevents coverage that the policyholder did not know about?

Using our Parent/Child Grade Contract as an example, imagine that the child is a freshman in high school. The child receives three "A's" and three "A-'s" on the first semester report card and gives it to the child's parents for review. The child expects $600 for the six "A's" on the report card. The parents say "good job," but do not pay the child because, they say, "Report Card" was defined in their contract as the final semester report card of the child's senior year and an "A" was defined as receiving 100% in a class.

The child did not present the final semester report card of the child's senior year and the child did not receive 100% in any class. The parents would have the burden of proving the exclusions. That might be easy to prove if they can point to the definitions section where "A's" and "Report Card" are defined in a way that excludes payment. If you heard that a freshman was going to get $100 per "A", but did not get paid because of how the parents defined "A's" and "Report Card", you might suggest that this does not sound fair. Seeking justice, you might want to know if there is a way to argue that the student should get paid the $600 because the Parent/Child Grade Contract was confusing and the outcome was unfair.

Applying this to the insurance contract, imagine that a policyholder turns in a notice of an occurrence to the insurance company because of a $1 Million occurrence. In response, the insurance company denies the claim because of a definition on page 93 of a 97 page policy. The policyholder never read page 93 of the policy and did not know about it. It seems that the insurance company satisfied the burden of proving that coverage is excluded because of the definition, but is this fair?

Different states vary on how they approach the situation where a policyholder misunderstands what is and is not covered by an insurance policy. Some states apply the *Reasonable Expectation Standard.* Some states apply the *Ambiguity Standard.* If you are a policyholder, you would prefer to have coverage where you reasonably expect coverage. If you are an insurance company, the reasonable expectation standard is somewhat terrifying. It is terrifying because the insurance company paid a team of attorneys to write the contract. They charged premiums based on the claims this contract says they should pay. The insurance company wants to pay according to the terms of the contract; not according to the reasonable expectations of an insured. If the terms of the contract need to be adjusted, the insurance company only wants the adjustment to be allowed when necessary to correct an ambiguous clause in the contract; not to bend to whatever a policyholder expected.

The Reasonable Expectation Standard

In our Parent/Child Grade Contract, you could argue that a child reasonably expected to get $600 when the child turned in a first semester report card with three "A-'s" and three "A+'s." The contract might say that there is only payment for "A's", and that "A-'s" and "A+'s" do not count as "A's". The contract might define "Report Card" as only the child's final semester report card. Even though a painstaking study of the Parent/Child Grade Contract might prove that no money is owed to the child, you could argue that this is not fair because the child reasonably expected payment.

Just like the child expected payment from the Parent/Child Grade Contract, an Iowa business purchased an insurance policy for theft, reasonably expecting to have coverage for theft. After a theft, the Iowa business learned that their insurance company was not going to provide coverage because it only paid for theft when there were visible signs of theft on the outside of the building. Perhaps the insurance company did this to limit coverage where there was a break-in and not where an employee accidently or intentionally left a door unlocked.

In the Iowa theft, the outside of the building did not have visible signs that thieves had broken into the building. There were clear signs of theft inside the building with some broken interior doors and, of course, missing goods. The insurance contract stated that the insurance company would only pay for theft where there were visible signs of theft on the outside of the building. With no visible signs of a break-in on the outside of the building, the insurance company denied coverage.

In response to the insurance company's denial of coverage, the judge in this case stated the following:

- "Few persons solicited to take policies understand the subject of insurance or the rules of law governing the negotiations, and they have no voice in dictating the terms of what is called the contract. They are clear upon two or three points which the agent promises to protect, and for everything else they must sign ready-made applications and accept ready-made policies carefully concocted to converse the interests of the company."
- "It is generally recognized the insured will not read the detailed, cross-referenced, standardized, mass-produced insurance form, nor understand it if he does."
- "One who applies for an insurance policy…may not even read the policy, the number of its terms and the fineness of its print being such as to discourage him."
- **"The objectively reasonable expectations of applicants and intended beneficiaries regarding the terms of insurance contracts will be honored even though painstaking study of the policy provisions would have negated those expectations."**

C&J Fertilizer, Inc. v. Allied Mutual Insurance Co, 22 Ill.227 N.W.2d 169 (Iowa 1975). The last sentence was restated by Professor (later Judge) Keeton and cited in *Western Alliance v. Jarnail Singh Gill*, 426 Mass. 115; 686 N.E.2d 997 (1997).

Why do I mention that the "Reasonable Expectation Standard" could be somewhat terrifying for an insurance company? The reason is that the insurance company pays attorneys to write their insurance policies and they have actuaries employed to quantify the risk of having to pay for damages according to the terms stated in the insurance policies. The actuaries help determine how much money an insurance company should collect in premiums to cover the cost of potential claims. They might determine that an insurance company could survive on collecting lower premiums if it imposes a clear exclusion for a type of activity that it considers too risky.

For example, an insurance company could decide to offer a policy for a mason that is half of the normal price because it excludes completed operations. It might provide great coverage while the mason is building a wall, but the policy would not provide any coverage once the wall is completed. A masonry company that believes its major risk of loss take place while it is building a wall, and not after a wall is completed, might appreciate the savings offered by such a policy.

Now imagine that after a wall is completed, it falls on a row of cars in a parking lot. The car owners all sue the masonry company. The masonry company reasonably expected coverage for its completed operations. It turns in the claim to its insurance company. Do you see why the "reasonable expectation" standard could be somewhat terrifying for an insurance company? The insurance company only charged half the normal premium because they did not think that they would have to pay for claims arising out of completed operations. The insurance contract clearly stated that completed operations were excluded. Now a court is telling the insurance company to pay the damages because **"the objectively reasonable expectations of applicants... regarding the terms of insurance contracts will be honored even though painstaking study of the policy provisions would have negated those expectations"** (*Ibid.*). The mason might have enjoyed the reduced premium for reduced coverage...until the mason had a claim. A court in a jurisdiction using the "Reasonable Expectation Standard" could force an insurance company to pay for damages beyond the scope of the written insurance contract if the court finds that the insured reasonably expected coverage. Paying beyond the terms of a contract—and potentially beyond the amount of premiums collected—would be terrifying for any business.

Ambiguity Standard

Instead of starting with the reasonable expectations of the insured, some states only look to the expectations of a policyholder when the terms of the insurance contract were somehow ambiguous. If the terms of the written contract are clear, the expectations of the parties are irrelevant. In these states, you start by looking at the ordinary meaning of the written contract. You only look to the reasonable expectations of the policyholder if a disputed term in the contract was somehow ambiguous. For example, The California Civil Code states the following:

1638. The language of a contract is to govern its interpretation, if the language is clear and explicit, and does not involve an absurdity.
1639. When a contract is reduced to writing, the intention of the parties is to be ascertained from the writing alone....
1649. If the terms of a promise are in any respect ambiguous or uncertain, it must be interpreted in the sense in which the promisor believed, at the time of making it, that the promisee understood it.

The promisor is the party that makes a promise. The promisee is the party that receives the promise. For insurance purposes, the insurance company is the promisor because it is making the promise to provide coverage. The policyholder is the promisee because the policyholder is receiving the promise that there will be coverage. When California Civil Code 1639 states that the intention of the parties of a written contract will be ascertained from the writing alone, it is saying that the courts will look to the written insuring agreement, exclusions, and exceptions to determine what promises the court should enforce. The court is not going to entertain questions about the reasonable expectations of the insured if the intentions of the parties can be ascertained in the writing.

California Civil Code 1649 tells us what to do if the intentions of the parties cannot be ascertained by the clear meaning of the writing. If the meaning of the contract is ambiguous, the court will look to the reasonable expectations of the insured at the time when the insured entered the contract.

Note that the code points out that we are not looking to the reasonable expectations of the insured at the time of the loss. It is not unusual for most policyholders to expect coverage at a time of loss. Instead, we are looking at the reasonable expectations of the insured at the time that the contract was formed. Using the masonry policy that excluded completed operations mentioned earlier as an example, we look to the expectations of the masonry business at the time the insurance contract was formed. Of course, if the policy clearly excluded completed operations, then there was no ambiguity, and we do not ask what the masonry business expected. We only look to the insured's expectations if a disputed term in a contract is ambiguous.

When is a term ambiguous? In its legal use, a term is ambiguous if the term can have more than one different meaning. For example, imagine that we enter a contract where I am going to sell you toy blocks. We enter a contract that states the following:

> Seller shall deliver one million blocks that are gray and white or checkered.

This statement is ambiguous because there are multiple meanings for what I could deliver to satisfy our agreement. To see how the contract is ambiguous, imagine that you want the blocks because you sell toy sets that come in solid gray, solid white, or completely checkered. I show this as Option A below. You do not have toy sets that have two-tone blocks that are both gray and white. You would have no use for such a two-tone block, but I do not know this. You agree to pay me $1 million for the one million blocks mentioned in our contract. In response, I deliver one million, two-tone, gray and white blocks.

You do not want to pay me because you have no use for the blocks that I delivered. You say that I did not follow the terms of the contract. I say that I did. Since we have a contract that could be interpreted in multiple ways, we say that the contract is ambiguous.

Contract Ambiguity Illustration[1]

Contract states: "Seller shall deliver one million blocks that are gray and white or checkered."

Seller can read the contract as meaning A, B, or C:

A. Ship gray blocks and white blocks, OR checkered blocks.

B. Ship blocks that are gray and white, OR checkered blocks.

C. Ship blocks that are gray and white, OR blocks that are gray and checkered.

Since the terms of the toy block contract can have multiple meanings, a court in an "Ambiguity Standard Jurisdiction" may look to the expectations of the parties at the time of contracting to determine the understanding of the parties. If there is no ambiguity, the court in such a jurisdiction would not look to the expectations of the parties. It would just look to the contract.

To further understand how an insurance policy provision could be ambiguous, imagine that you are a plumbing contractor and an insurance company sells you a policy that excludes roofing operations. The insurance company wants the exclusion to avoid the water damage claims that come from leaky roofs. You do not mind the exclusion because you do not work on roofs. You are a plumber.

What you might not realize unless you really are a plumbing contractor, or have paid attention to the roof of a single family residence, is this: toilets have roof vents. The vents help remove unpleasant gasses and help maintain the pressure necessary for proper flushing. When you install a new toilet as a plumbing contractor, you also install the small vent pipe that exits through the roof.

A homeowner hires you to install a new toilet in a house. You properly install the toilet with all of the necessary venting. After the next big rain, you get a complaint from the home owner. There is water leaking through the roof near where you installed the toilet's vent. You turn the claim into your insurance company and receive a letter that denies the claim because of the "roofing operations" exclusion. Unless the roofing exclusion is clearly defined to exclude everything that has anything to do with a roof, we have a potential contract ambiguity in an insurance policy. You thought the policy would cover you for your plumbing operations, and that the roofing exclusion just meant that the insurance policy would not cover you if you were ever hired to fix or install a roof. This was fine with you, so you thought, because you do not do roofing operations. You do plumbing. The insurance company, on the other hand, thinks the roofing exclusion means that it will not have to pay any claims that have anything to do with a roof. Because installing the toilet involved installing a vent pipe that went through the roof, the insurance company believes that any claim associated with that work should be excluded. We have a contract term that is ambiguous because it can be read to mean two different things. If this happened in a jurisdiction that uses the ambiguity standard to interpret contracts, the courts could look to the reasonable expectations of the insured at the time when the policy was purchased to help resolve the contractual misunderstanding.

We can contrast the plumbing contractor's policy ambiguity with the Iowa theft policy used to explain the "Reasonable Expectation Standard." Remember, the Iowa business had a theft policy that excluded theft unless there were visible signs of theft on the outside of the building. There were no visible signs of theft on the outside of the building. Iowa applied a "Reasonable Expectation Standard" that inquired into the policyholder's reasonable expectations. If the coverage dispute occurred in a jurisdiction that applied the ambiguity standard, we would never ask what the insured reasonably expected unless the terms in dispute were ambiguous[2]. In the Iowa case, the theft exclusion had a clear single meaning. In a jurisdiction using the ambiguity standard, there would be no inquiry into the reasonable expectations of the insured because there was no ambiguity. With no ambiguity, the clear exclusion would stand, and there would be no coverage for the theft.

---

[1]The person drafting the sales agreement in the Contract Ambiguity Illustration could have specified the contract terms unambiguously by using the language in A, B, or C below:
A. Seller shall deliver:
    1) Gray blocks and white blocks, or
    2) Checkered blocks.
B. Seller shall deliver balls that are:
    1) Gray and White, or
    2) Checkered.
C. Seller shall deliver balls that are:
    1) Gray and White, or
    2) Gray and Checkered.
[2] Even lacking an ambiguous term, all jurisdictions allow inquiry into the reasonable expectations of the insured in situations where the terms of a contract are unconscionable. An unconscionable term is one that is oppressive, unfair, and shocks the conscience of the court.

Chapter 2: Coverage A, Insuring Agreement

The CGL Policy is divided into three different coverage sections: Coverage A, Coverage B, and Coverage C. Each section begins with its own insuring agreement. The insuring agreement is the section in the policy where the insurance company agrees to pay in certain situations. Coverage A starts with a very broad insuring agreement. It then limits coverage by a series of exclusions that will be discussed in the next chapter.

Legally Obligated to Pay as Damages

Coverage A begins with a requirement that the CGL Policy will only pay for those damages for which the insured "becomes legally obligated to pay because of 'bodily injury' or 'property damages'."

> a. We will pay those sums that the insured becomes legally obligated to pay as damages because of "bodily injury" or "property damage" to which this insurance applies. (CG 00 01 04 13, ISO Properties, Inc., 2012, Page 1; Appendix Page 245).

This issue about whether the insured is "legally obligated to pay" is often overlooked until an insured is sued and learns that the insurance company is not providing a defense because the insured is not legally obligated to pay the damages. If the insured is not legally obligated to pay the damages, the insurance company will not provide coverage. This can be frustrating for an insured. The insured argues that it is a ridiculous lawsuit and that they need their insurance company to provide a defense. The lawsuit may be ridiculous and the insured may easily win, but the insurance company will not provide coverage for the defense when the insured is not legally obligated to pay the damages.

To understand how policyholders can be sued for something for which they are not legally obligated to pay the damages, we should look at how an insured may be found liable for damages. The most common way to determine if an insured is legally obligated to pay damages is to show that the insured was liable for the tort of negligence. A tort is a civil wrong for which lawsuits are filed in civil court. One can be found liable for the tort of negligence if the person had a duty to act like a reasonable person, breached the duty to act like a reasonable person, and this breach caused damages.

For example, reasonable chandelier-installers do not install chandeliers that fall from ceilings. If I install a chandelier and it falls and causes damages, then I could be liable for paying damages under the tort of negligence. If the chandelier fell because of a fire not caused by me, I would not be liable for negligence because my failure to act like a reasonable chandelier-installer (my breach) did not cause the damages. In order to be found liable for the tort of negligence, a plaintiff (that is, the injured party) needs to show that the defendant owed the plaintiff a duty, breached the duty, and that breaching the duty caused the plaintiff damages.

Negligence, Duty

Whether or not a defendant owed a plaintiff a duty is determined by a judge. The standard duty that is owed is to act like a reasonable person. However, a judge may determine that a defendant does not owe a plaintiff any duty at all. In deciding whether or not the defendant owed the plaintiff a duty, the judge may look at the foreseeability of the harm to the plaintiff by the defendant. One of the questions that a judge may ask in analyzing whether or not the harm was foreseeable, is to ask if the plaintiff was in the zone of danger. This serves to eliminate plaintiffs that may be too far removed from the conduct of the defendant.

For example, imagine that you are at fault in a car accident. Everyone is okay, but the accident caused a windshield to break and there is shattered glass everywhere. Somehow, a single shard of glass is picked up by a tornado. The tornado spins the glass around and then shoots it out, injuring a particularly unlucky person two miles away from your accident. The person injured by the glass two miles away sues you for negligence. We can say that you caused the injured person's damages because you were at fault in creating the broken glass that injured the person. However, a judge may not hold you liable for the injuries because the injured person was outside of the zone of danger. The zone of danger for a car accident is the area around the car; not two miles away. You can only be found liable for negligence if you owed the injured party a duty. You did not owe a duty to the plaintiff two miles away. Since you did not owe the injured person a duty, a judge should dismiss the negligence case that was filed against you.

Negligence, Breach

The element of breach is satisfied when the defendant fails to satisfy the duty that was owed to the injured party. First a judge determines that a driver owes a pedestrian a duty because the pedestrian was in the zone of danger. Next the judge says the driver owed the pedestrian a duty to act like a reasonable person. If the driver failed to act like a reasonable person, the element of breach is satisfied.

Negligence, Causation

In order to show that a defendant *caused* the damages, the plaintiff needs to prove that the defendant was the *Actual Cause* and *Proximate Cause* of the plaintiff's damages. **Actual Cause** is often called the "but for" cause because Actual Cause exists if you can say *"but for* the actions of the defendant, this would not have happened."* For example, *but for* me installing the chandelier without the necessary number of screws, it would not have fallen. My actions are considered the Actual

Cause of the chandelier falling because it would not have fallen but for my actions.

Proximate Cause requires a foreseeable link between the defendant's breach of the duty to act like a reasonable person, and the plaintiff's damages. For example, without requiring foreseeability, you might sue me for negligence, arguing that I wrote a boring book that caused you to fall asleep, which caused you to drop my book, which knocked over your drink, which stained your carpet. You could argue that this satisfies Actual Cause because *but for* my book, you would not have carpet damage. However, this would not satisfy the Proximate Cause requirement. Proximate Cause eliminates damages that are so far removed and unforeseeable that it is not fair to say that the defendant's actions caused the plaintiff's damages. In the case of the falling chandelier, it is foreseeable that not installing a chandelier properly could result in injuries to those sitting under the chandelier. Therefore, my actions are considered the Proximate Cause of the chandelier falling.

Negligence, Damages

Finally, in order for a defendant to be found liable for the tort of negligence, the plaintiff needs to prove that the defendant's breach of duty was the actual and proximate cause of the plaintiff's damages. If there are no damages, then the defendant will not be found liable for the tort of negligence. A defendant will only be found liable for negligence if the plaintiff can prove that the defendant owed a 1) Duty, that was 2) Breached, that 3) Caused, the plaintiff's 4) Damages.

To illustrate the importance of having to prove that the insured is legally liable for the damages, imagine a fencing contractor is hired to install all of the wooden fences in a new tract home development. There are 500 homes in the development. All that the fencing contractor does for the new tract development is install the wooden fences.

After five years, the houses in this development are showing some cracks in the stucco and concrete. This could be because these materials naturally crack and not because of anyone's negligence. Nevertheless, all 500 homeowners join a lawsuit seeking reimbursement for the cracked concrete and stucco. The lawsuit is filed against the developer, general contractor, and any subcontractor who ever touched the project. A polite person comes to the fencing contractor's door, hands the contractor a summons, and says, "You have been served."

The fencing contractor is being sued because he or she worked on the tract home development. The fencing contractor has a CGL insurance policy for the fencing business and hands the lawsuit over to the CGL insurance company. The insurance company may respond back that they are not going to defend the lawsuit because the fencing contractor is in no way legally liable for the alleged damages. Remember, the insurance company only provides coverage when an insured is legally obligated to pay damages. The fencing contractor only installed the wooden fences. There are no facts to suggest that installing a fence can make someone legally liable for the cracked concrete and stucco of these 500 homes. If the insured is not legally obligated to pay the plaintiff's damages, then the insurance company has no duty to defend. The insured still has a lawsuit in hand for which the insured needs a defense, but the defense will not come from the insurance company. The fencing contractor may need to hire an attorney—at the fencing contractor's own expense—to get dismissed from the lawsuit.

In reading about the importance of legal liability, you should not think that the insurance company can simply deny coverage until the insured proves that they are legally obligated to pay the damages. Whether or not the insured is liable for the tort of negligence ultimately may be determined at trial. It would not be fair for an insurance company to refuse to provide any defense until liability is proven. Once liability is proven, it is too late to provide a defense. The point of having an insurance company that will provide a defense is to have the attorneys available to hopefully prevent a court from finding the insured liable. The requirement of legal liability only stresses that if there is a lawsuit for which the insured is clearly not liable, then the insurance company does not have an obligation to defend or pay damages.

If there is a possibility that an insured is liable, the insurance company has a duty to defend its insured. In California, courts have emphasized that insurance companies have a duty to defend so long as there is the mere possibility or potential for coverage (*Montrose Chemical Corporation v. Admiral Insurance Company* (1995) 10 Cal. 4th 645).

Furthermore, any doubt as to whether the facts give rise to a duty to defend is to be resolved in the insured's favor. (See *Horace Mann Insurance Company v. Barbara B.* (1993) 4 Cal. 4th 1076; *Wausau Underwriters Insurance Company v. Unigard Security Insurance Company* (1998) 68 Cal. App. 4th 1030). The insurer also has a duty to defend when the insured would reasonably expect the insurer to defend...against the suit based on the nature and kind of risk covered by the policy. (*Foster-Garner, Inc. v. National Union Fire Insurance Company* (1998) 18 Cal. 4th 857). Together, these cases show that if there is a possibility of coverage, the insurance company has an obligation to defend. However, if the insured is clearly not legally obligated to pay the alleged damages, then the insured's insurance company has no duty to defend the insured in the matter.

Coverage Forms

Coverage A of the CGL Policy is written on three main different types of *coverage forms*. They are the Occurrence Form, Claims Made Form, and the Manifestation Occurrence Form. The insuring agreement of all three coverage forms require that the insured be legally obligated to pay the damages. If the insured is not legally obligated to pay the damages, then the insurance company is not obligated to pay the damages or provide a legal defense. However, after requiring legal liability, these forms differ in how coverage will be activated.

One way to understand the different coverage forms is to think of the insurance policies like a row of briefcases each filled with $1 Million. Inscribed on the front of each briefcase is a year representing a specific annual policy period. Each briefcase has a combination lock. If you have the right combination, you can open the briefcase and take as much money as you need to pay damages covered by that year's policy.

Which combination is the correct combination to open the briefcase of money depends on the policy's coverage form.

The Occurrence Form pays for *occurrences* that take place during a policy period.

The Claim's Made Form pays for *claims* that are made during a policy period.

The Manifestation Occurrence Form pays for occurrences that first manifest and appear during a policy period.

Each of these three policy forms will be discussed individually in this chapter.

Coverage A, Exclusions

The Occurrence Form

The Occurrence Form is designed to cover "bodily injury" and "property damage" to others caused by an "occurrence" that takes place during the policy period.

The standard ISO CGL Policy is written on what is called an Occurrence Form. It states that the insurance company "will pay those sums that the insured becomes legally obligated to pay as damages because of "bodily injury" or "property damage" to which this insurance applies" (CG 00 01 04 13, ISO Properties, Inc., 2012, Page 1; Appendix Page 245). The policy goes on to state that the "insurance applies to "bodily injury" and "property damage" only if:

1) The "bodily injury" or "property damage" is caused by an "occurrence" that takes place in the "coverage territory";
2) The "bodily injury" or "property damage" occurs during the policy period; and
3) Prior to the policy period, no insured...knew that the "bodily injury" or "property damage" had occurred, in whole or in part" (*Ibid.*)

In a nutshell, we can paraphrase the Occurrence Form CGL Policy as stating that it is designed to cover "bodily injury" and "property damage" to others caused by an "occurrence" that occurs during the policy period. In analyzing an Occurrence Form, you should notice that "bodily injury", "property damage", and "occurrence" are all in quotation marks. Quotation marks are used in an insurance policy to designate that the word or words within the quotation marks are defined elsewhere in the policy. Therefore, we should start with how the policy defines these terms.

"Bodily injury" means bodily injury, sickness or disease sustained by a person, including death resulting from any of these at any time" (*ibid. Page 13;* Appendix Page 265).

To help explain bodily injury, I could include a number of photos illustrating all kinds of bodily injury, sickness, disease, and any resulting death...but I do not think that this is necessary. The definition seems fairly clear and some readers could get squeamish looking through examples of injuries, illness, and death.

"Property damage" means:
a. Physical injury to tangible property, including all resulting loss of use of that property. All such loss of use shall be deemed to occur at the time of the physical injury that caused it; or
b. Loss of use of tangible property that is not physically injured. All such loss of use shall be deemed to occur at the time of the "occurrence" that caused it" (*ibid.* Page 15; Appendix Page 272).

To explain Paragraph a. of the definition of property damage, imagine that I go to an office building to do some catering and I burn down the building. The cost to rebuild the building is $1 Million and it is going to take one year to rebuild the building. The owner of the building is not going to be content with my insurance company just giving the owner $1 Million. During this year, the owner is not going to be able to collect any rent from the various tenants. Furthermore, there are a couple of tenants who might not want to come back to this location. The landlord might lose these tenants forever. The property damage to the building was physical injury to tangible (that is, touchable) property. There is also a dollar amount of future damages (losses) associated with the loss of use of the building. Damage to tangible property and loss of use of this tangible property are both included in the definition of property damage.

Paragraph b. of the definition of property damage addresses loss of use of tangible property that is not physically injured. What is loss of use of tangible property that is not physically injured? It happened when I caused the fire that burned down the office building. The fire department came and shut down the driveway and street next to the building in their efforts to fight the fire. There was smoke everywhere. Because of the smoke, the closed street, and the closed driveway, people could not get to the restaurants next door to the building that I burned down. The buildings next door are tangible property that are not physically injured. That is, you can touch them (they are tangible), and they did not experience any physical fire damage. Since these businesses were closed as a result of me starting the fire, they suffered *loss of use* of their tangible property. Loss of use of tangible property that is not physically injured is included in the definition of property damage.

What is an "occurrence"?

If the Occurrence Form is designed to cover "bodily injury" and "property damage" to others caused by an "occurrence", one of our first questions should be, "What is an 'occurrence'?" The ISO CGL Policy defines an occurrence as follows:

> "Occurrence" means an accident, including continuous or repeated exposure to substantially the same general harmful conditions" (*ibid.* Page 15; Appendix Page 271).

On the surface, this definition seems pretty straightforward. Imagine that I park my car in front a marking meter every day. If I accidentally bump my car into the parking meter and knock it over, it sounds like we have an occurrence because it was property damage caused by an *accident*. If I bump the same parking meter every day when I park my car, the parking meter is experiencing "continuous or repeated exposure to...the same...harmful condition" of me hitting the parking meter. If after a year of bumping the parking meter I finally knock it over, then we would have property damage (to the parking meter) caused by an occurrence. The occurrence was me accidently hitting the parking meter, and it includes the repeated exposure of me hitting the parking meter every day over the past year.

Now let us get back to the row of briefcases each filled with $1 Million. The Occurrence Form Policy would have a sign on the briefcase that would state something like, "Open if there was an occurrence during this policy period." There would be $1 Million available in the briefcase if the CGL Policy had $1 Million Occurrence Limits and $1 Million Aggregate Limits. The Occurrence Limit is the most the policy would pay for any one occurrence. The Aggregate Limit is the total amount the policy would pay, regardless of the number of occurrences. If you have an occurrence that is covered by the policy, you have the right combination to access the policy's $1 Million limits. Once the Aggregate Limit of $1 Million is paid, the briefcase is empty.

What is the right combination? Coverage A of the CGL Policy is designed to cover bodily injury or property damage caused by an occurrence during the policy period. If there is an occurrence during a policy period for which the insurance applies that is not excluded by the policy, you have the right combination to open the brief case.

Which policy will pay depends on when the occurrence happens. If you receive a lawsuit this year that says you caused covered occurrences in each of the last four years, you would have the correct combination to go to the four prior policy/briefcases. This means that you have access to a total of $4 Million because you are going to open four different briefcases that each have a maximum of $1 Million. Your current policy would not pay anything unless the occurrence

Coverage A, Exclusions

also took place during the current policy period. This is true even though you received the lawsuit (claim) this year. The correct combination is based on when the occurrence took place; not when the claim is made.

For example, imagine that my grandparents go to the same coffee shop every day for 20 years. They like this coffee shop because they use these special blue metallic cups that kind of make your lips tingle when you have your first few sips of coffee. The coffee shop has an Occurrence Form Policy with $1 Million per occurrence and per aggregate limits. After 20 years, my grandparents learn that it is not necessarily a good idea to drink coffee every day out of a metallic cup that makes your lips tingle. It turns out that the metal is dangerous and my grandparents are now experiencing various lip and throat cancers arising out of their contact with the metal cups over the past 20 years.

The Occurrence Form Policy states that it will pay Bodily Injury or Property Damage that occurs during the policy period. When did the bodily injury to my grandparents take place in the example above? I imagine that their attorney will think the bodily injury occurrence took place at least once during each of the past 20 years. (The attorney has 20 million reasons to find that an occurrence took place during each of the past 20 policy periods). The insurance company might have thought that the most they would pay for any one occurrence is $1 Million. It is true that the most they would pay for any one occurrence during any one year is $1 Million, but we have 20 annual policies each with $1 Million limits. All together, that would be $20 Million worth of coverage available for the 20 occurrences that took place over 20 different policy terms.

What is an Occurrence in Construction?

Too often I hear people in the contractors' insurance industry talk about how the CGL Policy will cover contractors for 10 years or that the CGL Policy they are selling is a 10-year statute of limitations policy. To insurance agents, contractors, or attorneys who repeat this, I suggest the following:

If an insurance agent tells you that you are covered in the future with your current occurrence policy, ask for this in writing along with a copy of the agent's own professional liability insurance policy, because the agent's professional liability policy may be the only policy that will provide you with future coverage.

The above statement is intended to make insurance agents feel uncomfortable and think about how they are presenting policies to their clients. Does the CGL Policy say that it covers occurrences 10 years in the future? Of course not. Does the CGL Policy say that it will cover contractors for any work that they do during the policy period up until the applicable state's statute of limitations? No. The CGL Policy states that it will pay those sums that the insured becomes legally obligated to pay as damages because of "bodily injury" or "property damage" that is caused by an occurrence that <u>occurs during the policy period.</u>[1]

---

[1]There are project specific policies that provide coverage for an extended period. Similarly, there are endorsements that can extend coverage for completed operations beyond the standard one year term. Some of these endorsements will say that the policy period for "products and completed operations" ends at the earlier of 1) The statute of limitations/repose applicable to claims or 2) 10 years after the date the Designated Project is completed. A statute of limitation is a law that requires claimants to file their lawsuits within a certain amount of time. These statutes vary by state and the type of work performed. For example, California might say that if you want to sue the contractor who installed the irrigation system on your new house, you need to sue the contractor within one year after the close of escrow. (Cal. Civil Code § 896 (g)(7)). If you decide to sue this contractor after the statute of limitation has passed, you will be barred from recovery. Project Specific Policies and specific project endorsements are not a part of the standard CGL Policy.

Does the Occurrence and Aggregate Limit for Products and Completed Operations Extend Coverage for Construction?

Some contractors—and insurance professionals—will argue that there must be coverage for the contractor's product and completed operations because the policy has a specific occurrence and aggregate limit for Products and Completed Operations. Limits show how much money is available to pay certain kinds of occurrences. These limits are subject to the policy's insuring agreement and exclusions. Limits do not change the provisions on who, or what, is insured or excluded in the policy.

If there is an occurrence during this policy year that arises out of work that the contractor has completed, then this year's CGL Policy will pay out of the Products and Completed Operations Limit. This is true even if the work was completed prior to this year's policy period. Coverage is triggered and paid out of the Products and Completed Operations Limit if there was an occurrence that occurs during the policy period arising out of Products or Completed Operations.

Imagine that a contractor has a CGL Occurrence Form Policy for the year 2014. If there is an occurrence after 2014 arising out of work that the contractor completed in 2014, the first question that the 2014 insurance company will ask is whether the occurrence took place during 2014. The insurance company is not asking when the contractor did the work. The insurance company is asking when the occurrence that caused the bodily injury or property damage took place. If there is no occurrence during the policy period in which the work was completed, then the policy in place when the work was completed has no duty to pay or defend.

To help explain occurrences in construction, let us start with a bodily injury occurrence example. Let us say that I am a mason and that in 2014 I built a wall. In 2015, the wall fell down and injured a person. They will be okay in a few months, but the injured person had to spend a few nights in the hospital and the bill is easily going to come in over $100,000. I had an Occurrence Form CGL Policy in 2014 and a separate

Occurrence Form CGL Policy in 2015. Which policy pays? Remember, the policyholder has the duty of proving that an occurrence took place during the policy period. Can the policyholder prove that bodily injury took place in 2015? Yes. Can the policyholder prove that bodily injury took place in 2014? No. The bodily injury was in 2015. The only way to get coverage out of the 2014 policy is to show that an occurrence took place during 2014. It seems clear that there was no bodily injury that took place in 2014.

What is an Occurrence in Construction Defect Claims?

In order to get coverage under an occurrence policy, you need to prove that an occurrence took place during the policy period. What if I built a wall in 2014 that was so bad that you think the construction itself was an occurrence? If you can prove that my constructing the wall was an occurrence, then you could possibly find coverage under the CGL Occurrence Form Policy that was in place at the time of construction. How do you prove that the construction of a wall was so bad that the negligent construction is itself an occurrence?

There are three main schools of thought on whether a defect in the workmanship by a contractor is ever, by itself, an occurrence. These schools of thought can be divided into the following categories:

1) Whether or not there was an occurrence depends on what property is damaged
2) If the damage was the result of the intentional act of construction, then it is not an occurrence
3) If the damage is the unintended result of faulty workmanship, it is an occurrence

1) Whether or not there was an occurrence depends on what property is damaged

One school of thought says that if there is damage to property other than to the contractors work, then there is an occurrence. If it is damage to the contractor's own work, then there is no occurrence. (For example, see *French v. Assurance Co. of America*, (4th Cir. 2006) 448 F.3d 693). I understand the need for courts to come up with a simple rule to apply, but determining whether or not there is an occurrence based on whether the damage was done to the contractor's work or someone else's work, is flawed for two reasons. 1) It ignores the substantive question as to whether or not there was an occurrence, and 2) It wrongfully forces the policyholder to prove the absence of an exclusion. Remember, the policyholder has the burden of proving that there was an occurrence. After the policyholder proves an occurrence, the insurance company then has the burden of proving the existence of any exclusion that might preclude coverage. The policyholder does not have the burden of proving that there is an occurrence for which there is no exclusion.

I suggest that the courts that follow this standard are confusing the burden of proof because what they are trying to do is apply the CGL Policy's exclusions for *damage to the policyholder's property, product or work* to the question of whether or not there is an occurrence. Broadly speaking, the CGL Policy is designed to cover bodily injury, property damage, or personal and advertising injury *to others.* If you build a wall and it falls on someone else's car, that would be property damage to others. Similarly, if the wall falls and injures a stranger walking down the street, that would be bodily injury to others. Both of these should be covered under the CGL Policy. However, if your wall falls and the only damage is to the wall itself, then there is no property damage or bodily injury to others. You could argue that the person who hired you to build the wall has suffered property damage, but the CGL Policy specifically excludes: j. that particular part of real property on which you or your subcontractor was performing operations, k. your product, and l. your work.

These exclusions suggest that what the CGL Policy is intending to cover is not a contractor's defective product or work, but the damage *resulting from* a contractor's defective work. Courts call this damage "resulting damage." Courts have held that the CGL Policy applies only to **resulting**

damage caused by the defective work of the insured. Coverage does not apply to the cost incurred to repair and replace the contractor's defective work. The risk of replacing or repairing defective materials or poor workmanship has been considered a commercial risk that is not passed onto a liability insurer (*F&H Construction v. ITT Hartford Ins. Co.* (2004) 188 Cal.App.4th 364, 372).

I can understand a state court wanting a simple rule for defining an occurrence in the construction defect setting. I can also appreciate that they have read the policy to see the exclusions for the contractor's property, product, and work. However, saying that there is only an occurrence if a policyholder can prove that the damage is not excluded, inappropriately adds the burden of disproving an exclusion on to the policyholder. The policyholder should only need to prove the existence of an occurrence. The burden of establishing the applicability of an exclusion falls on the insurance company, not the policyholder. Courts that fall into this first school fail to answer whether or not there was an occurrence, and inappropriately force the policyholder to prove that the occurrence is not excluded. Although this school of thought is based on what I believe to be faulty reasoning, if this is the rule in your jurisdiction, this is the rule that will be applied.

2) If the damage is the result of the intentional act of construction, then it is not an occurrence.

The second school of thought asks if the damage was the result of an intentional act. If it was the result of an intentional act, then it does not sound like an accident. If it was not an accident, then there is no occurrence. This position favors insurance companies and makes it difficult for a policyholder to find coverage for a construction defect because the act of construction is an intentional act. An example of an unintentional act would be something like an involuntary seizure. Involuntary seizures do not build buildings. Intentional acts build buildings.

This school of thought argues that since construction is an intentional act, it cannot be an accident. Because it is not an accident, it is not an occurrence. (For example, see *Kvaerner Metals Division of Kvaerner U.S., Inc. v. Commercial Union Insurance Co.* (Pa. 2006). 908 A.2d 888).

3) If the damage is the unintended result of faulty workmanship, it is an occurrence.

The third school of thought on whether a construction defect is an occurrence asks if the damage was the unintended result of the faulty workmanship. Remember that the CGL Policy defines an occurrence as an accident. This school of thought focuses on whether or not the damage was unintended. If it was unintended, it sounds like it was an accident. If the construction defect was an accident, then it sounds like an occurrence. This position favors coverage for the policyholders. (For example, see *United States Fire Insurance Co. v. J.S.U.B., Inc.*(Fla 2007). 979 So. 2d 871).

Whether or not a construction defect will be viewed as an occurrence or not will be determined based on which jurisdiction is reviewing the lawsuit. If a jurisdiction follows the first school of thought, then the construction defect will only be an occurrence if the damage involves work other than the work done by the policyholder. If a jurisdiction follows the second school of thought, the construction defect will probably *not* be an occurrence because construction is an intentional act, intentional acts are not accidental, and an occurrence must be an accident. If a jurisdiction follows the third school of thought, the construction defect probably *will* be an occurrence because the damage was unintended. If it was unintended, it was an accident, and that can make it an occurrence.

I offer information on all three schools of thought because of the fluid nature of construction defect litigation. States can change from one school of thought to another with the passing of a law or new court decision. For example, a state may pass a law making school of thought number one the law of that state. Similarly, a state court that has followed the second school of thought may decide that the third school of thought has the better legal arguments and write a decision changing their legal precedent from the second school to the third school of thought. The rule that is controlling in the jurisdiction at the time of the construction defect litigation will control whether or not the construction defect should be viewed as an occurrence. If it is not an occurrence, then the CGL occurrence policy will not provide coverage for the construction defect.

Sometimes insurance companies pay for things that are not covered by the policy.

Whenever I talk about occurrences with insurance professionals, invariably there is someone who wants to argue that I am misunderstanding the policy because this person has seen an insurance company pay for something that I am saying is not an occurrence. They tell me, "I have seen cases where insurance companies have paid for _____ and so the policy must cover _____."

In response, I ask them to send me copies of the cases and I realize two things: 1) We have a different meaning for the word "cases," and 2) Sometimes insurance companies pay for occurrences even when the insurance company should not have to pay.

1) We have different meanings for the word "cases."

In common usage, people might say something like, "He goes to the store in certain *cases.*" These people mean that the individual goes to the store in certain *situations*. When attorneys hear the word "cases," they are not just thinking about a situation where someone went to a store. For attorneys, a case is a legal dispute between parties for which a judge has made a ruling and to which other attorneys may refer. This is significant because the United States follows a Common Law legal system.

In a Common Law system, we look to the reasoning used in previous cases to resolve new disputes. The idea is that we expect similar cases to be resolved similarly. When a judge makes a decision, we say that the decision is a precedent that must be followed in future cases. Judges look to past cases for resolving future cases, and we can look to these same cases for guidance on how our own cases should be resolved. If there is a legal case that makes a decision defining when there is an occurrence, then everyone in that jurisdiction should be aware of the definition because this is going to be the definition used in future cases in that jurisdiction. If, however, we are not talking about a legal case, but simply a *situation* where an insurance company made some sort of payment, the insurance company's decision to make the payment forms no legal precedent by which future insurance companies should pay for occurrences.

2) Sometimes insurance companies pay for occurrences even when the insurance company should not have to pay.

Why would an insurance company pay for an occurrence for which it is not legally obligated to pay? The answer is simple: Sometimes it is cheaper to pay for an occurrence than it is to fight it. **The standard ISO CGL Policy pays for defense costs IN ADDITION to the policy's limits.** As I type this, there is a construction defect case being litigated in courtroom seven of the historic Riverside County, California Superior Court building. The case is expected to last six months. The six months in court are in addition to the *years* of discovery and motions that took place prior to getting to court. I know about this case because I am a local attorney and local attorneys know that courtroom seven is the courtroom of the Honorable Judge John Vineyard. Local attorneys know that his courtroom has been updated with the latest technology to make sure that it can handle the huge amount of electronic documents that will be reviewed in the case. We know that courtroom seven and Judge Vineyard will not be available to try new cases for quite a few months. And what can we all infer from what local attorneys know about this single construction defect case in Riverside County, California? THIS CASE IS EXPENSIVE.

Most insurance companies are businesses that seek to make a profit. Sometimes insurance companies face the decision to pay $1 million to settle a claim that they do not think they should have to pay, or spend $2 million going to court to prove that they should not have to pay the claim. In these situations, paying the claim is cheaper than fighting to not pay the claim.

All this is to say that we should be careful when we hear that there is a "case" where an insurance company paid for a certain type of claim or occurrence. This might not be a legal case with precedential value for future cases. It might just be a situation where an insurance company made a business decision to pay for something because paying was cheaper than not paying. You cannot depend on these decisions happening again. You should not refer to such "cases" as having anything to do with what the policy covers or how claims will be paid.

If the insurance company evaluates a similar situation and determines that not paying and litigating is now cheaper than paying, I think you should guess that the insurance company's business decision will be to decline coverage. Furthermore, if you are an insurance professional or attorney and you assure your clients that their claims will be paid like other claims that have been paid—even though the insurance policy clearly states that such claims are NOT covered—then you run the risk of your client suing you for misrepresenting coverage in the event that your client's insurance company denies the claim.

Problem: With the Occurrence Form Policy, there is no coverage for occurrences that take place after the policy period ends. **How do you retire after being in business with an Occurrence Form Policy?**

Imagine a man has been in the canned carrots business for the past twenty years. He sells quite a bit of canned carrots. He pays $50,000 per year for his annual CGL Occurrence Form Policy premium. He saved up sufficient assets to support what he expects to be 30 years of retirement. No one seems to want to buy his business and so he decides to just stop canning carrots, close up shop, and retire. He wants to retire before his next annual premium is due because he plans on using the $50,000 he would normally pay in premiums to spend on a year-long, round-the-world vacation that he has dreamt about for years. It sounds like the American Dream. He calls his insurance agent and cheers, "Cancel my policy because I am retiring and I have no more operations and no more liability exposure."

Before you get too excited—or jealous—for our imaginary canned carrots manufacturer, I have a question for you: When might he get sued for the can of carrots that is still on the shelf at the grocery store? What if the corn causes bodily injury next year...or the year after...or the year after? The occurrence policy pays for bodily injury caused by an occurrence that takes place during the policy period. If he cancels his policy in 2014 and never buys another insurance policy, he does not have a policy for occurrences that might take place in 2015, 2016, and beyond. If he wants to have coverage in retirement for bodily injury caused by his product or completed operations, he needs to either maintain a CGL Policy, or find a special, non-standard policy that will cover products or completed operations that may occur in the future. The standard Occurrence Form CGL Policy will not pay for bodily injury or property damage occurrences that take place after the policy period expires.

The Claims Made Form

Although the Occurrence Form CGL Policy is the most common form, the CGL Policy can also be purchased on a Claims Made Form. Like the Occurrence Form, the Claims Made Form begins by stating that the insurance company "will pay those sums that the insured becomes legally obligated to pay as damages because of 'bodily injury' or 'property damage' to which this insurance applies" (CG 00 02 12 04, ISO Properties, Inc., 2003, Page 1; Appendix Page 275). The Claims Form also shares the Occurrence Form's requirement that "bodily injury" or "property damage" is caused by an "occurrence" that takes place in the "coverage territory." How the Claims Made Form differs is in how coverage is triggered. In the Occurrence Form, coverage is triggered if the bodily injury or property damage occurs during the policy period. In the Claims Made Form, coverage is triggered if the claim for bodily injury or property damage is made during the policy period.

In a nutshell, we can paraphrase the Claims Made Form as stating that it is designed to cover "bodily injury" and "property damage" to others caused by an "occurrence" when the claim is made during the policy period.

The Claims Made Form is designed to cover "bodily injury" and "property damage" to others caused by an "occurrence" when the claim is made during the policy period.

The Claims Made Form uses the same definitions for "occurrence", "bodily injury", and "property damage" that we discussed for the Occurrence Form. Please refer to the prior section for these definitions.

Coverage Form Comparison

Occurrence Form	Claims Made Form
We will pay those sums that the insured becomes legally obligated to pay as damages because of "bodily injury" or "property damage" to which this insurance applies IF:	

	Occurrence Form	Claims Made Form
1	The "bodily injury" or "property damage" is caused by an "occurrence" that takes place in the "coverage territory";	
2	The "bodily injury" or "property damage" occurs during the policy period; and	A claim for damages because of the "bodily injury" or "property damage" is first made against any insured during the policy period or any Extended Reporting Periods; and
3	Prior to the policy period, no insured knew that the "bodily injury" or property damage" had occurred, in whole or in part.	The "bodily injury" or "property damage" did not occur before the Retroactive Date or after the end of the policy period.

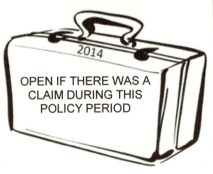

(Adapted from CG 00 01 04 13 and CG 00 02 12 04, ISO Properties, Inc.)

To explain the Claims Made Form, let us reconsider the example that we discussed for the Occurrence Form Policy: Every day for 20 years, my grandparents meet at the same coffee shop.

This time let us assume that the coffee shop has a Claims Made CGL Policy with $1 Million policy limits. Remember, my grandparents liked the coffee shop because the coffee shop used special blue metallic cups that kind of make your lips tingle when you have your first few sips of coffee. After 20 years, my grandparents learn that it is not necessarily a good idea to drink coffee every day out of a metallic cup that makes your lips tingle. It turns out that the metal is dangerous. My grandparents are now experiencing various lip and throat cancers arising out of their contact with the metal cups over the past 20 years.

When we discussed the Occurrence Form, we mentioned that my grandparents' attorney might think of 20 Million reasons to believe that the bodily injury *occurred* during every policy year over the past 20 years. This is because the Occurrence Form will pay for bodily injury or property damage that occurs during the policy period. If you can prove that it occurred during 20 different policy periods and each policy had $1 Million limits, then there is a possibility of recovering a total of $20 Million from the 20 annual Occurrence Form policies.

When it comes to the Claims Made Form, there is only going to be one policy in which the claim is made. The policyholder did not purchase coverage for every occurrence that might occur during a policy year. The policyholder purchased coverage for any claims that might be made during the policy year. If in year 20 there was a claim made for bodily injury, the most the policy would pay is the $1 Million limit from the one policy in which the claim was made. Because the risk of having a claim for any work you have done in the past increases over time, it is common for Claims Made policies to increase in price over time.

The Retroactive Date

In addition to the policy period dates, the Claims Made Policy also has an important date called the Retroactive Date. This date is important because in the Claims Made Form, the "bodily injury" or "property damage" has to occur after the Retroactive Date and before the end of the policy. The Retroactive Date is usually the date when the policyholder first purchased a Claims Made Form, so long as the policyholder maintained continuous coverage under a Claims Made Form after this first purchase. For example, let us say that I am a mason who purchased my first CGL Claims Made Policy on January 1, 2010. My first policy showed that my retroactive date was January 1, 2010. When I renewed my policy for 2011 and 2012, they also showed that my Retroactive Date was January 1, 2010. So long as I maintain continuous coverage with a Claims Made Form Policy, my Retroactive Date should continue to be January 1, 2010. If, however, there is a gap in time in which I do not have a Claims Made Form, then I will not have had continuous coverage. If I go to purchase a new Claims Made Form CGL Policy after a gap in coverage, I will get a new Retroactive Date.

The Claims Made Form CGL Policy says that it will only cover bodily injury or property damage that *occurs* after the Retroactive Date. Notice that the policy does not say that it only covers *work* done after the retroactive date. (This would refer to a "Prior Work Exclusion" that we will discuss under Coverage A Exclusions). The Claims Made Form CGL Policy does not exclude all work done prior to the Retroactive Date. It only requires that the occurrence take place after the Retroactive Date and before the end of the policy period.

What is the difference? Imagine that I have been building walls for ten years and I realize that I should probably get some liability insurance in case a wall falls down and hurts someone or something. In response, I purchase my first annual Claims Made CGL Policy on January 1, 2010. On February 1, 2010, a wall that I built in 2005 falls on a row of parked cars. I get sued the following month. Is there coverage under my 2010 Claims Made CGL Policy? To determine whether or not there is coverage under my Claims Made CGL Policy, let us answer three questions paraphrasing the insuring agreement:

1) Did a bodily injury or property damage occurrence take place in the coverage territory? **Yes.**

2) Was a claim for damages because of bodily injury or property damage made against any insured during the policy period? **YES.**

3) Did Bodily Injury or Property Damage occur after the retroactive date? **YES.**

Even though I built the wall before the retroactive date, there should be coverage for the claim that was made during this policy period because the bodily injury occurred after the retroactive date, and the claim was made during the policy period.

Now let us change the scenario to help explain the impact of a retroactive date. It is January 2010. Imagine that I have been building walls for ten years and I realize that I should probably get some coverage because I heard that a wall that I built in 2005 just fell and caused bodily injury and property damage at someone's New Year's Eve Party. The bodily injury and property damage occurred on December 31, 2009. In response, I purchase my first Claims Made Policy on January 1, 2010. That date is identified as my CGL policy's Retroactive Date. Three weeks later, I get sued for the bodily injury and property damage that occurred on December 31, 2009. Is there coverage under my 2010 Claims Made CGL Policy? To determine whether or not there is coverage under my Claims Made CGL Policy, let us ask the same three questions paraphrasing the insuring agreement:

1) Did a bodily injury or property damage occurrence take place in the coverage territory? **Yes.**

2) Was a claim for damages because of bodily injury or property damage made against any insured during the policy period? **YES.**

3) Did Bodily Injury or Property Damage occur after the retroactive date? **NO.**

My Claims Made CGL Policy will NOT provide a defense for this claim because the bodily injury or property damage occurred before the Retroactive Date. When analyzing whether or not a CGL Claims Made Policy will provide coverage, remember that the Retroactive Date requires that the bodily injury or property damage must take place after the Retroactive Date. The CGL Claims Made Form does not say that the work must take place after the Retroactive Date.

Professional Liability Policies.

It is common to see professional liability policies written on a Claims Made Form. You will see these policies written for accountants, attorneys, physicians, insurance agents, and really anyone who can be sued for providing advice that could financially harm another. A professional liability Claims Made policy is different than a CGL Claims Made policy. The CGL Claims Made Form is designed to cover claims of bodily injury or property damage that occur after the Retroactive Date. It does not matter if the work was done before the Retroactive Date as long as the bodily injury or property damage take place after the Retroactive Date.

In a professional liability Claims Made Policy, you are not looking for bodily injury or property damage. You are looking for a claim of financial injury arising out of an act, error, or omission done—or omitted—by the professional. The time when the work was done matters for a professional liability policy because the work is the event that triggers coverage. The negligent act or omission is the work that has to have been done after the retroactive date.

In both the CGL Claims Made Form and professional liability policies, the claim has to be made during the policy period. In the CGL Claims Made policy, the bodily injury or property damage has to occur after the retroactive date. In the professional liability policy, the act, error, or omission has to occur after the retroactive date.

Losing a Retroactive Date

I mentioned that the retroactive date is a date listed in the declarations and that it is usually the date when the policyholder first purchased and maintained continuous coverage under a Claims Made Form. What happens if a policyholder does not maintain continuous coverage?

Typically, when policyholders with a Claims Made Policy have a gap in coverage, they will get a new retroactive date when they purchase their next Claims Made Form Policy. The impact on the policyholders coverage is significant. For example, imagine that I purchased my first Claims Made Form CGL Policy in 2001 when I started building walls. In 2008, I do not have much work and so I decide not to purchase insurance. In 2014, I have an opportunity to build walls again and so I go out and purchase a new Claims Made Form CGL Policy. The retroactive date of my new policy is January 1, 2014. Later in 2014, I receive a lawsuit for a wall that fell down and caused bodily injury or property damage. If the bodily injury or property damage occurred prior to January 1, 2014, there will be no coverage for the claim.

Dangers of Changing Between Claims Made and Occurrence Forms

What would happen if a policyholder moves from a Claims Made Form CGL Policy to an Occurrence Form CGL Policy? For example, imagine that a business has a Claims Made Form in 2014 and moves to an Occurrence Form in 2015. There was a bodily injury occurrence that took place when a wall fell on a row of cars in 2014. The policyholder built the wall in 2005 and did not hear about the wall falling until being served with a lawsuit in 2015. If the policyholder turns in the claim to the 2015 Occurrence Form policy, the insurance company should decline coverage because the occurrence did not take place during their policy period (2015). If the policyholder turns in the claim to the 2014 Claims Made Form Policy, the insurance company should decline coverage because the claim did not

---

take place during their Claims Made Form Policy period (2014). The lawsuit was not served until 2015.

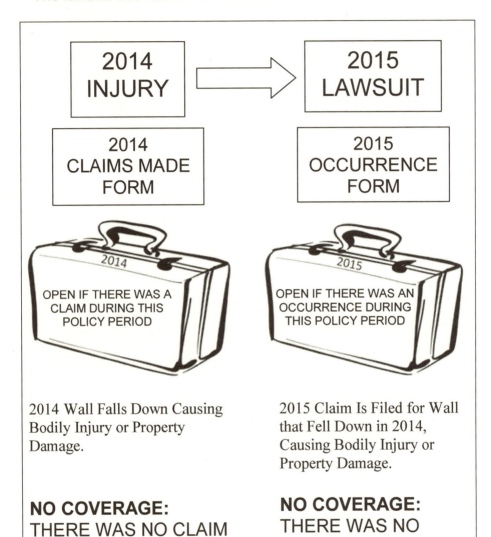

| 2014 INJURY | → | 2015 LAWSUIT |

| 2014 CLAIMS MADE FORM | | 2015 OCCURRENCE FORM |

2014

OPEN IF THERE WAS A CLAIM DURING THIS POLICY PERIOD

2015

OPEN IF THERE WAS AN OCCURRENCE DURING THIS POLICY PERIOD

2014 Wall Falls Down Causing Bodily Injury or Property Damage.

2015 Claim Is Filed for Wall that Fell Down in 2014, Causing Bodily Injury or Property Damage.

NO COVERAGE: THERE WAS NO CLAIM CURING THE POLICY PERIOD.

NO COVERAGE: THERE WAS NO OCCURRENCE DURING THE POLICY PERIOD.

Tail Coverage

One of the problems with the Claims Made Form CGL Policy is that there is no coverage for claims made after the policy period ends. To help correct this problem, the standard CGL Claims Made Form Policy offers extended reporting periods. The policy has an automatic Extended Reporting Period (ERP) and a Supplemental Extended Reporting Period (SERP). Sometimes these are referred to as a Short Tail (ERP) and Long Tail (SERP) because they extend the reporting period past the main body of the policy.

The Problem: With the Claims Made Form Policy, there is no coverage for claims made after the policy period ends.

The Solution: TAIL COVERAGE (Extended Reporting Period and Supplemental Extended Reporting Period)

The Extended Reporting Period (ERP) Short Tail:

The ERP (Short Tail) is provided without additional charge and it automatically extends the reporting period for 60 days after the end of the policy. The ERP extends the reporting period out five years after the policy period expires, but the occurrence has to be reported to the insurance company within 60 days after the end of the policy period. With this in mind, I think it is safer to think of the ERP (short tail) as an automatic 60 days of time in which you can report an occurrence, and not think about it as a five year tail. That is, if you do not report an occurrence within the first 60 days after the policy expires, then you do not have five years to report new claims. If you report an occurrence during the first 60 days after the policy expires (or during the policy period), then you have up to five years to report any claims arising out of the occurrence.

It is also important to note that the ERP extends the reporting period only. It does NOT reinstate or increase the Limits of Insurance. It does NOT extend coverage. The Claims Made Form still only covers claims made during the policy period for occurrences that take place between the

---

retroactive date and the policy's expiration date. Once the policy period expires, the ERP (and SERP) may extend the time in which a policyholder can report a claim for an occurrence, but the occurrence still had to take place before the policy period expired. The Claims Made Form CGL Policy does not provide coverage for occurrences that take place after the policy period expires.

> IMPORTANT: The Extended Reporting Period does not extend the policy period or scope of coverage provided. The Claims Made Form CGL Policy only covers claims that are made for occurrences that take place between the retroactive date and the policy's expiration date.

Supplemental Extended Reporting Period (SERP) (Long Tail /Lifelong Tail)

Unlike the ERP, the Supplemental Extended Reporting Period (SERP) is not automatic or free. If you want the SERP, you are going to need to endorse the policy and pay an extra charge. The SERP begins when the ERP ends. As stated above, the ERP requires that you report claims within 60 days of the end of the policy period. If you want the SERP, you need to notify the insurance company in writing within this first 60 day ERP period. The SERP provides supplemental aggregate limits that are "equal to the dollar amount shown in the Declarations in effect at the end of the policy period" (CG 00 02 12 04 ISO Properties, Inc., 2003, p 13 of 17). However, this limit only applies to claims first received and recorded during the SERP and will be "excess over any other valid and collectible insurance available" once the SERP begins (*ibid*). The additional premium will not exceed 200% of the annual premium for the policy. Like the ERP, the SERP does not extend coverage. It only extends the reporting period. The Claims Made Policy still only covers claims made during the policy period for occurrences that take place between the retroactive date and the policy expiration date. However, unlike the ERP, the SERP does reinstate the limits. The SERP limit will be excess over any other insurance, it may cost two times (200%) more than the original policy, and you still do not have coverage for occurrences that take place after the original policy period expired.

How do you retire after being in business with a Claims Made Form Policy?

Let us revisit the same scenario that we used when analyzing someone retiring with a CGL Occurrence Form Policy. We imagined a successful canned carrot businessman who was paying $50,000 for his annual CGL Occurrence Form policy premium. This time, imagine that he is paying $50,000 per year for his annual CGL Claims Made Form Policy premium. He has been in the canned carrots business for the past twenty years. He saved up sufficient assets to support what he expects to be 30 years of retirement. No one wants to buy his business, so he is just going to stop canning carrots and retire. He decides to get a lifetime tail (SERP) for his Claims Made Form CGL Policy. This costs him 200% of his annual premium which means he pays $100,000 to retire. That is painful, but he feels a little comfort because he thinks that he is covered for any claims that might be made against his business during the rest of his life.

If you read the description of the ERP and SERP above, you know the retiring canned carrot businessman has a problem. He is not covered for any claims that might be made against him during the rest of his life. The ERP and SERP do not extend coverage. They only extend the reporting period. The occurrence still needs to take place before the policy's expiration date. If, however, claims are made against him over the rest of his life based on bodily injury occurrences that took place before his policy period expired, then his insurance policy with the SERP will respond to the future claims arising out of occurrences that took place during his policy period. If he wants to have coverage in retirement for bodily injury caused by his products or completed operations, he need to either maintain a CGL Policy, or find a non-standard policy that will pay for products or completed operations that may occur in the future. Both the standard Occurrence Form CGL Policy and the Claims Made Form CGL Policy will not pay for bodily injury or property damage occurrences that take place after their policy periods expire.

Manifestation Occurrence Policy

- The <u>Occurrence Form Policy</u> is designed to cover *occurrences* that take place during the policy period.
- The <u>Claims Made Form Policy</u> is designed to cover *claims* that are reported during the policy period.
- The <u>Manifestation Occurrence Form Policy</u> is designed to cover occurrences that **first manifest during the policy period**.

The ***Manifestation Occurrence Policy*** is designed to cover occurrences that first manifest during the policy period. Different policies might have different definitions of "manifest." Sometimes it is defined as "to become apparent to a common observer." Sometimes "manifest" is defined as the time when an occurrence is reported to the insurance company. However manifest is defined, it is clear that it can only **FIRST** manifest once.

To explain the Manifestation Occurrence Form, let us reconsider the example that we discussed for both the Occurrence Form and Claims Made Form CGL Policies: Every day for 20 years, my grandparents meet at the same coffee shop.

This time let us assume that the coffee shop has a Manifestation Occurrence Form CGL Policy with $1 Million policy limits. Remember, my grandparents liked the coffee shop because the coffee shop used special blue metallic cups that kind of make your lips tingle when you have your first few sips of coffee. After 20 years, my grandparents learn that it is not necessarily a good idea to drink coffee every day out of a metallic cup that makes your lips tingle. It turns out that the metal is dangerous. My grandparents are now experiencing various lip and throat cancers arising out of their contact with the metal cups over the past 20 years.

When we discussed the Occurrence Form, we mentioned that my grandparents' attorney might think of 20 Million reasons to believe that the bodily injury *occurred* during every policy year over the past 20 years. This is because the Occurrence

Form CGL policy will pay for bodily injury or property damage that occurs during the policy period. If you can prove that it occurred during 20 different policy periods and each policy had $1 Million limits, then there is a possibility of recovering a total of $20 Million from the 20 annual Occurrence Form policies.

When it came to the Claims Made Form, there was only going to be one policy in which the claim was made. The policyholder did not purchase coverage for every occurrence that might occur during a policy year. The policyholder purchased coverage for any claims that might be made during the policy year. If in year 20 there was a claim made for bodily injury, the most the policy would pay is the $1 Million limit from the one policy in which the claim was made.

Like the Claims Made CGL Policy, the Manifestation Occurrence Policy would only pay $1 million in the above example. This is because the occurrence could only *first* manifest itself during one policy. Only the policy in which the occurrence first manifests itself would be obligated to provide coverage. If, in the example above, all of the policies were Manifestation Occurrence policies and the bodily injury first manifested during 1965, then the 1965 policy would be the only policy to pay. If it manifests itself again in 1966 or in later years, this would not be the first manifestation of the occurrence. Only the policy in which the occurrence first manifested itself would have the obligation to provide coverage.

Although the amount paid with the Claims Made CGL Policy Form and the Manifestation Occurrence CGL Policy Form are the same in these example, how coverage is activated differs. With both the Occurrence Form and Manifestation Occurrence Form CGL policies, we ask when the bodily injury or property damage occurred or first occurred. With the Claims Made Form CGL policy, we ask when the claim for the bodily injury or property damage was made.

Coverage Form Comparison		
Occurrence Form	Manifestation Occurrence Form	Claims Made Form
We will pay those sums that the insured becomes legally obligated to pay as damages because of "bodily injury" or "property damage" to which this insurance applies IF:		
1 The "bodily injury" or "property damage" is caused by an "occurrence" that takes place in the "coverage territory";		
2 The "bodily injury" or "property damage" occurs during the policy period; and	The "bodily injury" or "property damage" first manifests and appears during the policy period; and	A claim for damages because of the "bodily injury" or "property damage" is first made against any insured during the policy period or any Extended Reporting Periods; and
3 Prior to the policy period, no insured knew that the "bodily injury" or property damage" had occurred, in whole or in part.		The "bodily injury" or "property damage" did not occur before the Retroactive Date or after the end of the policy period.
(Adapted from CG 00 01 04 13 and CG 00 02 04 13, ISO Properties, Inc.)		

As you can see from the above comparison, the only difference between the Occurrence Form and the Manifestation Occurrence Form is it item #2. The Occurrence Form pays for occurrences that occur during the policy period. The Manifestation Occurrence Policy pays for occurrences that first manifest during the policy period. As mentioned above, this can make a large impact on coverage for exposures that are ongoing and continuous. This also impacts the number of policies that might be triggered because, although you might be able to argue that an occurrence took place during multiple occurrence policies, an occurrence can only *first* appear and become apparent during one Manifestation Occurrence Policy.

The Occurrence Form CGL Policy pays from the policy(ies) in force when the occurrence took place.
The Manifestation Occurrence Form CGL Policy pays from the policy in force when the occurrence first manifests and appears.

Manifestation Occurrence Policies in Construction Defect Litigation. In our discussion of what constitutes an occurrence for construction defect claims, I suggested that different jurisdictions use one of three different definitions for what constitutes an occurrence. How a jurisdiction defines an occurrence impacts whether or not a construction defect will be viewed as an occurrence. The first school of thought may determine that a construction defect is an occurrence if the damage is not to the policyholder's work, but it is damage to others *resulting from* the policyholder's defective work. The second school is unlikely to view construction defect as an occurrence because a construction defect is the result of the intentional act of construction. The third school is likely to view a construction defect as an occurrence so long as the result was unintended. (See page 36ff).

With this background, we can see that in certain circumstances in certain jurisdictions, a construction defect could be considered an occurrence. In determining the impact of the Manifestation Occurrence Policy, we need to dig deeper into the definition of a construction defect. A construction defect can be either a *patent defect* or a *latent defect*. A patent defect is one that is readily discoverable or "apparent by a reasonable inspection" (Code of Civil Procedures § 337.1(e)). A latent defect is one that is NOT readily discoverable or apparent by a reasonable inspection.

Now that we know the difference between a latent and a patent defect, let us revisit the key difference between the Occurrence Form and the Manifestation Occurrence Form:

OCCURRENCE FORM:	MANIFESTATION OCCURRENCE FORM:
The "bodily injury" or "property damage" occurs during the policy period; and	The "bodily injury" or "property damage" first manifests and appears during the policy period; and

As you can see, the Manifestation Occurrence Form is designed to cover only "bodily injury" or "property damage" that first manifests and appears during the policy period. Since a latent defect is one that, by definition, is not readily discoverable or "apparent by a reasonable inspection," the Manifestation Occurrence Form would not provide coverage for latent defect occurrences even in a jurisdiction that views latent defects as occurrences. The only construction defects for which the Manifestation Occurrence Policy would provide coverage would be for patent defects because only patent defects would have the ability to become manifest and appear during the policy period.

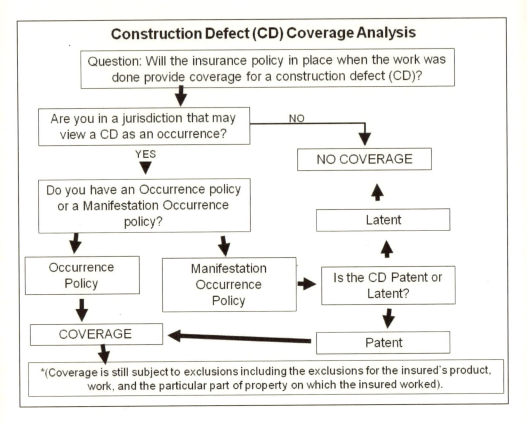

Construction Defect (CD) Coverage Analysis

Question: Will the insurance policy in place when the work was done provide coverage for a construction defect (CD)?

Are you in a jurisdiction that may view a CD as an occurrence?

NO

YES

NO COVERAGE

Do you have an Occurrence policy or a Manifestation Occurrence policy?

Latent

Occurrence Policy

Manifestation Occurrence Policy

Is the CD Patent or Latent?

COVERAGE

Patent

*(Coverage is still subject to exclusions including the exclusions for the insured's product, work, and the particular part of property on which the insured worked).

Manifestation Occurrence in the Conditions and Definitions

Remember that when I introduced the five basic elements of the CGL Policy, I included Conditions and Definitions. The reason for this becomes apparent in how I have seen some policies adjust coverage through the policy definitions. An insurance company may market their policy as an Occurrence Form, but have definitions that make it a Manifestation Occurrence Policy. For example, a policy might have a standard Occurrence Form insuring agreement, but then define an "occurrence" as "bodily injury or property damage that first occurs and become manifest during the policy period." Even though the insuring agreement and certificate of insurance might call the policy an "Occurrence Form," the definitions section—often at the end of the policy—essentially made it a Manifestation Occurrence Policy. Similarly, if an Occurrence

Form Policy has a condition that says, "coverage is void if you do not notify the carrier within thirty days of an occurrence," it sounds like the conditions created a Claims Made Form that is forcing you to report a claim within thirty days of an occurrence.

INSURING AGREEMENT SUMMARY

Remember that I introduced the CGL Policy like a row of briefcases each filled with $1 Million. Inscribed on the front of each briefcase was a year representing a specific annual policy period. Each briefcase had a combination lock. If you had the right combination, you could open the briefcase and take as much money as you needed to pay damages covered by that year's policy.

The combination that was the right combination depended on the type of policy. The standard CGL Policy is written on what is called an Occurrence Form. This form is designed to pay for occurrences that take place during the policy period. You can also purchase a CGL Policy that is written on a Claim's Made Form. The Claim's Made Form pays for claims that are made during the policy period. More recently, the Manifestation Occurrence Form was created. The Manifestation Occurrence Form is often referred to as simply an "Occurrence Form" on certificates of insurance, but it has wording that limits payment only to those occurrence that first manifests and appear during the term.

As we went through the various insuring agreements and a few introductory definitions and conditions, I hope that you can see that the insuring agreement creates the terms by which you are granted access to a briefcase. Moving beyond the insuring agreement, we will now explore some exclusions. These exclusions protect the briefcases by defining those specific occasions when someone should be granted access to the briefcase of money.

Coverage A Insuring Agreement Overview

An insurance policy is like a briefcase full of money. The coverage form is the combination needed to open it.

Occurrence Form	Claims Made Form

Manifestation Occurrence Form	Occurrence Form with extra Definitions/Conditions

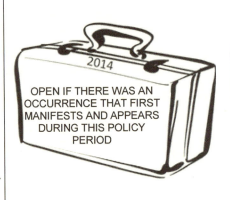

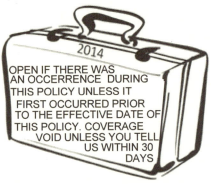

Chapter 3: Coverage A, Exclusions

When I introduced the insuring agreement, I described insurance policies as a row of briefcases filled with money. Each has a combination lock. If you have a bodily injury or property damage occurrence that takes place during the policy period, then you have the correct combination to open your standard CGL Occurrence Form Policy. If you look at the insurance policy as a briefcase of money, you can think of the exclusions as additional locks that you need to unlock before you get the money. That is, you had the correct combination because there was an occurrence during the policy period, but you cannot open the briefcase if the exclusions prevent you from opening the briefcase.

Exclusions limit the insuring agreement by removing certain things that the insurance company thinks should be outside the scope of the insuring agreement. This is especially important for Coverage A in the CGL Policy because Coverage A provides coverage on a "covered unless excluded basis." That is, there is a relatively short insuring agreement that provides broad coverage, and then there are specific exclusions that remove things that the insurance company does not intend to cover. This is important to note because sometimes a policyholder will demand, "Tell me where in my insurance policy it says that I am covered for _____."

In the blank, you can insert the thing that is really important for the policyholder. For example, let us say that the policyholder in this case is a maker of kites. The kite-making policyholder wants to see where in the policy it says there is coverage for kites. I will save you a little time that you might otherwise waste searching the CGL Policy, and just let you know that you will not find the word "kite" listed in a standard CGL Policy. Does this mean that there is no coverage for kite flying operations? Not at all. If there is Bodily Injury or Property Damage for which the CGL Policy applies, there will be coverage unless coverage is excluded. The person doing kite-flying operations should be pleased not to see the word "kite" in the policy because it means that the person did not find a specific exclusion for kites. The CGL Policy provides coverage unless it is excluded. If we did not find an exclusion for kite-flying operations, there should be coverage for bodily injury or property damage caused by kite-flying operations.

In case you were wondering, I have never had the above conversation with a kite-maker, but I have had this conversation with a plumber. The plumber wanted to see where in the policy it said that the plumber was covered for plumbing. There is no place in a standard CGL insuring agreement that says there is coverage for plumbing. However, although I have never seen a kite-flying exclusion, I have seen insurance companies insert an exclusion for water damage caused by plumbing!

The plumber found a policy that did not have a plumbing exclusion. This is good news for the plumber, but then the plumber wanted to see where in the policy it said that he was covered for plumbing. Again, you will not find plumbing in the insuring agreement. The only place you might find the word plumbing is if an insurance company adds it to the exclusions. Although it was frustrating for the plumber, not finding the word "plumbing" in the policy was actually great news because it meant that there was not an exclusion for plumbing. The CGL Policy provides coverage unless it is excluded, and since we did not find an exclusion for plumbing, there should be coverage for bodily injury or property damage caused by plumbing.

Coverage A of the CGL Policy provides coverage for Bodily Injury or Property Damage unless it is excluded.

How many exclusions are there in a CGL Policy? We will discuss the exclusions that are a part of the standard ISO CGL Policy (a. – q.), but the exact number varies by insurance policy. There can be as many exclusions as the insurance company thinks is necessary to ensure that they only pay for the risks associated with the premium they charge. For example, let us imagine that you asked me to write an insurance policy for you to cover any property damage or bodily injury that you might cause to others while reading this book. You suspect that there is a risk of you falling asleep while you are reading this book. If this causes you to spill your drink and ruin your rug, you may want a policy in place to provide coverage for the rug damage. You convince me that there is a great need for this policy because of all of the people who could fall asleep reading my book. In response, I write an insurance policy, collect some money, and somehow get my policy approved by the Department of Insurance in my state.

I established this insurance company assuming that the main financial risk is that I might have to pay for an occasional rug damaged when a sleeping reader spills a drink. But, what if you are reading by candle light and knock over a candle that burns down a city block? What if people determine that my book is the perfect size for throwing, and youth start roaming the streets with bundles of my books to throw at other people? It sounds like I need to add an exclusion for fire and maybe an exclusion for the intentional act of throwing my book. My example may seem ridiculous, but I have seen a CGL insurance policy that had 45 pages of great-looking coverage followed by 45 pages of exclusions. The exclusions largely removed the great coverage that was listed in the first 45 pages. This 90 page policy was the thickest policy on my desk, but the exclusions made it the thinnest policy in terms of what coverage would be provided in the event of an occurrence. If you want to know what is covered by a CGL Policy, you need to read the exclusions to know what is not covered by the policy.

Can I get a policy without exclusions?

The short answer to this question is probably, "No. You cannot get a CGL Policy without any exclusions." Even if you could get such a policy, you probably would not want to pay for it. To explain why, imagine that we create two businesses. One will be a low risk business and the other will be a high risk business. For the low risk business, we open a store that sells comic books. For the high risk business, we open a business that sells skateboards and handguns.

Both stores have a chance of someone getting injured on the premises. We saved money for years to start these stores. We do not want to lose everything in the event that a court finds us liable for someone's bodily injury at a store. To help offset this risk of loss, we decide to purchase a $1 Million CGL Policy to be able to compensate customers who might suffer bodily injury or property damage at the store.

Now let us stand in the shoes of the insurance company and compare the risks of these two companies. The insurance company calculates that there is a 1 in 1,000 chance that someone might have a $1 Million injury because of the comic book store next year. This means that if the insurance company sold insurance policies to 1,000 comic stores and charged $1,000 in premium per policy, it would collect the $1 Million needed to pay for the 1 store in 1000 that might have a claim next year. (1,000 policies x $1,000 premium = $1 Million). By charging $1,000 per year in premium, the insurance company has enough money to pay one, $1 Million claim next year.

The insurance company determines that there is a greater risk of injury at the skateboard and hand gun store than at the comic store. It decides that the skateboard and handgun store has a 1 in 100 chance of getting dragged into a $1 Million liability lawsuit next year. The insurance company decides to insure 100 of these skateboard and handgun stores, charging $10,000 per year for the CGL Policy. (100 policies x $10,000 premium = $1 Million). By charging $10,000 per year in premium, the insurance company collected the $1 Million it might need to pay the $1 Million claim that it could have next year.

The people who look at statistics and do the math to determine the appropriate premiums for a given risk are called actuaries. If you are reading this and you are an actuary, I may have offended you with my quick risk analysis and premium calculations. The big picture is that there is an appropriate amount of premium that needs to be collected to be able to cover the potential claims.

What do actuaries, a comic shop and a skateboard and handgun shop have to do with exclusions? Remember, Coverage A of the CGL Policy provides coverage for bodily injury or property damage unless it is excluded. Therefore, if there is no exclusion for bodily injury arising out of skateboards and handguns, they are included. What if an insurance company realizes that more stores are getting claims relating to skateboards and handguns than anticipated? The insurance company could respond by raising premiums on all of its policies by 50% to make sure that it has the money needed to pay the claims.

If you are a comic book store that has nothing to do with skateboards and handguns, you might not be happy with this 50% increase. You do not think you should be punished for skateboard and handgun exposures because this has nothing to do with you. You might want to have the insurance company add a Skateboard and Handgun Exclusion to your policy. By doing this, you and the insurance company are agreeing that there will not be coverage for bodily injury or property damage arising out of skateboards and handguns. With the exclusion, you might be able to enjoy lower premiums because the insurance company may charge less knowing that it will not have to pay for any claims arising out of skateboards and handguns. Exclusions are a great way to reduce one's premium by eliminating coverage for exposures that do not relate to the policyholder's operations.

What are the really bad exclusions?

To policyholders, the "really bad exclusion" is the exclusion that prevents them from getting coverage. With that in mind, you could say that all exclusions are significant because you do not know what unfortunate, unforeseen occurrence might happen. If you do not know what might happen, you do not know what exclusion might exclude coverage. For example, most businesses might not care if they have a policy that excludes any claim involving a dog...unless they end up having a claim involving a dog.

With that said, not all exclusions are created equally. The standard Insurance Service Office (ISO) CGL Policy includes 17 standard exclusions that they label exclusions a through q. I will describe these 17 exclusions as "Standard Exclusions." After these 17 exclusions, I will provide some additional exclusions that are not always a part of the standard CGL Policy, but happen frequently enough that you should be aware of them. Although I stress that just because a policy contains an exclusion does not make it a bad policy, it should go without saying that the more exclusions a policy contains, the more likely a claim will be denied because of an exclusion.

Standard Exclusions

a. Expected or Intended Injury

The first exclusion on most CGL policies is the exclusion of coverage for Expected or Intended Injury. I hope that the existence of this exclusion does not disappoint or surprise you. In general, insurance is designed to provide coverage for accidents that you do not foresee happening. If you are expecting or intending to cause someone bodily injury, and then you plan on turning over the claim to your insurance company when you get sued, you may want to spend more time reading books by criminal defense attorneys than books like this one by an insurance/civil litigation attorney. That is, insurance is not a get out of jail free ticket. You cannot just go to the police and say that you intentionally caused someone bodily injury, and then offer them your insurance policy, pay the deductible, and think that everything will be fine.

To help understand what the policy means by "expected" or "intended" injury, let us look at the tort of trespassing because it also includes an intentional act. People can be found liable for trespassing if they intentionally enter the land of another person without permission. Let us say that the room you are in right now is your land and the boundary line between your land and someone else's land is the line dividing your room and the room next to you. If I intentionally step across that line in to your room without permission, I could be liable for trespassing. I have intentionally entered the land of another (your land) without permission. That is all that is necessary to find me liable for trespassing. Notice that I am not asking whether or not I intended to trespass. It does not matter if I know whether or not it is your land, or whether or not I intended to trespass. We are just analyzing whether or not my actions were intentional, and whether or not I intentionally entered your land.

To contrast this with an unintentional act, imagine that I have an epileptic seizure that forces me to fall across the boundary line of your room. I would not be found liable for trespassing because I did NOT intentionally enter your land. My action of entering your land was completely unintentional because it was the result of an involuntary epileptic seizure. Similarly, if someone shoves me into your room against my will, I should not be found liable for trespassing because I did not intend to enter your land. (The person who shoves me could be liable for trespassing because this person intentionally caused something—me—to enter your land without permission).

Now that we understand the difference between an intentional and an unintentional act, we need to understand what it means to intend or expect that you will cause bodily injury or property damage. **In its legal meaning, if you intend to do something, you either desired the consequences, or there was a substantial certainty that the consequences would occur.** For example, imagine that I live near a busy interstate highway and I think it would be fun to hit golf balls onto the highway. I am thinking of how high the balls will bounce off of the pavement; not about the possibility of hitting a car. I decide to hit balls on to the highway. This causes bodily and property damage to others. I might argue that I did not *intend* to hit any of the cars on the highway. That is, it was not my desire. Maybe my specific desire was to bounce the balls in between the cars. Even though I did not desire the consequence of hitting the cars, a court would say that hitting the cars was the result of my intentional act because the act was intentional (e.g., it was not the result of a seizure), and there was a substantial certainty that my actions (hitting golf balls on to a busy highway) would have the consequence of causing bodily injury or property damage to the drivers and vehicles on the highway.

It is with this understanding of intentionality that we should approach the exclusion for bodily injury or property damage when the injury or damage is expected or intended. Imagine that I see a train coming toward you that you do not see. I tackle you to save you from the train. I saved your life, but in the process, I dislocated your shoulder. You sue me for bodily injury. Did I intend to cause you bodily injury? Well, I may not have desired the consequence of hurting you, but I did intentionally tackle you and knew to a substantial certainty that you getting tackled on hard pavement would cause you injury. We do not ask whether or not I intended or expected the extent of bodily injury or property damage that I caused. We just ask if I expected or intended the bodily injury or property damage. The CGL Policy excludes bodily injury or property damage that the insured expects or intends.

Reasonable Force Exception

There is often an exception to this exclusion that allows coverage for bodily injury if the expected or intended act by the insured was caused by the insured using reasonable force to protect persons or property. To explain this exception, imagine that you are employed as a bouncer at a large bar and concert venue. Your job is to keep people from beating each other up in the crowd, and away from the musicians on stage. One night there is a particularly unruly patron who is threatening the safety of others. You intervene to tackle the unruly patron. During the tackle, the unruly patron is injured and sues you and the business.

Did you intend your action of tackling the patron? Yes. Did you desire or know to a substantial certainty that your actions may result in bodily injury? Yes. Your employer's CGL Policy starts by saying that if you expect or intend to injure someone, there is no coverage. However, there is an exception that will provide coverage if the bodily injury is the result of reasonable force that was used to protect persons or property. If you used reasonable force to protect persons or property, then the bar/concert venue's CGL Policy should provide coverage.

What is Reasonable Force?

Anytime you are wondering if something is reasonable in the eyes of the law, I want you to think of an imaginary person that a jury creates during jury deliberations. This imaginary person has all of the life experiences of the jury members. It has the jury's history of making good decisions, and the jury's history of making bad decisions. Once created, the jury then asks how this imaginary person would have behaved if put in the situation faced by the defendant on trial. Did the defendant behave as the imaginary reasonable person, or did the defendant fail to act like this reasonable person?

In our case of the bar bouncer tackling the unruly patron, we need to ask if it would be reasonable for the jury's imaginary reasonable person to use the force that the bar bouncer used if the imaginary reasonable person was faced with the same facts and threats that the bar bouncer faced. If the jury determines that the imaginary reasonable person would have behaved as the bouncer behaved, then the bar bouncer behaved reasonably. The Expected or Intended Exclusion starts by saying that coverage is excluded if the insured expected or intended the bodily injury. However, coverage for bodily injury is not excluded if it was the result of the insured using reasonable force to protect persons or property.

b. Contractual Liability

The CGL Policy begins with a broad exclusion for any contractual liability. The policy then provides some exceptions where the policy will provide some coverage. To give an idea of why there would be a broad exclusion for contractual liability, it is helpful to begin with an understanding of contract law.

A contract exists when there has been an exchange of promises to do or not do certain things. In order for a contract to be enforceable, there must be an **offer**, **acceptance**, and **consideration**. The **offer** needs to contain sufficiently definite terms that are communicated in a way that invites the other person to accept the offer. **Acceptance** exists where the person who received the offer accepts the terms of the offer. **Consideration** exists where both parties agree to do something that they are not already obligated to do in exchange for the other party's performance. Consideration is often referred to as a "bargained for exchange."

For example, let us say that I communicate to you that I would sell you this book for $10.00. The terms are sufficiently definite: this book and $10.00. You accept this offer. You may have accepted by silently giving me $10.00 or you might have yelled, "I accept." Either way, we have an offer and acceptance. Consideration exists because there is bargained for exchange. You did not have to give me $10.00. I did not have to sell you my book. We agree on the terms and we have offer, acceptance, and consideration. At this moment, we have formed a contract.

How we end up in court with contract law is when at least one party to the contract feels that the other party has broken his/her promise. When a party breaks a promise expressed in the contract, we say that the party who broke the promise "breached the contract." For example, in the above exchange, let us say that you gave me an envelope that contained a $5.00 bill instead of a $10.00 bill. We had a contract for $10.00. You broke your promise. It may have been an accident that can be corrected easily, but it is still a broken promise.

Maybe it turns out that you were not the only person who made a mistake. I said that I would give you "this book" for $10.00. If you receive a book at your home and it turns out to be a different, perhaps especially uninteresting book, you have a right to call me up and tell me that I broke my promise to you. As children, we may have screamed, "You broke your promise" and beg a parent or teacher for justice. As adults, we say, "You breached your contract," and we ask the courts for justice. And what is justice? In our examples, we want the terms of the contract fulfilled. I want $10.00. You want this book.

The reason that the CGL Policy begins by stating that contractual liability is excluded is because contractual liability could be about almost anything. Imagine that you want a new roof on your house and I am a roofer. You and I are both fans of the Dallas Cowboys football team. You received several bids from other roofers. They want to charge $75,000. I say that I will do it for $100,000, but that if the Cowboys win the Super Bowl this year, your roof will be free. You like to gamble and love the Cowboys. You accept my offer. At that moment, we have an offer, acceptance, and consideration. A contract has been formed. If it turns out that the Cowboys win the Super Bowl and you ask for your $100,000 back, I may not have it ready for you. In response, you may want to sue me in court or file a claim against my CGL Policy. The policy is going to look at the claim and see that it arises out of Contractual Liability. The policy will then apply the Contractual Liability Exclusion, and deny payment for the claim.

Exceptions to the Contractual Liability Exclusion
There are two exceptions to the Contractual Liability Exclusion: Liability the insured would have had in the absence of a contract and 2) Liability assumed in an "insured contract".

Exception 1: Liability the insured would have had in the absence of the contract.
Imagine that a roofer signs a contract to install a roof at an office building. It turns out that the roofer is not very good at operating the crane necessary to lift a bunch of tiles on to the roof. The roofer drops a pallet of tiles across four parked cars, causing $100,000 in damage to the four cars. There was a contract, but the liability is not arising out of the fact that there was a contract. There is liability because the roofer caused property damage. Since the roofer may be liable absent the existence of the contract, the policy will not exclude coverage simply because there was a contract.

Exception 2: Liability assumed in an "insured contract".
If the liability results from an "insured contract", then the policy may pay for the third party's attorney fees, litigation expenses, and defense costs IF these expenses were also assumed in the "insured contract". Sometimes people get excited that there is coverage for an "insured contract" before asking the basic question, "What is an 'insured contract'?"

A little trick for understanding policies is understanding the use of quotation marks in an insurance policy. These are not used for irony or emphasis. The quotation marks are used in an insurance policy to designate that the word or words within the quotation marks are defined elsewhere in the policy. Therefore, when we read that an "insured contract" is not excluded, we need to go to the definitions section to find the definition of an "insured contract."

The standard CGL Policy defines an "insured contract" as six specific kinds of contracts: Lease of Premises, Sidetrack Agreements, Easement/License Agreements, An Obligation as required by ordinance to indemnify a municipality, Elevator Maintenance Agreements, and Tort Liability Assumed by the Named Insured.

a)   Lease of Premises

Landlords often require tenants to sign a lease agreement before the tenant can occupy the landlord's premises. This is a contract for a lease of premises. The contract often includes words stating that the tenant will hold the landlord harmless and indemnify the landlord in the event that one of the tenant's customer's is injured in the tenant's office, and then sues the landlord. Imagine that you own a building and I rent a space in your building to open an ice cream shop. Someone slips in the ice cream, is injured, and sues you because you are the building owner. You then remind me that I have a duty to defend you and make you whole because of the hold harmless agreement that I signed with my lease. There is no reason for me to have to pay to defend you in this lawsuit except for the contract we signed for the lease of premises.

The CGL policy starts by saying that liability arising out of a contract alone is excluded, but then says there is an exception for an "insured contract". A contract for a lease of premises is included in the definition of an "insured contract". That *hold harmless agreement* was part of my contract for a lease of premises. Since there was liability arising out of a lease agreement and a lease agreement is an "Insured Contract," the CGL Policy should provide coverage.

b)   Sidetrack Agreement

A sidetrack is a railroad spur that connects a business to a main railroad. You can imagine that if I am manufacturing something in Michigan that I want to deliver to Florida, Texas, and California, it would be convenient for me to have a special railroad track that branches off of the main track and into my heated warehouse. This way I can send the goods throughout the country by rail from the comfort of my own heated warehouse. Just as the landlord wanted the tenant to sign a hold harmless agreement in case the landlord gets sued because of the tenant, the railroad company is going to want me to sign something accepting liability associated with the railroad spur connected to my business location.

This should make sense. What looks to business owners like a practical way to distribute goods across the country, looks to children like something to climb on or push. If there are any injuries associated with such an adventure, you can imagine that the railroad company would get sued. If sued, the railroad company would look at the sidetrack agreement with the business and hand over the lawsuit to the business. The business would have to defend and indemnify the railroad company in accordance with the terms of the sidetrack agreement.

In this situation, there is no reason for the business to have to pay to defend the railroad in the lawsuit except for the sidetrack agreement. The policy starts by saying that contractual liability is excluded, but then says there is an exception for an "insured contract". Since our example has liability arising out of a sidetrack agreement, and a sidetrack agreement is an "Insured Contract," there should be coverage from the CGL Policy.

c) Easement/License Agreement

An easement and license agreement are similar to a lease in that they deal with rights to someone else's property. The difference is that a lease allows one to take possession of property. Easements and license agreements do not grant possession of property. Instead of granting possession, easements and license agreements allow one to enter, use, or access the property of another person.

Imagine that you own the land between a parking lot and my office. People can take the sidewalk to walk around your land, but they prefer walking through your land on the well-worn path between the parking lot and my office. You ask me to sign an easement agreement that gives me and my customers a right to use the small path through your land that connects the parking lot and my office. I sign the agreement and then, of course, someone trips on the easement and sues you. They sue you because they were injured on your land. You then give the lawsuit over to me so that I can defend you. The only reason I have to defend you is because of the easement agreement that I signed. The policy started by excluding any contractual liability, but provided an exception for an "insured contract". Since this example has liability arising out of an easement agreement and an easement agreement is an "insured contract", there should be coverage from my CGL Policy.

d) An Obligation as Required by Ordinance to Indemnify a Municipality.

The phrase, "an ordinance to indemnify a municipality" is unnecessarily complicated. For our purposes, an ordinance is a law, indemnification means to make someone whole, and a municipality is a city. Therefore, this paragraph is talking about "a city law that requires someone to make the city whole." For example, let us say that a city passes a law that requires businesses to take care of the sidewalks in front of their businesses. The law states that if someone is injured on a sidewalk in front of a business and sues the city, the business must make the city whole. Imagine that someone is injured because they slipped on a sidewalk in front of a bank. The person who slips sues the city. The city turns over the lawsuit to the bank. The bank is only getting dragged into the lawsuit because of the city ordinance that requires the business owner to indemnify the city. Since this obligation is included within the definition of an "insured contract", there would be coverage for liability arising out of this obligation as required by ordinance to indemnify a municipality.

e) Elevator Maintenance Agreement

If you have an elevator in your building, you may have to sign an Elevator Maintenance Agreement. If someone gets injured in an elevator and sues the elevator maintenance company, you may find that the contract that you signed makes you responsible to hold the elevator maintenance company harmless for any bodily injury or property damage associated with the elevator.

Imagine that there is a fancy restaurant on the top floor of a skyscraper. The restaurant signs an elevator maintenance agreement with an elevator maintenance company. Someone uses the elevator to transport expensive wine to the fancy restaurant. The elevator malfunctions and all of the bottles of wine break. The person transporting the wine sues the elevator maintenance company. The elevator maintenance company gives the lawsuit to the restaurant so that the restaurant will defend and indemnify the elevator maintenance company according to the terms of their elevator maintenance agreement. The restaurant's liability only exists because of this contract, and contractual liability is excluded in the CGL Policy. However, since an Elevator Maintenance Agreement is included in the definition of an "insured contract", there would be coverage for the liability arising out of the Elevator Maintenance Agreement.

f)   Tort Liability Assumed by the Named Insured

The definition of an "insured contract" includes "tort liability assumed by the named insured." A tort is a civil wrong. The most common tort for insurance matters is the tort of negligence. One can be found negligent if the person had a duty to act like a reasonable person, breached the duty to act like a reasonable person, and this breach caused damages. For example, reasonable chandelier-installers do not install chandeliers that fall from ceilings. If I install a chandelier and it falls and causes damages, then I could be liable for paying damages under the tort of negligence. If the chandelier fell because of a fire not caused by me, I would not be liable for negligence because my failure to act like a reasonable chandelier-installer (my breach) did not cause the damages. In order to be found liable for the tort of negligence, a plaintiff needs to show that the defendant owed the plaintiff a duty, breached the duty, and that breaching the duty caused the plaintiff damages.

When would one assume tort liability by contract? The most common examples are Hold Harmless Agreements and Indemnification Agreements. A **Hold Harmless Agreement** is an agreement where one party agrees to hold another party harmless for any liabilities associated with the agreement. An **Indemnification Agreement** is an agreement where one party agrees to indemnify another. In contract law, to indemnify means to make the other party to a contract "whole." The indemnitor gives the promise to make someone else whole. The indemnitee receives the promise to be made whole. In the indemnification agreement, the indemnitor agrees to indemnify (or make whole) the indemnitee.

For example, imagine that you want me to install a new chandelier in your office. You ask me to hold you harmless and indemnify you. I install the new chandelier, and then it falls. Everyone escaped unharmed except a visitor named Smith. Smith left a $1000 computer in the room, and it is destroyed. Smith asks you for $1000. You give Smith the $1000. I agreed to indemnify you (make you whole), and so I have to give you $1000 for the $1000 you gave to Smith. I also have agreed to hold you harmless. This means that if this ends up being a bigger lawsuit that gets brought against you, I cannot say that it is all your fault and has nothing to do with me. I have agreed to hold you harmless for whatever damages arise out of my work on the chandelier.

My agreement to hold you harmless and indemnify you is a contract where I have agreed to assume tort liability. The tort in question is the tort of negligence. You are being sued because you had a duty to act like a reasonable business owner and reasonable business owners do not have chandeliers that fall from ceilings. I am only getting dragged into the lawsuit between you and Smith because of my contract with you. My CGL Policy starts by excluding contractual liability. However, I will have coverage in this situation because the CGL Policy has an exception that provides coverage for "insured contracts", and "tort liability assumed by contract" is considered an "insured contract". When I signed the hold harmless and indemnity agreements with you, I assumed tort liability by our contract. This created an exception to the CGL Policy's contractual liability exclusion, granting coverage for the tort liability I assumed.

The importance of Tort Liability Assumed by Contract

Some insurance policies do not contain all six definitions for the "insured contract". Sometimes they will only have five exceptions and leave out "Tort Liability Assumed by Contract." Sometimes they will only have one exception, and it will be "Tort Liability Assumed by Contract." You have broader coverage if you have a policy that includes "Tort Liability Assumed by Contract" in the definition of an "insured contract".

For example, imagine that there is no provision for a "lease" under an "insured contact". Even without the lease, the landlord's contract with the tenant to indemnify and hold the landlord harmless still sounds like the named insured's contract to assume the tort liability of the landlord. Therefore, if you have a policy that does not include lease of premises in the definition of an "insured contract", you still may pick up any tort liability associated with the lease if the "insured contract" includes "Tort Liability Assumed by Contract." However, if you have a policy that does not include "Tort Liability Assumed by Contract" in the definition of an "insured contract", then there is no coverage for liability arising out of the many hold harmless and indemnity agreements the insured may sign.

c. Liquor Liability

The standard CGL Policy excludes "Bodily Injury" or "Property Damage" for which the insured is held liable because of:

(1) Causing or contributing to the intoxication of any person;
(2) The furnishing of alcoholic beverages to a person under the legal drinking age or under the influence of alcohol; or
(3) Any statute, ordinance or regulation relating to the sale, gift, distribution or use of alcoholic beverages.
(CG 00 01 04 13, ISO Properties, Inc., 2012, Page 2; Appendix Page 247).

There is an important exception to this exclusion. The exception clarifies that the exclusion above only applies if the insured is "in the business of manufacturing, distributing, selling, serving or furnishing alcoholic beverages" (*ibid.*). If you are in the business of alcohol, you need to look for a special liquor liability policy that will add the coverage removed by this exclusion. If you are not in such a business, this exclusion does not apply to you.

Liquor liability that you have when you are not in the alcohol business is often called "Host Liquor Liability." As a host, you may serve alcohol to your guests. Your conduct will not be subject to this exclusion unless you are in the "business of manufacturing, distributing, selling, serving or furnishing alcoholic beverages" (*ibid.*).

When is a business in the business of manufacturing, distributing, selling, serving, or furnishing alcoholic beverages? Sometimes this is not as obvious as it may seem. Years ago there was a social club in the northeastern United States where older men would often gather for a drink, or two. Drinks were free for members at the club's dimly lit bar. The annual membership dues were expensive. Almost as if their business model included wanting to be listed in an insurance or legal publication someday, this social club also had a shooting range. Here is a scenario where there is a social club that has expensive membership dues, free drinks, and a shooting range. What could go wrong, right? Well, imagine that there is bodily injury relating to the shooting range that was also related to the club "causing or contributing to the intoxication of any person" or "furnishing alcoholic beverages to a person under the...influence of alcohol." In response, the CGL Policy denies coverage for the claim. The social club then argues that they should have coverage because they fit within the exception to the Liquor Liability exclusion because they are not in the business of "selling, serving or furnishing alcoholic beverages."

Was this social club in the business of serving alcohol? They would argue that they are not in the business of alcohol because they do not charge any money for alcohol. How could they be in the business of alcohol, they would argue, if their drinks are free? Of course, the insurance company would argue that they are in the business of alcohol because club members pay significant membership fees so that the members can enjoy the "free" alcohol at the club.

What is at stake? If they are in the business of alcohol, the Liquor Liability exclusion would preclude any coverage for liability because liability arose out of the club contributing to the intoxication of the person who was involved in the incident. If the club is not in the business of alcohol, then this exclusion does not apply, and there would be coverage for the bodily injury occurrence that arose out of the social club's operations.

d. Workers' Compensation and Similar Laws

The standard CGL Policy excludes coverage relating to worker's compensation laws. The reason for this is because if a business has employees, the business needs to comply with a state's worker's compensation laws. The most common way to comply with state worker's compensation laws is to get a worker's compensation insurance policy. The CGL Policy inserts this exclusion to make it explicit that the CGL Policy will not cover occurrences that should be covered under a worker's compensation policy. If a business wants coverage to satisfy worker's compensation laws, the business needs to purchase a worker's compensation policy.

Another way to think about this exclusion is to remember my definition of liability being "bodily injury and property damage *to others*." Worker's compensation insurance policies are designed to provide coverage for an employee's injuries, illness, occupational diseases, or death arising out of the employee's employment. If you call me and say, "*My* employee was just injured on the job and I need to file a claim with *my* CGL Policy," I may remind you that liability policies are not intended for *your* employees. Liability policies are designed to provide coverage for bodily injury or property damage that you might cause to third parties. If you injure someone else's employees, you can call your CGL Policy. If one of your own employees gets injured, you need to call your worker's compensation insurance policy. Any obligation arising out of worker's compensation laws is excluded from the CGL Policy.

e. Employer's Liability

The standard CGL Policy excludes employer's liability. Just as businesses can purchase Worker's Compensation Insurance to cover worker's compensation exposures, businesses can purchase Employer's Liability Insurance to cover employer's liability exposures. In most states, employer's liability policies are included along with a Worker's Compensation Insurance policy. The difference is that whereas a Worker's Compensation Insurance policy is designed to provide coverage relating to an injured employee, the Employer's Liability policy is designed to provide coverage to a third party that is injured (usually financially) because of an injury, sickness, or death of an employee.

There is an important exception to the Employer's Liability Exclusion in the standard CGL Policy. The exception states, "This exclusion does not apply to liability assumed by the insured under an 'insured contract'"(*ibid.*). Therefore, if Employer's Liability arises out of an "insured contract", then there will be coverage for the Employer's Liability under the CGL Policy. You may remember from pages 76-82 that there are six specific contracts that are included in the definition of an "insured contract". If there is a contract for employer's liability that falls within the definition of an "insured contract", then the CGL Policy will provide coverage for the employer's liability. Since this means that there is a possibility of employer's liability coverage under the CGL Policy, I will explain what is covered under a standard Employer's Liability policy.

Employer's Liability policies often provide coverage in four main areas:

1) Third Party Claims (Also called Action Over Claims)
2) Care and Loss of Services
3) Consequential Bodily Injury
4) Dual Capacity Claims

---

1) Third Party Claims (Also called Action Over Claims)

In a third party (action over) claim, an injured worker sues a third party in addition to filing a worker's compensation claim. The third party then files a claim against the injured employee's employer. The claim for the injured employee that comes from the third party is called a third party claim, or an action over claim.

For example, imagine that an employee in a processing plant removes the safety guard from a piece of machinery. The employee does this with the supervisor's knowledge. The employee gets injured while using the machine without the safety guard. The employee files a claim against the employer's worker's compensation insurance company. While home recovering and watching advertisements for attorneys on day time television, the employee decides to file a claim against the manufacturer that made the machine that caused the employee's injuries. The claim against the manufacturer could be that the machine was too dangerous or did not have sufficient warnings, and this is what caused the employee's injuries.

In response, the machinery company may sue the injured worker's employer for negligence. The manufacturer sues the injured worker's employer because the manufacturer would argue that the employer was negligent in hiring, training, or supervising the employee. This negligence caused the injuries to the employee.

Worker's Compensation Insurance is designed to provide payments to an injured employee. Here we have a situation where the employer needs to provide money for damages and a legal defense costs not directly to an employee, but to the third party (i.e. the machinery company) that is being sued because of the employee's injuries. Since we have injuries to a third party arising out of injuries to an employee, this is considered a third party/action over employer's liability claim. If there was an "insured contract" for employer's liability between the manufacturer and employer, then the employer's CGL

Policy could provide coverage for the employer's liability exposure.

A similar situation arises when an employee of a subcontractor is injured on a job and files Worker's Compensation with his/her employer AND sues the General Contractor for having an unsafe workplace. The General Contractor might sue the subcontractor for negligently training or supervising the subcontractor's employees on the job site. The Employer's Liability policy of the subcontractor would defend the subcontractor against this suit from the general contractor. If the subcontractor had an "insured contract" with the general contractor whereby the subcontractor assumed employer's liability exposures, then this exposure could be covered under the CGL Policy.

2) Care and Loss of Services

Employer's Liability claims that fall under Care and Loss of Services are usually claims filed by a spouse or another family member of the injured employee.

For example, imagine that a parent is injured at work. Prior to the injury, the parent used to drive children to and from school, prepare meals, and perform household chores. As a result of the injury, the parent can no longer perform these tasks. Since the injured parent can no longer do these things, the injured worker's spouse or other family members may have to take on additional tasks associated with not having the parent available to do the things the parent always did. The uninjured family members may need to hire a house cleaning service, driver, and household maintenance person just to help fill the roles that are not being filled by the now injured parent or spouse. These are financial damages suffered by family members of an injured employee. The injured employee could file a claim for worker's compensation insurance. The family members could file an employer's liability claim for the care and loss of services they suffer as a result of the injuries to the employee. If this liability is assumed under an "insured contract", then this could be covered under the "insured contract" exception to the CGL Policy's employer's liability exclusion.

3) Consequential Bodily Injury

Employer's Liability claims arising out of Consequential Bodily Injury are liability claims filed against an employer by a family member of an injured employee for injuries a family member suffers as a consequence of the employee's injury. Remember, the injured employee will get compensation from worker's compensation insurance. But what about an employee's family member who might be injured as a result of the employee's injury? The family member is not an employee, and so the family member will not be able to collect from worker's compensation insurance. Employer's Liability addresses the need to compensate a family member who might be injured as a result of an employee's injury.

For example, my grandmother had cancer. My grandfather took care of her while she was battling cancer. He would help her walk from her bed to her favorite chair. When she got too weak to walk to her favorite chair, he would carry her. At one point, my grandfather admits that there was a day when he felt "dizzy." He was a proud man and did not want to admit that there was anything weak about him, but the family knew that what grandpa described as "feeling dizzy," the medical community calls a heart attack. He was stressed from caring for his dying wife, and one day on a walk, he "felt dizzy," collapsed on a sidewalk, strangers called an ambulance, and we were fortunate to have him revived to spend a few more decades with us.

To help explain coverage for Consequential Bodily Injury under the Employer's Liability policy, imagine that my grandmother's cancer was an occupational disease caused by her employment. Imagine that she worked at a chemical factory and it was determined that her work with the chemicals caused her cancer. She would be able to file a claim against her employer's worker's compensation insurance. Her husband suffered injuries (a heart attack, ambulance ride, surgery, hospital stay, rehabilitation, etc.) as a consequence of his wife's occupational disease. A husband cannot file a claim against his wife's worker's compensation insurance if he is not an employee. He would need to file an Employer's Liability claim against the employer. Under the Employer's Liability policy, a family member of an injured employee may recover financial damages for the family member's consequential bodily injury. The Employer's Liability policy may also provide the legal team needed to defend against frivolous lawsuits for consequential bodily injury. Employer's Liability is excluded under the CGL Policy unless the exposure arises out of an "insured contract". In this example, if the employer and employee had an "insured contract" (perhaps in an employment agreement) that extended Employer's Liability to the employee's spouse, then this exposure could be covered under the CGL Policy.

4) Dual Capacity Claims

Dual Capacity Claims arise when an employer may be liable for an employee's injuries as both an employer and also from a separate source of liability. If the employer is liable for the injuries because of the employer's role as the employer, then compensation would come from the worker's compensation insurance policy. However, if the employer's liability exists for a reason other than the employer is the employer, there could be a "Dual Capacity Claim" that could trigger coverage under an Employer's Liability Policy.

For example, think of an employee who works at a stepladder manufacturing company. To assemble the last ladder of the day, the employee needs to get a part from the shelf that is just out of reach. What will the employee do to get a part off a shelf that is a little too high to reach? The employee will grab a ladder so that the employee can reach the part. What kind of ladder will the employee grab when the employee works at a stepladder manufacturing company? The company does not want to keep ladders from the competition in the ladder manufacturer's warehouse. The employee will grab a ladder made by the employer.

The good news about working at this ladder company is that the pay is good and the people are really nice. The bad news about the ladder company is that they do not make a very good ladder. When the employee climbs up the ladder to get the part that was just out of reach, the ladder collapses, injuring the employee.

This sounds like a typical workplace injury, and so the employee files a worker's compensation claim against the employer. In addition, however, the employee files a claim against the manufacturer of the ladder. Someone who is injured because of a defective product would certainly have a right to file a claim against the manufacturer of the defective product, but here the manufacturer of the defective product is also the employer of the injured employee.

This is a classic example of a Dual Capacity Claim because the employer's liability exists for a reason other than simply being the injured employee's employer. Liability arises because the employer is a manufacturer of a defective product. The employee files a worker's compensation insurance claim against the employer because the employee was injured on the job. The employee files a separate claim against the employer in its capacity as the manufacturer of the ladder.

The claim against the employer is a dual capacity claim that would be covered under an Employer's Liability policy. The CGL Policy would exclude any liability associated with Employer's Liability UNLESS liability arises out of an "insured contract". If the employer and employee had an "insured contract" relating to employer's liability, then the CGL Policy could provide coverage for this dual capacity exposure just as the policy would provide coverage for anyone injured by the insured's product.

As I mentioned above, **Employer's Liability is excluded in the CGL Policy.** You do not expect to get home or auto insurance from your CGL Policy. You should not expect Employer's Liability from your CGL Policy either. However, there is an exception to the Employer's Liability Exclusion. The CGL Policy states that **the Employer's Liability Exclusion does not apply to liability assumed by the insured under an "insured contract".** This means that, under the standard ISO CGL Policy, you could get the above Employer's Liability coverage if liability arises out of an "insured contract".

f. Pollution

Before providing some exceptions, the CGL Policy starts with a broad exclusion eliminating coverage for any bodily injury or property damage "arising out of the actual, alleged or threatened discharge, dispersal, migration, release or escape of 'pollutants'" (CG 00 01 04 13 ISO properties, Inc., 2012, Page 3; Appendix Page 248). To understand how broad this definition is, you need to look at how the policy defines "pollutants." The standard CGL Policy defines "pollutants" as "any solid, liquid, gaseous or thermal irritant or contaminant, including smoke, vapor, soot, fumes, acids, alkalis, chemicals and waste. Waste includes materials to be recycled, reconditioned or reclaimed" (CG 00 01 04 13 ISO properties, Inc., 2012, Page 15; Appendix Page 271).

I include the full definition because I want you to think about how broad this definition really is. To see if a business has a pollution exposure, you can ask two questions:

1) Does the business work with anything that has any particulate matter?
2) Could the particulate matter be an irritant or contaminant?

Pollution Exposure Analysis

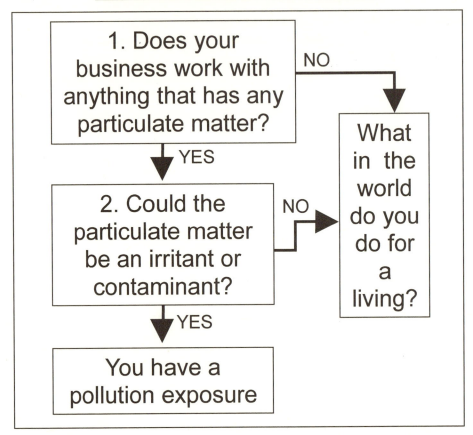

In the flowchart, I am trying to be humorous when I ask, "What in the world do you do for a living?" But I want to challenge you to think of any business that does not have anything to do with any particulate matter. Even if I just write books all day, I am going to use some sort of computer. I may print out some rough drafts that will produce the tangible risk exposures of ink and paper. Even if I do not print out rough drafts, I will still see them on the screen of glass, plastic, and circuits that I call my monitor. I hear that these electronic devices may contain heavy metals that can contaminate soil. Even if I think I am reducing my pollution exposure by using pencil and paper instead of a computer, my pencils and paper still have particulate matter. I do not know how I can write a book without using something that is a solid, liquid, or gas. If you are a business with a CGL Policy, I am going to say that you are dealing with something that is a solid, liquid, or gas.

Question two in my pollution analysis asks whether this thing that you have could be an irritant or a contaminant. To help you think of irritants and contaminants, I think it is helpful to think of weeds. I define something as a weed when it is a perfectly good plant that happens to be where you do not want it. For example, my mother lived in Sweden for a year. In the spring—which I think was the first week of July that year—she was walking with a Swedish friend as they came upon a hillside full of yellow flowers. Upon closer inspection, my mom realized that the flowers that created this beautiful yellow hillside were all dandelions. Their conversation went something like this:

Mom: In the U.S.A. we pull out those flowers.
Swede: Why would you pull out a perfectly good flower?
Mom: We consider them weeds and pull them out of our lawns.
Swede: Why?
Mom: I don't know.

In addition to making a beautiful yellow hillside, it turns out that dandelions are also edible and their leaves are sometimes used in salads. However, if you are in the U.S.A. and have neighbors who care about their uniformly green lawns—and if you want to maintain a positive relationship with your neighbors—I do not recommend that you cultivate dandelions.

The yellow flowers transform into delicate white globes of seeds. Children like to pick these, make a wish, and then blow into the dandelion, exploding the globe and scattering the seeds. As adults, you may need to find other ways to make your wishes come true, because if you cultivate dandelions and think it is fun to scatter their seeds in the wind, your neighbors may just wish that you were no longer their neighbor.

What do dandelions have to do with pollution? I will ask my first pollution question: Are dandelions a solid, liquid, or gas? Yes. Here is my second question: Are they an irritant or a contaminant? Before you answer, imagine you have a farm where you grow sod for sports fields. I buy the farm upwind from you and decide to grow dandelions. I think you are going to answer, yes, dandelions could be a contaminant.

In September 2013, a pipeline burst dumping 233,000 gallons into Honolulu Harbor. The spill killed more than 20,000 fish. Pictures of dying fish filled the news. The pipeline that burst was not carrying oil. The pipeline was carrying molasses from a processing plant on the island of Oahu to cargo ships bound for California.

The cleanup was costly. In addition to the cleanup costs, the pipeline company agreed to pay a total penalty of $1 million along with pleading guilty to two counts of violating the Rivers and Harbors Act of 1899. I share this because we may not generally think of molasses as a pollutant, but molasses is a solid, liquid, or gas. If you could ask the fish—or the U.S. Attorney in Hawaii—I think you would also agree that molasses is an irritant or contaminant.

At this point, you should realize that just about every business has a pollution exposure and that the CGL Policy excludes coverage for pollution. Fortunately, the CGL Policy provides some exceptions to the CGL Policy's pollution exclusion.

Exceptions to the Pollution Exclusion:

Exception 1: Bodily Injury from Heating and Air Conditioning Systems (CG 00 01 04 13 ISO properties, Inc., 2012, Page 3; Appendix Page 248).
The CGL Policy WILL cover bodily injury that happens within a building when it is caused by smoke or fumes produced or originating from equipment used to heat, cool, or dehumidify a building. This may seem like an obvious thing for a CGL Policy to cover, but remember that pollution includes gaseous irritants like smoke and vapor. Imagine that you are in

a building where something is going wrong with the heating or air conditioning. Some sort of smoke or gas is coming into your room. Your throat is starting to hurt. Your eyes are starting to water. Maybe you have to go to the hospital.

You might not have thought about it this way, but you were experiencing a pollution exposure. If this pollution exposure occurred to a guest at a hotel, the hotel guest might ask the hotel to pay for the medical bills and hospital bills. The guest experienced a pollution exposure. The CGL Policy starts by excluding all pollution coverage, but then adds coverage back for bodily injury from heating and air conditioning systems. Therefore, the guest could file a claim against the CGL Policy of the hotel, and it should not be excluded because of this exception to the pollution exclusion.

Exception 2: You are a contractor and the discharge, dispersal, seepage, migration, release or escape of pollutants happens at your Additional Insured's premises (CG 00 01 04 13 ISO properties, Inc., 2012, Page 3; Appendix Page 249).

The second exception to the pollution exclusion provides coverage for pollution if the insured is a contractor and the pollution takes place at a premises where the contractor is working for someone who was named as an Additional Insured for ongoing operations on the contractor's CGL Policy. This exception to the pollution exclusion goes on to emphasize that the occurrence must not take place at a location that the named insured ever owned, occupied, rented, or loaned to any insured (other than the additional insured).

This exception is seeking to ensure that coverage is limited to bodily injury and property damage to *others*. If this exception provided coverage back to property that the named insured owned, then it would not be providing coverage to *others*. It would be providing coverage for the insured. However, if a contractor is working at a separate location, for a separate individual or entity that is named as an Additional Insured, then that Additional Insured will have coverage for bodily injury or property damage for which the named insured is liable, even if it involves something of a particulate matter that is an irritant or contaminant.

For example, imagine that you hire me to remodel your house. You require that I name you as an Additional Insured using Additional Insured Endorsement CG 20 10 04 13 Additional Insured—Owners, Lessees or Contractors— Scheduled Person or Organization. This endorsement adds you as an insured on my insurance policy with regard to my ongoing operations. (For more information on Additional Insured Endorsements, read *Understanding Named, Automatic, and Additional Insureds in the CGL Policy* by Dwight M. Kealy; available at www.GoGetCE.com).

In the Charlie Brown cartoons by Charles M. Schulz, there was a character named Pig Pen who always had a cloud of dust surrounding him. Imagine that this is how I look as the contractor working on your house. The only difference is that the cloud that follows me is full of saw dust, drywall, bits of your old granite countertops, and 1950's insulation. This cloud drifts over to your neighbor's house. Your neighbor gets sick, goes to the hospital, and then demands that you pay for the medical bills.

In response, you turn to my CGL Policy, which is kind of your CGL Policy because you are named as an additional insured with regard to my ongoing operations. The CGL Policy starts by excluding all pollution exposure and defines pollution broadly as any liquid, solid, or gas that is an irritant or contaminant. The cloud that I created contained particulate matter, and clearly your neighbor—and your neighbor's physicians—viewed this cloud as an irritant. Therefore, the cloud that I created would be excluded from the CGL Policy if it were not for the exception that provides coverage for the **discharge, dispersal, seepage, migration, release or escape of pollutants caused by a contractor at an Additional Insured's premises.** Since your neighbor's pollution exposure falls within this exception to the pollution exclusion, there could be coverage under my CGL Policy.

Exception 3: Escape of Fuels from "Mobile Equipment"

The CGL Policy's pollution exclusion contains an exception that will provide coverage for pollution exposures caused by the escape of fuels from "mobile equipment". To understand the exception, we need a little background on how the CGL Policy handles autos and "mobile equipment". The CGL Policy excludes liability exposures caused by autos. It covers liability exposures caused by "mobile equipment".

What is the difference between an auto and mobile equipment? An auto is a land motor vehicle designed to be operated on public roads that is subject to state financial responsibility laws. Being "subject to state financial responsibility laws" usually means that it has a license plate and a current sticker from the state's department of motor vehicles. Mobile equipment, on the other hand, includes vehicles like fork lifts and tractors that are not designed for public roads, stay on or adjacent to the insured's property, and are not subject to state financial responsibility laws.

The pollution exception for the **Escape of Fuels from "Mobile Equipment"** provides coverage for the escape of fuels, lubricants or other operating fluids which are needed for the functions necessary for the operation of the mobile equipment and escape from the part of the equipment designed to hold, store, or receive them (CG 00 01 04 13 ISO properties, Inc., 2012, Page 3; Appendix Page 249). For example, imagine that a contractor takes a barrel of oil to a jobsite. The barrel leaks, contaminating the ground. Oil meets the definition of a pollutant because it is a solid, liquid, or gas...and it is a contaminant. Therefore, the pollution exclusion excludes property damage caused by oil. However, instead of a barrel that leaked oil at a jobsite, imagine that oil leaked from a tractor's engine at a jobsite. In this case, the oil leaked from "the part of the equipment designed to hold" the oil, and the oil was a fluid "necessary for the operation of the mobile equipment." It was not just oil leaking from a barrel that the contractor took to the jobsite. Since this was pollution escaping from the part of "mobile equipment" designed to hold the oil and necessary for the mobile equipment's functions, this exception to the pollution exclusion applies. Therefore, there would be coverage for the exposure under the CGL Policy.

Exception 4: That New Carpet Smell
The fourth exception is for bodily injury or property damage within a building caused by the release of "gases, fumes, or vapors from materials brought into that building in connection with operations being performed by the named insured or contractor working for the named insured" (*ibid).* For example, imagine that you had a contractor come to your building yesterday and the contractor installed new carpet. It looks great. It has that great new carpet smell. However, as the day goes on, some of your co-workers have headaches. Some go to the hospital. You are not feeling well either. It is determined that the "new carpet smell" was actually toxic fumes coming from the new carpet. This is a pollution exposure because it a contaminant or an irritant of a particulate matter (fumes). This would be excluded by the CGL Policy except for this exception that brings back coverage for the release of "gases, fumes, or vapors from materials brought into a building in connection with operations being performed by the named insured or contractor working for the named insured" (*ibid.*). Since the bodily injury caused by the new carpet smell fits within this pollution exception, there would be coverage for the exposure under the CGL Policy.

Exception 5: Hostile Fire
The standard CGL Policy has an exception to the pollution exclusion that will provide coverage for pollution resulting from a hostile fire. I think it helps to think of a hostile fire as a perfectly good fire where you do not want it. A fire in a fireplace is not a hostile fire. A controlled burn that is in the area where it is intended to burn, is not a hostile fire. A hostile fire is a fire that has escaped its intended boundaries, or where no fire was ever intended.

For example, imagine that I am doing some work at a hotel by an interstate highway. There is a highway off-ramp by the hotel and a number of restaurants and small businesses. It turns out that I am not very good at doing the work at the hotel, and somehow I negligently start a fire. Damage to the hotel would be covered as property damage to others under the CGL Policy. However, I have another problem: smoke. Smoke is stopping traffic on the interstate highway. Across the street, a restaurant and another hotel have to shut down because of all of the smoke. The highway patrol close the highway exit so that no cars can enter or leave the highway. In addition to the cost to rebuild the hotel from the fire that I caused, a number of businesses want me to reimburse them for a day of lost business because I caused the fire, that caused the smoke, that shut down their businesses.

The pollution exclusion starts by removing any coverage for property damage arising out of pollution. Pollution includes smoke. This exception to the pollution exclusion provides coverage if there was property damage caused by a hostile fire. However, this situation leads to another question involving the businesses that suffered a loss of business when the police closed the highway exits: did the businesses suffer property damage? To answer this, we need to recall that the definition of property damage includes the "loss of use of tangible property that is not physically injured" (CG 00 01 04 13 ISO Properties, Inc., 2012. Page 15; Appendix Page 272).

In this situation, the other businesses were not physically injured, but there was a loss of use that would count as property damage. Therefore, we have property damage caused by a pollutant. Pollution would be excluded except that there is an exception for pollution arising out of a hostile fire. The CGL Policy should provide coverage for both the businesses that suffered direct physical damage as well as those businesses that suffered loss of use as a result of the hostile fire.

g. Aircraft, Auto, or Watercraft

The standard CGL Policy "excludes bodily injury or property damage arising out the ownership, maintenance, use or entrustment to others of any aircraft, "auto" or watercraft owned, or operated by or rented or loaned to any insured" (CG

00 01 04 13, ISO Properties, Inc., 2012, Page 4; <u>Appendix Page 250</u>). The exclusion applies even if the claim against the insured is for negligence in the supervision, hiring, employment, training, or monitoring of others. What the exclusion is trying to say is that the standard CGL Policy is not intended to cover bodily injury or property damage arising out of aircraft, auto, or watercraft; period. If there are damages to others arising out of an auto accident, you should contact the auto insurance policy. If you try to come back to the CGL Policy and say that the CGL Policy should pay because the insured negligently hired the driver who caused the accident, the CGL Policy will still deny coverage. The starting point for the CGL Policy is that there is no coverage for bodily injury or property damage arising out of aircraft, autos, or watercraft. There are, however, some interesting exceptions.

Exception 1: Watercraft while ashore on premises you own or rent

The aircraft, auto, and watercraft exclusion has an exception that will provide coverage for bodily injury or property damage to others caused by watercraft on the premises the insured owns or rents. This exception suggests that although the policy may not want to have anything to do with whatever liability exposures watercraft may experience at the dock or out on the water, liability exposures on the policyholder's dry land are exposures a CGL Policy will consider. You can think of this exception as simply allowing the slip and fall coverage that you would expect a CGL Policy to cover on the policyholder's premises. Instead of a customer slipping on the floor of a store, this exception contemplates coverage for a customer slipping on a watercraft while it is ashore on the policyholder's premises.

In case you are wondering what kind of liability could arise out of parked watercraft, imagine that you are a child. Adults might view a watercraft ashore as a boat conveniently stored at a business location. For children, this is not an owner avoiding dock fees. This watercraft is a playground pirate ship waiting for sword fights, mast swinging, and maybe even a walk out on the plank. We have some liability exposures.

If a bunch of neighbor children walk on to your property and decide to re-enact a pirate scene on your parked boat, there is a possibility that there could be bodily injury to the child forced to walk the plank. There is also the possibility that the boat could cause property damage to others when the children realize that they can push your boat down the hill in your parking lot using the boat's unguided trailer wheels. If the rolling boat ends up damaging customer cars that are parked on your premises, this could be property damage to others by the watercraft that was once ashore peacefully on your premises.

The insurance policy has the aircraft, auto, and watercraft exclusion so that it will not be involved with liability from vehicles that move in air, land, or sky. However, the CGL Policy is designed to cover bodily injury or property damage to others that takes place on the insured's premises. This exception will allow for coverage *even* if it is the result of a watercraft ashore on the policyholder's premises.

Exception 2: Non-owned watercraft less than 26 feet long not used to carry persons or property for a charge.

This exception is giving a little coverage back for liability you might encounter while actually traveling on the water. The exception only applies to boats under 26 feet that are not being used to carry persons or property for a charge. For example, San Diego Harbor has a number of places where you can rent a boat and take it out on the harbor. As an office team-building exercise, you could give your driver's license and credit card to a boat rental facility, tell them that you know how to sail, and then sail away with a 25 foot sailboat with a handful of your favorite (or least favorite) co-workers. While out on the water, you may realize something that you should have realized back at the dock: You don't know how to sail. You aim for a dock connected to a restaurant where people can sit and wave to the passing boats. The casual single-handed wave of the customers turns into the double-handed waves of panic as they realize that you are about to crash into the restaurant. You and your co-workers exit the boat in your company shirts to evaluate the damage to the restaurant. The restaurant owners notice your company shirts and sends your company a bill to repair the restaurant.

Since the boat was under 26 feet and you were not transporting people or cargo for a fee, there would be coverage under the CGL Policy. You should note that there would not be coverage for the boat itself because the boat was in your care, custody, or control (see exclusion j). Remember, the CGL Policy is a *liability* policy that is providing bodily injury and property damage to *others*. It is not designed to provide coverage for you, your injured employees, or anything in your care, custody, or control. This means that if you destroyed the 25 foot sailboat, you may have to buy a new sailboat to reimburse the sailboat rental company.

However, there would be coverage for the bodily injury or property damage that you caused to *others* when you ran the boat into the dock and restaurant. This exception to the watercraft exclusion provides bodily injury or property damage *to others* caused by non-owned watercraft that are less than 26 feet long that are not used to carry persons or property for a charge.

Exception 3: Parking an auto on or next to premises you own or rent.

This exception can appear to give some coverage for valet parking. So long as you do not want coverage for the vehicle you are parking, this could be true. The standard wording provides that the auto exclusion does not apply to "parking an 'auto' on, or on the ways next to, premises you own or rent, provided the 'auto' is not owned by or rented or loaned to you or the insure" (CG 00 01 04 13, ISO Properties, Inc., 2012, Page 4; Appendix Page 251).

The first thing to realize is that this coverage is *not* for vehicles that the named *insured* owns, rents, or borrows. This

---

Coverage A, Exclusions

is for bodily injury or property damage to others caused by a vehicle the insured is parking.

The second thing to understand is that this is for parking an auto on or next to the premises of a business. If someone is in the auto business and driving cars around and testing them, this does not provide the coverage the business needs.

The third thing to note about this exception is that because of Exclusion j. there is no coverage for "Personal property in the care, custody, or control of the insured" (CG 00 01 04 13, Insurance Services Office, 2012, Page 5; Appendix Page 252). This applies to cars that are being parked because they are personal property in the care of the insured.

Together these three things mean that if you are parking cars for your company's office party and you park the visitors' cars on or next to your office premises, you should have coverage if you cause bodily injury or property damage to others. However, there will be no coverage for the car that you are driving because there is no coverage for the car that is in your care, custody, or control.

For example, imagine that you own a business and you are going to have an office Christmas party. I am your employee. Parking is available in the back of your building, but you want people to come to the well-decorated grand entrance in the front of your building. You instruct everyone to come to the front of your building, get out of their cars, and give their keys to me. I will drive their cars around to the back parking lot for the duration of the party. When people are ready to leave, they will tell me which car is their car. I will then run behind the building, jump in their car, and drive it around to the front for them. I am essentially a valet parker for the night.

The parking lot in the back gets full, and so I decide to park cars on the street in front of your building. I am parking a beautiful, $100,000 vehicle. I get in an accident with another vehicle. I cause $100,000 in bodily injury and property damage to the other car and its occupants. The vehicle I am driving is completely totaled. This exception will provide coverage for the $100,000 of bodily injury and property damage to the vehicle I was *not* driving. However, this exception will not provide coverage for the $100,000 in damage to the vehicle I was parking because the vehicle I was parking was in my care, custody, or control, and property in an insured's care, custody, or control is excluded.

Exception 4: Liability under an "insured contract" for the ownership, maintenance or use of aircraft or watercraft.

The CGL aircraft, auto, and watercraft exclusion provides an exception that will provide coverage for liability arising under an "insured contract" for the ownership, maintenance or use of aircraft or watercraft (CG 00 01 04 13, ISO Properties, Inc., 2012, Page 4; Appendix Page 251). We discussed the definition of an "insured contract" under exclusion b. Contractual Liability. You may recall that Contractual Liability is excluded unless liability arises out of an "insured contract", and that an "insured contract" is defined as six specific types of contracts. As an example, let us imagine the insured entered an "insured contract" by agreeing to assume the tort liability of another party. The most common tort liability that would be assumed for insurance purposes would be the tort of negligence. When would someone assume tort liability of someone else in connection with the use of aircraft or watercraft?

Imagine a realtor specializes in selling waterfront properties. All of the properties that the realtor sells have docks. The realtor contracts with a boat operator to take a group of potential buyers to see a bunch of nice homes that the realtor will access by dock. The boat operator requires that the realtor sign a document that will hold the boat owner harmless for any damage the boat might cause while the realtor is out showing homes to clients. When approaching the nicest, most expensive dock, the engine stops and the boat operator is unable to stop the boat from continuing to—and through—the nicest dock on the water. The boat operator gets sued and then turns the lawsuit over to the realtor to defend, and indemnify the boat operator according to the terms of their contract. This contract would be an "insured contract" because the realtor assumed the tort liability of another party. The CGL Policy starts by excluding any liability for autos, aircraft, or watercraft, but provides this exception to provide coverage for liability under an "insured contract" for the ownership, maintenance or use of aircraft or watercraft. Here, since there was an "insured contract" for the ownership, maintenance, or use of watercraft, there should be coverage from the CGL Policy to defend and indemnify the boat operator according to the terms of the realtor's CGL policy.

Exception 5: Mobile Equipment

The aircraft, auto, and watercraft exclusion is designed to make it clear that the CGL Policy is *not* the policy you should look to for bodily injury or property damage arising out of the use of aircraft, autos, and watercraft. However, this exception makes it clear that the CGL Policy *is* the policy you should look to for bodily injury or property damage to others arising out of the use of mobile equipment.

For example, imagine that a large sports utility vehicle (SUV) is speeding through an alley behind your business. Your employee is driving a forklift, unloading a delivery truck in the alley. The forklift is raised to a height of exactly six feet. The SUV speeds through the alley and does not see the forklift. The height of the SUV *was* a few inches over six feet. Yes, I said that the SUV *was* a few inches over six feet. Now the height of the SUV and the height of the raised forklift are both exactly six feet high. When the SUV sped under the forklift, the forklift peeled back the top of the SUV like you might open a can of sardines. The good news is that everyone is okay. The bad news is that when you drive quickly under a metal forklift that is a few inches shorter than the height of your SUV, you risk having the forklift rip off the top few inches of your SUV.

In such a case, the claim dispute would be between the auto insurance policy for the SUV and the CGL Policy of the company using the forklift. The auto insurance policy would represent the SUV because the SUV is an auto. The CGL Policy would represent the interest of the company using the forklift because the forklift is mobile equipment, and the CGL

Policy is designed to provide coverage for bodily injury or property damage arising out of the operation of mobile equipment. The aircraft, auto, and watercraft exclusion makes it clear that the CGL Policy is not designed to pay for bodily injury or property damage arising out of the ownership or use of aircraft, auto, and watercraft. The mobile equipment exception to the exclusion makes it clear that the CGL Policy is designed to pay for bodily injury or property damage arising out of the ownership or use of mobile equipment.

We should note that this exception does not provide coverage for the mobile equipment. This exception allows coverage for bodily injury or property damage to *others* caused by mobile equipment. If the forklift mentioned above was damaged in the accident with the SUV, there would be no coverage for the forklift under the CGL Policy. The forklift was in the care, custody, or control of the business owner. This is excluded. What is covered, however, is bodily injury or property damage to others caused by the mobile equipment.

Is it an Auto or Is it Mobile Equipment?

If the CGL Policy provides coverage for bodily injury or property damage to others arising out of mobile equipment, but excludes this coverage for autos, it is important to know the difference between an "auto" and "mobile equipment". Once when I was showing slides illustrating the difference between mobile equipment and autos for an insurance class, a student remarked, "You can tell the difference between autos and mobile equipment because mobile equipment is yellow and autos are different colors." The student was joking, but it is a simple way to introduce the distinction between autos and mobile equipment. The mobile equipment pictures that I was showing were of yellow construction vehicles: backhoes, tractors, etc. The autos were all different colors. John Deere's green tractors are a reminder that not all mobile equipment is yellow, but it is an entertaining place to start. When you think of mobile equipment, think of vehicles that are principally used off road or equipment used for making roads.

---

h. Mobile Equipment

I just explained that Mobile Equipment is covered under the CGL Policy, and that "autos" are not. Now I introduce a standard CGL Policy exclusion for "Mobile Equipment." What does this mean? When you read this exclusion, you find that it excludes mobile equipment in only two situations:

1) The transportation of "mobile equipment" by an auto, and
2) The use of "mobile equipment" in, or while in practice for, any prearranged racing, speed, demolition, or stunting activity (CG 00 01 04 13, Insurance Services Office, Inc., 2012, Page 4; Appendix Page 251).

Exclusion 1: The transportation of "mobile equipment" by an auto.

The reason that the transportation of mobile equipment by an auto is excluded is because this coverage would come under the auto policy. For example, I saw a photo of a commercial flatbed truck carrying a tractor. The tractor that was being carried had a large hydraulic bucket that could be raised and lowered. The photo was memorable because it pointed out a good rule of thumb for anyone who might consider towing or carrying large mobile equipment. The rule is this: **If you are going to tow large tractors under low bridges, you should make sure that the tractor's arms and buckets are as low as possible before going under the bridges.** The operators in the photo that I saw had forgotten to lower the bucket. It looked like the vehicles were moving at about 60 miles per hour when the high tractor bucket hit the low bridge. The tractor bucket cut through about half of the bridge before coming to its final resting place. The cost to repair the bridge looked like it would be significant. Even though the damage to the bridge was caused by mobile equipment and property damage caused by mobile equipment is normally covered under the CGL Policy, this exclusion clarifies that bodily injury or property damage is excluded when caused by mobile equipment while it is being towed or carried by an auto.

In contrast, let us imagine that the damage to the bridge was caused by mobile equipment in a different way. Instead of mobile equipment being carried or towed by an auto, imagine that the tractor was working near the bridge and the driver accidently ran the mobile equipment into the bridge, causing damage to the bridge. This damage *would* be covered under the CGL Policy because it was property damage to others caused by the policyholder's mobile equipment. This exclusion only applies when the mobile equipment is being towed or carried by an auto. When the mobile equipment that was being carried by an auto sliced through half of the bridge, there was no coverage from the CGL Policy because the CGL Policy specifically excludes bodily injury or property damage caused by mobile equipment when it is being carried or towed by an auto.

Exclusion 2: The use of "mobile equipment" in, or while in practice for, any prearranged racing, speed, demolition, or stunting activity.

The next exclusion for mobile equipment might seem like one that may not be a problem for most businesses, but they still need to be aware of it. It is the exclusion of mobile equipment while racing. Preparing for a race, as well as any demolition and stunting activities, are also excluded. What I want you to consider is the fun team-building exercises a business might host. Maybe the business shuts down the office early one day, has a barbeque, and holds a contest to see who can move a pallet of goods the fastest with a forklift. It sounds like a fun way to practice, refine, and show off one's skills. However, if it looks like a prearranged racing or speed activity, any bodily injury or property damage to others as a result of the exercise would be excluded.

i. War

Standard insurance policies of all kinds exclude war. I think the main reason is because war is unpredictable. Insurance companies have actuaries who look at statistical data to calculate the risk of having to pay claims. With this, they have in mind the understanding that people, and their governments, will do what they can to avoid claims and prevent losses. But, what if the saying "All is fair in love and war" is true? How do you anticipate the costs that may be associated with war? What kind of premiums would an insurance company have to collect to have the capital sufficient to rebuild and pay for the loss of use after General Sherman's march toward Georgia in the U.S. Civil war, or to rebuild Pearl Harbor or Hiroshima after the attacks in World War II? Besides the great extent of damage, there is also the possibility that the government may make a strategic decision to withdraw support to one area in exchange for pursuing a course of action elsewhere. These sorts of strategic decisions are outside of the scope of what the standard CGL Policy actuaries are evaluating. The CGL Policy makes it explicit that there is no coverage for "bodily injury or property damage, however caused, arising, directly or indirectly out of War...warlike action...or [any] insurrection, rebellion, [or] revolution" (CG 00 01 04 13, ISO Properties, Inc., 2012, Page 4; Appendix Page 251).

Does the exclusion for war exclude bodily injury and property damage caused by riots or terrorism? Coverage for certain acts of terrorism can be purchased (or declined) separately, but bodily injury or property damage caused by domestic riots is *not* removed by the war exclusion. The discussion on insurance coverage for damages caused by domestic riots is usually discussed under a property policy where property owners are seeking coverage for property that may be damaged in a riot. Remember, in the CGL Policy, coverage is offered where the insured is legally obligated to pay for damage to the *property of others*. There is no coverage to the property of the insured in the CGL Policy. Furthermore, coverage is only triggered if the "insured becomes legally obligated to pay...damages because of bodily injury or property damage" (CG 00 01 04 13, ISO Properties, Inc., 2012, Page 1; Appendix Page 245).

How would a policyholder become legally obligated to pay damages arising out of a domestic riot? If I am a mason who is building a brick wall and rioters take my bricks to throw at windows, am I legally obligated to pay for the broken windows? As discussed under negligence (<u>page 22ff</u>), one can be found liable for the tort of negligence if the person had a duty to act like a reasonable person, breached the duty to act like a reasonable person, and this breach caused damages.

It would be difficult to find that a mason had a duty to the owner of the damaged building because the mason should only have a duty to act reasonably toward foreseeable plaintiffs within the zone of danger. The zone of danger for bricks would be where bricks could fall—not where they can be carried or thrown by strangers.

Even if a judge determines that the mason did have a duty to the owner of the building that was damaged by the mason's bricks, we still need to ask if the mason acted reasonably. If the mason lined up the bricks and handed them out to passing rioters like children handing out lemonade at a lemonade stand, then yes, I would say that the mason failed to act like a reasonable mason. However, if the bricks were reasonably protected and the rioters stole them, then it would be difficult to say that the mason failed to act reasonably. If the mason did not fail to act reasonably, then the mason did not breach the duty to act like a reasonable person, and the mason would not be found liable for negligence.

Even if the mason did not act reasonably in keeping rioters from using the mason's bricks, the mason would still only be liable if the mason was the actual and proximate cause of someone else's property damage. The actual cause is easy to satisfy because you can say that *but for* the mason bringing bricks into the area, the brick would not have been thrown through the window. That is sufficient to show actual causation.

However, proximate cause deals with foreseeability. Can you say that it is foreseeable that neighboring properties will be damaged by the mason's bricks when a mason brings bricks to a job site to build a wall and a riot breaks out, rioters steal the mason's bricks, and use the bricks to damage property? The foreseeable dangers from bricks are that they could fall from the wall and hurt someone. Their zone of danger is fairly small. It is not foreseeable that they would be stolen, removed from their location, and then be used as a projectile to cause property damage to others.

Finally, the rioters' criminal act of stealing and damaging property could be sufficient to show that the mason bringing the bricks to the jobsite was *not* the proximate cause of the damage. Whenever there is an intervening criminal act that causes the damages, courts are unlikely to find that there was proximate cause sufficient to show that the defendant is liable for the damages. Even if the mason behaved unreasonably, there was an intervening criminal act by another party that was intentional, willful, reckless, malicious, wanton, or depraved. These criminal acts will break the causal connection between the possibly negligent act of the mason and the property damage caused by the rioters. If the mason is not the proximate cause of the damages, then the mason will not be found liable for the tort of negligence.

War is excluded in the CGL Policy. Bodily Injury or Property damage caused by riots is not excluded by the CGL Policy, but it would be unlikely that a policyholder would be found liable for a riot in which the insurance company would be obligated to pay damages.

There are at least two more coverage reasons why rioting would probably not be covered under Coverage A of the CGL Policy: 1) There is no coverage if there is no occurrence. An occurrence is an accident. Rioting does not sound like an accident. 2) Exclusion a. eliminated coverage for expected or intended injury. If an insured is the actual and proximate cause of damage caused by rioting, it seems that the behavior would be the result of an act where the insured expected or intended injury. If the damage was the result of the insured expecting or intending injury, there is no coverage).

j. Damage to Property

Exclusion j. Damage to Property makes it clear that the CGL Policy is designed to cover bodily injury and property damage *to others*. It is not designed to cover bodily injury and property damage to the named insured. Exclusion j. Damage to Property clarifies this in two ways: 1) Excluding property that the named insured owns, rents, or occupies, and 2) Excluding that Particular Part of Real Property.

Property Damage Exclusion 1: Property that the Named Insured Owns, Rents, or Occupies

Property loaned to the insured or in the named insured's care, custody or control is also excluded. If you want coverage for your property, then you need to get a property policy that would provide coverage for your property. If you want coverage for your cargo or inventory or tools, you are going to need the appropriate property, cargo, or inland marine coverage to cover these items of property.

For example, if you are an insured and you have a stack of vases that fall and injure a customer, the CGL Policy would provide coverage for the bodily injury to the customer. However, the CGL Policy does not provide coverage for the vases that broke when they crashed to the ground. These vases would be your property. The CGL Policy is not designed to provide coverage for *your* property. It is designed to cover property damage to others caused by you.

Exception: Damage to Premises Rented to You

The CGL Policy makes an exception to the Property Damage exclusion for **"Damage to Premises Rented to You."** This is a separate, often reduced, limit that provides limited coverage for:

"...'property damage' to any one premises, while rented to [the insured], or in the case of damage by fire, while rented to [the insured] or temporarily occupied by [the insured] with permission of the owner" (CG 00 01 04 13, Insurance Services Office, 2012).

While a standard CGL occurrence limit might be $1 Million, the reduced "Damage to Premises Rented to You" limit is often only $100,000 or $50,000. Notice that the limit does not say that it will pay for the insured's personal property, inventory, or furniture. It is only paying for damage to any one premises while rented to the insured. The individual or entity that benefits from this coverage is not the insured, but the owner of the premises. However, this limit is necessary because the exclusion begins by stating that there is no coverage for damage to property that the insured owns, rents, or occupies. A landlord might require some coverage for the premises being rented to the insured. The "Damage to Premises Rented to You" exception provides limited coverage for damage to property rented to the insured.

Property Damage Exclusion 2: That Particular Part of Real Property

The Property Damage Exclusion excludes:

1) "that particular part of real property on which you or any contractors or subcontractors working directly or indirectly on your behalf are performing operations" and
2) "that particular part of any property that must be restored, repaired or replaced because 'your work' was incorrectly performed on it."

(CG 00 01 04 13, Insurance Services Office, Inc., 2012, Page 5; Appendix Page 252).

1) "That particular part of real property on which you or any contractors or subcontractors working directly or indirectly on your behalf are performing operations."

To explain "that particular part of real property," imagine that you hire me to change out the light switch in your office. The cost for the switch is $4.95. It turns out that I do not do a very good job changing the light switch. Somehow the wires get crossed, and my work ends up starting a fire that causes $500,000 in damage to your building. You contact my CGL Policy, and they say that they will pay for $500,000 minus $4.95. Why did they subtract $4.95? They subtracted $4.95 because of the exclusion for the particular part of property on which I was performing operations. The particular part of property on which I was performing operations was that $4.95 switch that caused the fire.

You may not be upset about not having coverage for the $4.95 switch after my insurance policy paid you $499,995.05, but what if instead of me installing a light switch, I installed your roof. The roof costs $500,000. The building costs $3 Million. If just the roof collapses and there is no damage to the building, then the insurance company would exclude coverage for the roof because that was the particular part of property on which I was doing work. If, on the other hand, the roof collapsed, causing the whole building to be destroyed, then the insurance company should pay for the $3 Million (subject to policy limits) to rebuild the building minus the $500,000 to rebuild the particular part of property—the roof—on which I was doing work. If the only damage is to the particular part of real property on which I was doing work, there will be no coverage from the insurance company.

2) "That particular part of any property that must be restored, repaired or replaced because 'your work' was incorrectly performed on it."

Imagine that you hire a contractor to make a custom door for your office. You want the door to be very smooth. In an effort to make the door extra smooth, the contractor keeps sanding the door until the door is so thin that the contractor's sander breaks a hole through the door. The door now needs to be repaired or replaced.

This exclusion removes any coverage for that particular part of property that must be restored, repaired or replaced because of the insured's incorrect work on it. This means that the policy will not fix or replace the door broken by the contractor's work. This property damage exclusion is often cited along with the CGL Policy's exclusions for k. Damage to Your Product, and l. Damage to Your Work.

k. Damage to Your Product, and

l. Damage to Your Work

Coverage A of the CGL Policy excludes damage to the insured's product and the insured's work. I think the best way to think about the exclusions for "Your Product", "Your Work", and exclusion's j.'s "particular part of property on which the insured is working", is to think about them together in the context of a contractor building a wall. Many contractors may be surprised to find that the walls they build are not covered by the CGL Policy the way they may think they are. This is because although the CGL Policy may cover bodily injury or property damage *to others resulting from* your product or work, the policy specifically excludes damage to your property, product, or work.

If the contractor's property, product, and work are excluded, what does the CGL Policy cover for contractors?
Broadly speaking, the CGL Policy is designed to cover bodily injury, property damage, or personal and advertising injury *to others.* If you build a wall and it falls on someone else's car, that would be property damage to others. Similarly, if the wall falls and injures a stranger walking down the street, that would be bodily injury to others. Both of these should be covered under the CGL Policy. However, if your wall simply falls and the only damage is to the wall itself, then there is no property damage or bodily injury to others. You could argue that the person who hired you to build the wall has suffered property damage, but the CGL Policy specifically excludes: j. that particular part of real property on which you or your

subcontractor was performing operations, k. your product, and l. your work.

Resulting Damage

What the CGL Policy is intending to cover is not your defective product or work, but the damage *resulting from* your defective work. Courts call this damage "resulting damage." Courts have held that the CGL Policy coverage applies only to **resulting damage** caused by the defective work of the insured. Coverage does not apply to the cost incurred to repair and replace the contractor's defective work. The risk of replacing or repairing defective materials or poor workmanship has been considered a commercial risk that is not passed onto a liability insurer. *F&H Construction v. ITT Hartford Ins.Co. (2004) 188 Cal.App.4th 364, 372.*

Imagine that a particularly bad painter is hired to paint all of the interior walls in a hotel. When "finished," it looks like the painter used colored pancake batter instead of paint on the walls. Sometimes the paint looks thick and lumpy. Sometimes it looks like it is still wet and running down the walls. Everyone over the age of five years old who sees the walls agrees that the walls need to be repainted. The cost to repaint all of the walls is $100,000.

The painter also regularly spilled paint, causing $100,000 in damage to the carpets. Combining the cost to repaint and clean up the carpets, the hotel wants $200,000 for its damages. As a way to get the $200,000, the hotel files a claim against the painter's CGL Policy. There should be coverage for the $100,000 in damage to the carpets because this damage resulted from the contractor's work on the walls. (I am assuming that the contractor was not intentionally painting the carpet). However, the $100,000 in damage to the walls will be excluded as the contractor's product, work, or that particular part of property on which the contractor was performing operations.

Contractors can feel confident that the CGL Policy provides coverage for bodily injury or property damage to others *resulting from* the contractor's completed operations. The CGL

---

116   Coverage A, Exclusions

Policy even has a designated Products and Completed Operations Limit for these kinds of occurrences. The contractor—and insurance professionals—just need to understand that: 1) The limit does not remove the exclusions for the insured's product or work, and 2) The limit does not change that the policy responds to *occurrences* that occur during a policy period—not *work* that takes place during a policy period.

m. Damage to Impaired Property or Property Not Physically Injured

The standard CGL Policy has an exclusion for 1) Damage to Impaired Property or 2) Property Not Physically Injured.

1) Damage to Impaired Property

The CGL Policy defines "impaired property" as "tangible property, other than 'your product' or 'your work', that cannot be used or is less useful because it incorporates 'your product' or 'your work' that is known or thought to be defective, deficient, inadequate or dangerous" (CG 00 01 04 13 ISO Properties, Inc., 2012, Page 13; Appendix Page 268). You can think about impaired property like a small piece that goes inside a cell phone. If one piece in that phone does not work, the whole phone may not work.

Let us imagine that I am the manufacturer of one small piece in a customer's cell phone. It turns out that after 100 days, my piece stops working. When my piece stops working, the customer's phone stops working. The customer wants the phone repaired or replaced. But there is a problem from an insurance perspective. Is anything wrong with the customer's phone? I know it does not work, but is there any bodily injury or property damage? No, it sounds like the phone is a perfectly good piece of metal, glass, and plastic. It could be a great paperweight or look perfect in an art museum someday. It just does not work as a phone. It is a product that does not work because it incorporates an insured's defective product. By definition, this is "impaired property" and the policy excludes damage to impaired property.

2) Damage to Property that is not Physically injured.

What does the policy intend by excluding damage to property that is not physically injured? I heard of this exclusion being used for a claim involving a tile roof. There was a condominium association along the coast of Southern California that decided to change the roof tiles on all of the condominiums. Sometimes a tile roof can look red. Sometimes a tile roof can look more like orange or pink. Evidently, a condo owner came home one evening and looked up to see that the reddish roof that had once beautifully contrasted with the Pacific Ocean, was now a hideous pink roof. He sued the roofing contractor. The roofing contractor turned in the claim to the roofing contractor's CGL Policy. The problem for the roofing contractor was not just that there was no "resultant damage" as discussed under exclusions k and l. Here, there was no damage at all. It was a perfectly good pink tile roof. The roof was "property [that was] not physically injured", and the CGL Policy specifically excludes coverage for property that is not physically injured. There was no coverage from the CGL Policy for the roofing contractor who was sued for installing the perfectly good pink roof.

n. Recall Of Products, Work Or Impaired Property

The standard ISO CGL Policy excludes Recall of Products, Work, or Impaired Property. We discussed under exclusion m that "impaired property" would include items like a cell phone that does not function because it incorporates a defective part. We imagined that I was the manufacturer of the small defective part that made the whole phone inoperable.   My part did not start a fire or anything that would cause bodily injury or property damage to others. My part just did not work, and when my part did not work, then the whole cell phone did not work.

The cell phone is considered the "impaired property" because it is tangible property that is not my product, but cannot be used or is less useful because it incorporates my defective, deficient, inadequate, or dangerous part (CG 00 01 04 13 ISO Properties, Inc., 2012, Page 13; Appendix Page

268). If there are a million cell phones (or cars or airplanes!) that may not function properly because of my defective part, you can imagine that we might want to correct the problem as quickly as possible before anyone gets hurt because of the impaired property. With Exclusion n. Recall Of Products, Work Or Impaired Property, the CGL Policy makes it clear that it will not pay for the costs associated with recalling any products, work, or impaired property that may need to be recalled because of a "known or suspected defect, deficiency, inadequacy or dangerous condition in it" (CG 00 01 04 13 ISO Properties, Inc., 2012, Page 5; Appendix Page 253).

CGL Policyholders should be aware of this exclusion because the costs of a product recall can be huge. In 1982, Johnson & Johnson recalled all 31 million bottles of Tylenol that it had manufactured. It did this because someone in Chicago took Tylenol off the shelves, added cyanide to the Tylenol, and then put the bottles back on the shelves. Several people died after taking the Tylenol. The 31 million bottles had a retail value of over $100 million in 1982.

In 2000, the National Highway Traffic Safety Administration noticed a problem with the tire tread on Ford SUVs fitted with Firestone tires. Almost 20 million tires were recalled and one source states that, as a result, Ford ended up losing around $3 billion. Between 2010 and 2015, Toyota had a series of recalls that called back more than 10 million vehicles for flaws that led to unintended acceleration. In addition to the cost to recall the vehicles, Toyota also agreed to a $1.2 billion settlement (http://www.bloomberg.com/news/articles/2014-04-09/toyota-recalls-6-76-million-vehicles-worldwide-including-rav4).

Product recalls are so common that there is now a government website where people can go to see which products are being recalled: www.recalls.gov.

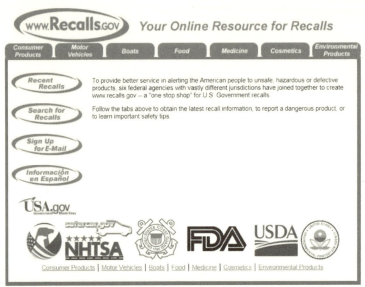

Recalls have affected all kinds of businesses from toy manufacturers to lettuce growers. CGL Policyholders need to understand that the cost of a product recall can be significant and that the standard CGL Policy will not cover the cost of a product recall. The standard CGL Policy specifically excludes coverage for "damages claimed for any loss, cost, or expense incurred by you or others for the loss of use, withdrawal, recall, inspection, repair, replacement, adjustment, removal or disposal of the insured's product, work, or impaired property" (CG 00 01 04 13 ISO Properties, Inc., 2012, Page 5; Appendix Page 253).

o. Personal and Advertising Injury

The standard CGL Policy excludes "Personal and Advertising Injury" under Coverage A of the CGL Policy. For those who realize that the standard CGL Policy has a policy limit for Personal and Advertising Injury, this may seem somewhat confusing. Why would an insurance policy offer a limit for "Personal and Advertising Injury" only to remove any coverage for this in the exclusions? Here we need to remember that we are just talking about the exclusions under Coverage A of the CGL Policy. The reason that the CGL Policy excludes "Personal and Advertising Injury" under coverage A is

---

that the CGL Policy provides coverage for "Personal and Advertising Injury" under Coverage B of the CGL Policy. Coverage A provides for Bodily Injury and Property Damage that is caused by an occurrence during the policy period that is not excluded.

Remember, the importance of studying Coverage A's exclusions is that there is coverage unless coverage is excluded. Coverage B, on the other hand, does *not* provide coverage on a "covered unless excluded" basis. Instead, Coverage B provides coverage for "Personal and Advertising Injury" in only seven specifically defined situations. The seven personal and advertising injuries that are covered under Coverage B are: 1) false arrest, 2) malicious prosecution, 3) wrongful eviction/wrongful entry, 4) slander or libel that disparages a person's goods, products, or services, 5) publication that violates a person's right of privacy, 6) use of another's advertising idea in your advertisement, or 7) infringing upon another's copyright, trade dress or slogan in your advertisement (CG 00 01 04 13 ISO Properties, Inc., 2012, Page 15; Appendix Page 271).

When you have a personal and advertising exposure, you need to realize that Coverage A excludes this exposure. If you need coverage for personal and advertising injury, you will need to see if there is coverage under the specific offenses named in Coverage B of the CGL Policy.

p. Electronic Data

The standard CGL Policy excludes coverage for Electronic Data. This means that there is no coverage for "damages arising out of the loss of, loss of use of, damage to, corruption of, inability to access, or inability to manipulate electronic data" (CG 00 01 04 13 ISO Properties, Inc., 2012, Page 5; Appendix Page 253). As a way to explain the exposure that the CGL Policy is trying to eliminate, I want you to think about a 10-year old laptop computer. When it was purchased 10 years ago, it was not the most expensive laptop. It was just an average laptop at the time. The owner of this laptop is a technology company. Ten years ago they hired three young programmers.

Each programmer works eight hours per day on the same laptop. Worker one works from 8:00 a.m. to 4:00 p.m.. Worker two works from 4:00 p.m. to Midnight. Worker three works from Midnight to 8:00 a.m.. Each programmer gets paid $100,000 per year, so the technology company is paying $300,000 per year to have these three programmers enter information into this laptop. The technology company pays these three programmers to enter data into this same laptop for ten years. After ten years, the technology company has paid $3 million in salaries for the information now stored on this one, ten year old laptop computer.

Now imagine that I am a caterer who is paid to deliver food to these programmers. I spill soup on the laptop. The laptop is destroyed. The technology company wants me to pay $3 million. What should my CGL insurance policy pay? Well, first of all, should my CGL Policy pay at all? I would say, "Yes" because my business operations caused property damage to someone else and this occurred during the policy period. The next question would be: How much should my CGL insurance policy pay?

To calculate the damages to property, we need to have an estimate of the value of a ten year old laptop. I would think $30 would be a generous payment for a ten year old laptop. Even if the insurance company generously pays for a brand new laptop, it could probably do so by adding a zero or two to reach a payment amount of between $300 and $3,000. This should be sufficient to purchase a brand new laptop that is technologically superior to the now destroyed ten year old laptop. A generous payment of $3,000 is a long way from the $3 million in damages that the technology company thinks it suffered as a result of my negligent catering operations. The CGL Policy eliminates any discussions on the value of electronic data by simply excluding electronic data from the policy. The CGL Policy may pay to replace a computer. The CGL Policy may even pay for damages caused by the loss of use of a computer. The CGL Policy will *not* pay for any electronic data.

q. Recording And Distribution of Material in Violation of Statutes.

The government passes laws to provide boundaries between what society considers appropriate and inappropriate conduct. For example, a state might set the maximum legal speed limit at 65 mph. Imagine that you have a fast new car and instead of 65, you decide to drive 165 mph. The good news is that you did not get into an accident. There are no injuries and everyone is fine. Your car is also fine. You are even somewhat exhilarated. The bad news is that the police caught you driving 165 mph. Your car is at the police impound lot, and you are in jail. You are facing a $5,000 fine. For some reason, your first call is to your insurance company and you ask if you can just pay the deductible on your auto insurance policy to get out of jail. Although our focus is on the CGL Policy and not auto insurance, I hope you can see that calling your insurance company to bail you out when you intentionally violate a law, is at best misguided. Laws exist to provide boundaries. When you cross the boundaries, you can face punishment. The financial punishments imposed for violating laws can be severe. The CGL Policy uses its final standard Coverage A exclusion to point to some specific laws for which there will be no coverage.

The specific laws addressed in Exclusion q. Distribution of Material in Violation of Statues are:

1) The Telephone Consumer Protection Act (TCPA), 2) the Controlling the Assault of Non-Solicited Pornography And Marketing Act of 2003 (CAN-SPAM), and 3) The Fair Credit Reporting Act (FCRA) / Fair and Accurate Credit Transactions Act (FACTA).

What was the purpose of the TCPA and CAN-SPAM Acts? Businesses are always looking for efficient ways to market to potential consumers. They found that instead of the expense of mailing letters that consumers may not open, they could send thousands of emails or faxes with the touch of a button. The two acts provide guidelines and prohibitions against these unwanted calls, faxes, and emails. To give you an idea of the extent of the cost that could be involved, in August 2014, the insurance company MetLife agreed to pay $23 Million to settle blast-faxing litigation. Exclusion q. Recording and Distribution of Material or Information in Violation of Law, makes it clear that the standard CGL Policy excludes any bodily injury or property damage arising directly or indirectly out of any action or omission that violates or is alleged to violate the TCPA or CAN-SPAM acts.

To give you an example of the liability that could arise with just one violation of TCPA or CAN-SPAM, below is a letter that a law firm sent to a business for sending the lawyer's client an unsolicited fax. While reading the letter, imagine that you had sent a similar fax to hundreds or thousands of potential clients.

A LAW OFFICE
100 ANYTOWN
ANY CITY, ANY STATE, U.S.A.

TEN (10) DAY NOTICE OF SUIT

Our Law Firm represents [the person who received your fax], who was faxed 1 unsolicited business solicitation by or on behalf of your company. We have enclosed a copy of the facsimile transmission sent to my client on or about the following date: [date] to facsimile number [number of person who received fax].

This letter is to provide formal notice of our client's intent to sue under the *Federal Telephone Consumer Protection Act 47 U.S.C. Section 227 and the FCC regulations promulgated under the statute.* This statute and regulations prohibit fax transmissions without prior express permission. The regulations also require a header on each fax including the date and time the fax was sent as well as identifying the sender and the fax number of the sender. The statute and regulations provide for a minimum $500.00 (FIVE HUNDRED US DOLLARS) statutory recovery for each violation if the above provision or regulations are violated. Our client has calculated 1 violation of the statute. Further, if it is legally determined that this violation was willful or knowing, as defined in the Telecommunication Act, the recovery will be tripled for each violation. Let our Law Firm assure you that it is impossible to send a facsimile transmission "unknowingly" or "unwillfully"—faxes do not spontaneously occur.

Thus, the 1 unsolicited facsimile transmission is subject to treble [triple] damages, attorney fees, and court costs.

You are further given notice that to the extent that you are in possession and/or control documents, or other evidence relevant to this matter, you are under a continuing legal duty to secure such documents or evidence from loss, alteration, or destruction. Failure to do so may result in sanctions, forfeiture of legal rights, and a separate action for spoliation of evidence.

Our client is willing to settle this matter for $500.00 (Five Hundred US Dollars) if a cashier's check for the above amount is received within ten (10) calendar days of the date of the letter. If for any reason you feel that you have not violated the TCPA, and/or intend to settle this matter promptly out of court, please contact our Law Firm, in writing, with those reasons within the aforementioned ten (10) day period. If settlement is not possible, a lawsuit shall be immediately initiated hereafter. The suit shall be for the statutorily imposed treble damages of $1,500.00 (One Thousand and Five Hundred US Dollars) plus attorney fees and court costs.

If you are a business owner, you may find the above letter annoying. It appears that someone had just been collecting faxes or emails and then handed them over to an attorney to go try to collect some money. It almost feels like what the attorney is doing is spam, but the attorney would argue that he or she is just giving notice of a potential lawsuit. Giving notice of a potential lawsuit is certainly not illegal and the attorney did not send the notice as an unsolicited fax. The attorney sent it through the U.S. mail in a way that did not violate TCPA or CAN-SPAM.

Although you may be willing to ignore a threat to get sued over one transmission to see if the plaintiff will really sue you, you need to be aware that the damages for multiple transmissions could add up quickly. With the touch of a button, a business can send out hundreds of thousands of faxes or emails through a fax or email service provider. If the damages are $500 per transmission, then the second that it cost you to send the 100,000 transmissions might have cost you $500 x 100,000 = $50,000,000! This exclusion in the CGL Policy makes it clear that there will be no coverage for violations of the TCPA, CAN-SPAM, FCRA, or FACTA.

Non-Standard Coverage A Exclusions

At this point in the book we turn from what I called the "Standard Exclusions" to what I am calling the Non-Standard Exclusions. I do not mean to suggest that these additional exclusions are any worse than the standard exclusions. After all, the standard exclusions prevented coverage for things like the insured's property, product, and work. That seems pretty significant. However, I differentiate between the standard exclusions and non-standard exclusions because the insured— or the insured's insurance broker, client, or attorney—will probably not be aware of the non-standard exclusions without reading the policy. The standard exclusions exist in the Insurance Service Office's (ISO) standard, unendorsed CGL Policy. Insurance professionals should be familiar with ISO's standard CGL Policy exclusions. However, non-standard exclusions, as their name implies, are not standardized. They could exclude anything. If you are encountering a policy that adds exclusions to the ISO CGL Policy, or a policy that does not use the ISO CGL wording at all, it is important to read the exclusions to see what the policy will not cover.

Defense Costs Inside Limits

Although not technically an exclusion at all, an increasing number of CGL policies are excluding defense costs. The policies exclude defense costs with a short statement that tells the policyholder that "defense expenses are included within the policy's limits of liability." At first glance, this may not seem like a big deal to an insured because the insured can look at the certificate of insurance and see that the policy has $1 million limits, and maybe $1 million limits is all that the insured wanted to see. However, to understand the significance of the exclusion, you need to understand that **the standard ISO CGL Policy pays defense costs IN ADDITION to the policy limits.**

The provision where defense costs are paid in addition to the limits is found in the Supplementary Payments section of the standard ISO CGL Policy. Here you will find that the insurance company agrees to pay all expenses it incurs with respect to any claim the insurance company investigates, settles, or for any suit against an insured. The policy goes on to say that "These payments will not reduce the limits of insurance." (CG 00 01 04 13, ISO Properties, Inc., 2012, Page 9; Appendix Page 259).

> ***IMPORTANT:** If an insurance policy is using its own policy wording instead of the standard ISO policy wording, you should look under the Supplementary Payments section to make sure that the policy has not removed the standard ISO wording that states, "These payments will not reduce the limits of insurance." This is the sentence that ensures that defense costs are paid in addition to the policy limits. Without this sentence, defense costs could reduce policy limits.
>
> A policy that does not pay for defense costs in addition to the limits may not have an exclusion that alerts the policyholder to the defense costs being inside the limits. An exclusion is only necessary to remove something that is promised in the insurance policy. If the policy does not promise that defense payments "will not reduce the limits of insurance," then it does not need a separate exclusion removing the promised coverage. If they never made the promise, they do not need an exclusion to take away the promise.

To understand the impact of a policy that includes defense costs within the policy limits, imagine that you own a business and you have CGL Policy with limits of $1 million. Now imagine that you are sued for $10 million for damages arising out of your operations. You give the lawsuit to your insurance company and they hand it over to a law firm to defend you. It is a complex lawsuit. The law firm assigns a team of attorneys to work on the lawsuit. They work on it for many years, and they do a great job. The law firm is able to reduce your damages from the original $10 million down to only $1 million in damages.

Here is the potentially bad news: It cost the law firm $1 million to defend and resolve your law suit. If you have a standard ISO CGL Policy, this is not bad news at all. The standard ISO CGL Policy pays defense costs IN ADDITION to damages. This means that you would still have the $1 million limit available to pay the remaining $1 million in damages. The defense costs did not affect your limit.

If, however, you have a policy where the defense costs are included inside the policy limits, then the law firm already spent the $1 million limit that you had for coverage. When the law firm spent the one millionth dollar from the policy, they spent the last dollar you had available for coverage. The good news is that your policy paid for the attorneys to get your damages reduced from $10 million to $1 million. The bad news is that you purchased a policy where defense costs were included in the limit, and the law firm used up this limit to defend you. You now owe $1 million in damages, and you do not have any more money in the policy to pay for these damages.

As a practical footnote for the above, what would have happened if you had a policy that would not pay for defense costs at all and only paid for damages? In a policy without defense costs at all, you may have suffered a judgment of $10 million. If you had $1 million in limits that could only go to pay damages and not defense, then you would end up $9 million short of the judgment. I offer this footnote to emphasize the importance of having defense costs. People often buy a CGL Policy because they want the insurance company to pay for the defense and damages that arise out of running a business. Policyholders just need to be aware of whether or not defense costs are included in the policy limits. If defense costs are included in the limit, then defense costs will reduce the limit available to pay damages.

Prior Work Exclusion

The prior work exclusion is an exclusion that removes coverage for any work that occurred prior to a specific date listed in the exclusion. The date listed is usually the date when the policy started. Therefore, the exclusion usually removes coverage for any work that was done prior to the beginning of the policy period. To understand the impact of this exclusion, it is helpful to review what the CGL Policy covers without the exclusion.

Remember that the CGL Occurrence Form Policy is like a row of briefcases each filled with $1 million. Inscribed on the front of each briefcase is a year representing a specific annual policy period. Each briefcase has a combination lock. If you have the right combination, you can open the briefcase and take as much money as you need to pay damages covered by that year's policy.

These briefcases represent a row of Occurrence Form CGL insurance policies that each have $1 million Occurrence Limits and $1 million Aggregate Limits. The Occurrence Limit is the most the policy will pay for any one occurrence. The Aggregate Limit is the total amount the policy will pay, regardless of the number of occurrences. If you have an occurrence that is covered by the policy, you have the right combination to access the policy's $1 Million limits. Once the Aggregate Limit is paid, the briefcase is empty.

What is the right combination? Coverage A of the CGL Policy is designed to cover bodily injury or property damage caused by an occurrence during the policy period. If there is an occurrence during a policy period for which the insurance applies that is not excluded by the policy, you have the right combination to open the brief case.

Which policy will pay depends on when the occurrence happens. If you receive a lawsuit this year that says you caused covered occurrences in each of the last four years, you would have the correct combination to go to the four prior policy/briefcases. This means that you have access to a total of $4 million because you are going to open four different briefcases that each have a maximum of $1 million. Your current policy would not pay unless the occurrence also took place during the current policy period. This is true even though you received the lawsuit (claim) this year. The correct combination is based on when the occurrence took place; not when the claim is made.

This brings us back to the importance of the Prior Work Exclusion. An increasing number of CGL policies for contractors contain a Prior Work Exclusion. The Prior Work Exclusion changes the combination on the briefcases so that there is no coverage for any occurrences arising out of work that the contractor completed prior to the policy period. If a 2014 policy had a Prior Work Exclusion, it is saying that it will not cover any occurrences arising out of work done prior to 2014. This is true even if the occurrence takes place during 2014. The exclusion creates a wall between the 2014 briefcase and all prior briefcases.

Speaking of walls, imagine that you are a mason, and in 2013, you built a wall. In 2014, the wall fell on a person causing bodily injury. You get sued. You go to the 2014 briefcase, enter the combination, and you get a letter back apologizing that you do not have the correct combination. There is no coverage because, although there was an occurrence during the 2014 policy period, the policy/briefcase contained a Prior Work Exclusion. This exclusion excludes any work that you did prior to the 2014 policy. You built the wall in 2013, and so there is no coverage from the 2014 CGL Policy with the Prior Work Exclusion.

You then try to open the 2013 policy/briefcase. Once again you get a letter back apologizing that you do not have the correct combination. The 2013 letter is shorter. It just says that they only pay occurrences that occur during the 2013 policy period, and your occurrence took place in 2014.

PRIOR WORK EXCLUSION WARNING: If a 2014 policy has a Prior Work Exclusion, there is no coverage for occurrences that take place during 2014 that arise out of work the insured did prior to 2014. The 2014 policy will deny coverage because, even though the occurrence took place during 2014, the policy excludes occurrences arising out of your prior work. Previous policies will deny coverage because they only pay for occurrences that take place during their policy periods, and the 2014 occurrence did not take place during their policy periods. If you are wondering if a policy with a Prior Work Exclusion is right for you or someone else, you should evaluate the insured's risk of being sued for any work that the insured has ever done in the past.

The prior work exclusion is one of the exclusions most likely to result in litigation against an insurance professional for selling a CGL Policy. The cause of action against the insurance professional would be for negligence in selling someone an insurance policy with a prior work exclusion. One of the lead cases involving a broker who sold a policy with a prior work exclusion is *San Diego Assemblers, Inc. v. Work Comp for Less Insurance Services, Inc.* (2013) 220 Cal.App.4th 1363, 63 Cal.Rptr. 3d 621).

In the San Diego Assembler's case, an insurance broker sold a policy that contained a Prior Work Exclusion to a contractor. The contractor did work on a restaurant in 2004. In 2008, the broker sold the contractor a policy that contained a Prior Work Exclusion. In 2008, "an explosion and resulting fire occurred at the restaurant, causing substantial property damage" (*San Diego Assemblers, Inc. v. Work Comp for Less Insurance Services, Inc*). The 2008 policy did not pay for the damage because that policy had a Prior Work Exclusion. The 2004 policy did not pay because the occurrence did not take place during the policy period. The insurance company for the restaurant paid to rebuild the restaurant and then wanted to get reimbursed by the contractor's CGL insurance company. The restaurant's insurance company sued the broker who sold the contractor the policy with the prior work exclusion, arguing that there would be coverage to reimburse them *but for* the insurance broker's failure to get a policy that did not exclude prior works. In order to succeed, the restaurant needed to show that the broker was negligent in selling the contractor a policy that excluded prior works.

In determining whether or not the broker was negligent, the court looked at the following three factors:

a) Did the broker misrepresent the nature, extent or scope of the coverage being offered or provided?
b) Did the insured request a particular type or extent of coverage?
c) Did the broker assume an additional duty by either express agreement or by "holding himself out" as having expertise in a given field of insurance being sought by the insured?

If you are an insurance professional getting sued for negligence in California, the three factors above will determine whether or not you breached the duty that you owed your client. If the answer to these questions are "no," then you owe only the "limited duty...'to use reasonable care, diligence, and judgment in *procuring* the insurance requested by an insured'" (*San Diego Assemblers, Inc. v. Work Comp for Less Insurance Services, Inc.*(2013); *Pacific Rim Mechanical Contractors, Inc. v. Aon Risk Ins. Services West, Inc.* (2012). This implies that if the answer is "yes" to any of the three questions above, the broker may owe the client a greater duty.

In the San Diego Assembler's case, the California Appellate court found that the insurance broker was NOT negligent when the broker sold the contractor a policy that contained the Prior Work Exclusion. The court stated that the "broker never misrepresented any coverage contained in [the client's] policies and never failed to obtain the coverage the client requested." Furthermore, "after learning of the denial of coverage, [the client] did not ask Broker why Broker had not obtained a different type of policy for [the client] and [the client] had no criticisms of Broker's failure to do so....[The client] did not ask Broker to change any of [the client's] policies to include the coverages excluded... because the coverages were cost-prohibitive" (*San Diego Assemblers, Inc. v. Work Comp for Less Insurance Services, Inc.*).

I share the above discussion from the court because it is tempting for brokers to look quickly to see whether or not the insurance broker won instead of looking at the court's rationale. The above case does not give a green light for selling insurance policies that contain a Prior Work Exclusion. The court decided that the broker in this specific case was not negligent in selling the policy because the broker did not breach the duty of providing reasonable care. In a different situation where a broker misrepresents the policy, knows about the special needs of the client, or "holds him/herself out" as a having specific expertise for this kind of insurance, the case could have been decided otherwise. The prior work exclusion is appearing in CGL policies with greater frequency—especially with CGL policies for contractors. Insurance professionals should understand the exclusion, and realize that litigation against brokers who sell policies with the exclusion is also appearing with greater frequency.

The Sunset Provision

Whereas the Prior Work Exclusion is designed to eliminate exposures from the past, the Sunset Provision is designed to reduce exposures in the future. Imagine that you are the insurance company that owns that row of briefcases, each filled with $1 million. That is your money. Over the years, maybe you have had to pay some money out of the briefcases for covered occurrences, but hopefully there is still some money in those briefcases. At some point, you would like to put some of that money in your own pocket. You risked money. Now you are looking for your reward. But what if someone sues today for an occurrence that took place four years ago, or ten years ago? If a policyholder has the right combination to open the briefcase from four or ten years ago, you need to make sure the money is available for the policyholder. Does the insurance company need to keep the money available in the briefcases forever?

The Sunset Provision changes the briefcase/policy combination so that there is no coverage available if the policyholder does not report a claim within a certain amount of time. A two year sunset will say that there is no coverage unless the policyholder reports a claim within two years of the end of the policy period. A three year sunset requires reporting the claim to the insurance company within three years, and so on. After the designated period of time in the Sunset Provision has passed, the sun has set on the policyholder's opportunity to file a claim against the policy.

Imagine that the 2012 policy/briefcase has a two-year Sunset Provision and you are an electrician. You were working on a project in 2012 when a pedestrian was injured on the jobsite. The pedestrian eventually sues the project's owner, developer, and general contractor. More time passes and then you get added as a defendant in the lawsuit. The 2012 briefcase holds the money to pay damages for 2012 occurrences. If you notify your 2012 policy within the two year Sunset Provision (2013, 2014), you have the right combination to open the policy/briefcase. When you celebrate the arrival of 2015, two years will have passed since the end of your 2012 policy. As the apple drops to ring in the New Year in New York, the sun sets on your policy. Not only has the combination been changed on the briefcase, the insurance company owner walked into that room, picked up the 2012 briefcase, and walked out with it. If you are the insurance company, it's a Happy New Year. You finally get to enjoy whatever money is left in the 2012 briefcase. If you are the policyholder, the sun has set on your opportunity to file a claim against the 2012 policy.

Depending on your state and its applicable statutes of limitation, the Sunset Provision may not be as scary as it sounds. This is because a statute of limitation is essentially a Sunset Provision imposed by law. Just like the CGL Sunset Provision required notice of a claim within a certain amount of time, statutes of limitation require people to file their lawsuits within a certain amount of time. For example, California requires that if you want to sue the contractor who installed the irrigation system on your new house, you need to sue the contractor within one year after the close of escrow. (Cal. Civil

Code § 896 (g)(7)). If you decide to sue this contractor after the statute of limitation has passed, you will be barred from recovery.

Statutes of limitation vary by state and the type of work performed. If an insured always does work that has a statute of limitation shorter than the insured's policy's Sunset Provision, the insured may not have a problem with the Sunset Provision. The insured just needs to remember that there is no coverage for claims made after the sunset period ends. If an insured is wondering if a policy with a Sunset Provision is right for them, they should evaluate their risk of being sued after the sunset period ends. The insurance company will not accept claims after the sunset period.

Classification Limitation

The Classification Limitation exclusion states that coverage is only provided for those operations specified in the insurance application. This is significant because remember, Coverage A of the CGL Policy provides coverage on a "covered unless excluded basis." The classification limitation changes this to limit coverage to only the work that falls within the specific business description listed in the insurance application. Anything outside this description would be excluded.

For example, imagine that you were doing mostly tile flooring installation when you got your policy and the declarations page says "flooring" for your "Business Description." You are doing great work at someone's house, and the homeowner asks if you would do some framing for a remodel in another area of the house. Framing is not flooring. If there is a claim arising out of framing, the policy may exclude coverage because you are doing work that is not consistent with the classification in the policy declarations.

This exclusion is one of the exclusions that might be a big deal for certain businesses, but not a big deal at all for others. The insurance company may offer a policy at a discounted price in exchange for making sure that they will not cover exposures outside of your business description. If you are an insured who is sure that you will not want to do any work outside of your business description, you may decide that the policy with a classification limitation is fine with you. However, for the contractors and various businesses that might have the people and relative expertise to pick up work in an area outside of their specific business description, they need to understand that this exclusion may preclude coverage for any occurrences arising from work in any area outside of the specific business description listed on the insurance policy.

Total Pollution Exclusion

The standard ISO CGL Policy excluded pollution under "exclusion f. pollution." With this in mind, some people will see the non-standard "Total Pollution Exclusion" and dismiss it as insignificant because they will assume that all policies exclude pollution. However, there is a difference between "exclusion f. pollution," in the standard ISO CGL Policy, and the non-standard "Total Pollution Exclusion."

The standard CGL pollution exclusion provided a number of exceptions where there would be coverage for pollution. The non-standard "Total Pollution Exclusion" removes these exceptions. You should note, however, that the non-standard "Total Pollution Exclusion," will not list the exceptions it removed. Instead, the "Total Pollution Exclusion" may be an endorsement that simply states that the CGL Policy's Pollution Exclusion has been removed and "replaced with the following wording." The "Total Pollution Exclusion" may then go on to list the exact wording that you read in the standard CGL Policy's pollution exclusion, minus the exceptions.

Remember, the standard ISO CGL Policy starts by excluding all pollution, but then provides exceptions to the exclusion. The exceptions provide coverage for pollution exposures in limited situations. A policy with a "Total Pollution Exclusion" starts and finishes with a complete exclusion for any bodily injury or property damage "arising out of the actual, alleged or threatened discharge, dispersal, seepage, migration, release or escape of" "any solid, liquid, gaseous or thermal irritant or contaminant, including smoke, vapor, soot, fumes, acids, alkalis, chemicals and waste" (CG 00 01 04 13 ISO properties, Inc., 2012, Pages 3, 15; Appendix Pages <u>248</u>, <u>271</u>). There are no exceptions.

By removing the exceptions, the "Total Pollution Exclusion" eliminates the following instances when the standard CGL Policy would provide pollution coverage.

1) **Bodily Injury from Heating and Air Conditioning Systems.** The standard CGL Policy WILL cover bodily injury that happens within a building that is caused by smoke or fumes produced or originating from equipment used to heat, cool, or dehumidify a building. A CGL Policy with a "Total Pollution Exclusion" would not cover this exposure because smoke is defined as a pollutant, and pollution is excluded without any exceptions.

2) **You are a contractor and the discharge, dispersal, seepage, migration, release or escape of pollutants happens at your Additional Insured's premises.** The second exception to the exclusion provides coverage for pollution if the insured is a contractor and the pollution takes place at a premises where the contractor is working for someone who was named as an Additional Insured for Ongoing Operations on the contractor's CGL Policy. A CGL Policy with a "Total Pollution Exclusion" would not cover this exposure because pollution is excluded without any exceptions.

3) **Escape of Fuels from "Mobile Equipment".** The standard CGL Policy's pollution exclusion contains an exception that will provide coverage for pollution exposures caused by the escape of fuels from "Mobile Equipment". A CGL Policy with a "Total Pollution Exclusion" would not cover this exposure because the escape of fuels would be a pollutant, and pollution is excluded without any exceptions. This can be significant because auto policies are designed to cover auto exposures, and the CGL Policy is designed to cover bodily injury and property damage arising out of "Mobile Equipment". If

there is property damage relating to "Mobile Equipment", the CGL Policy is the one that should respond. In a policy with a "Total Pollution Exclusion," there will be no response for damages arising out of the escape of fuels from "Mobile Equipment" because the escape of fuels would be a pollutant, and pollution is excluded without any exceptions.

4) **That new carpet smell.** The fourth exception is for bodily injury or property damage within a building caused by the release of "gases, fumes, or vapors from materials brought into that building in connection with operations being performed by the named insured or contractor working for the named insured" (CG 00 01 04 13, ISO Properties, Inc., 2012 page 3; <u>Appendix Page 250</u>). A CGL Policy with a "Total Pollution Exclusion" would not cover this exposure because the "gases, fumes, or vapors" would be defined as pollutants, and pollution is excluded without any exceptions.

5) **Hostile Fire.** The standard CGL Policy has an exception to the pollution exclusion that will provide coverage for pollution resulting from a hostile fire. The significant pollution exposure from a hostile fire is smoke damage. A CGL Policy with a "Total Pollution Exclusion" would not cover this exposure because smoke is a defined as a pollutant, and pollution is excluded without any exceptions.

For example, imagine that you are a contractor and you cause a fire that causes smoke. This smoke forces people to the hospital. This would be excluded as a pollution exposure under a policy with the "Total Pollution Exclusion." Under a standard ISO CGL Policy, this would not be excluded because of the exception above for a Hostile Fire caused by the insured's operations. Similarly, if a contractor brings in new carpet with that great "new carpet smell" that forces people to go to the hospital because the fumes are too strong, this would be excluded under a policy with a total pollution exclusion. It would not be excluded by the standard ISO CGL Policy because of the standard policy's exception that provides coverage for fumes or vapors released from materials brought into a building in connection with operations being performed. (For more information on the impact of the "Total Pollution Exclusion," please refer to <u>page 94</u> and following for the section on the exceptions to the standard ISO CGL Policy's pollution exclusion. The exceptions in the standard ISO CGL Policy provide coverage for pollution exposures. The "Total Pollution Exclusion" removes the exceptions so that pollution is completely excluded without any exceptions).

Chapter 4: Coverage B, Personal and Advertising Injury

The standard CGL Policy contains a section called Coverage B. This section provides coverage for "Personal and Advertising Injury." Coverage B has its own insuring agreement and exclusions. A common mistake that policyholders make about personal and advertising injury is assuming that the insurance company and the policyholder have the same thing in mind when they refer to "Personal and Advertising Injury". You will notice that "Personal and Advertising Injury" is listed in quotation marks in the CGL Policy. This means that the term is defined elsewhere in the policy. People could read through the entire Coverage B insuring agreement and be really excited about the coverage afforded for what they think is personal and advertising injury, only to find out that the insurance policy defines "personal and advertising injury" as something else.

"Personal and Advertising Injury" is defined as seven specific offenses. If there is a personal and advertising offense involving something other than one of these seven enumerated offenses, then the policy will not consider it to be a personal and advertising injury. If the policy does not view it as a personal and advertising injury, the policy will not provide coverage for the offense.

Before spending time on these seven personal and advertising injuries, we need an overview of the Coverage B insuring agreement. Like Coverage A, Coverage B begins by promising to pay "those sums that the insured becomes legally obligated to pay as damages." If the insured is not responsible for paying the damages, then the insurance company does not need to stand in the insured's place to provide a defense or pay damages on behalf of the insured. The insurance company's obligation to defend or indemnify the insured only exists when the insured is responsible. (For more information, please refer to Coverage A, Legally Obligated to Pay as Damages, on <u>page 21ff</u>).

Unlike Coverage A, Coverage B does not talk about occurrences. Instead, it talks about offenses. The insuring agreement states that "This insurance applies to 'personal and advertising injury' caused by an offense arising out of your business but only if the offense was committed in the 'coverage territory' during the policy period" (CG 00 01 04 13, ISO Properties, Inc., 2012, Page 6; Appendix Page 254).

Whether or not there will be coverage under Coverage B depends on how an insured can answer a series of four questions. If the insured can answer "yes" to all four questions, then Coverage B should be activated. After the insured satisfies the burden of answering "yes" to the four questions, the burden shifts to the insurance company to try to prove that there is no coverage because of a Coverage B exclusion. If the four questions are answered "yes," and there is no applicable exclusion, then there should be coverage under Coverage B.

The four questions that an insured must answer affirmatively to get coverage under Coverage B are as follows:

Coverage B Activation Questions

1. Is the insured legally obligated to pay damages because of "personal and advertising injury"?

2. Is the "personal and advertising injury" offense included in the policy's definition of "personal and advertising injury"?

3. Was the offense committed in the coverage territory?

4. Did the offense take place during the policy period?

Intentional Acts

A common theme of the "personal and advertising injury" offenses is that they are based on intentional acts. This differs from Coverage A where most of the exposure arises out of the unintentional tort of negligence. As discussed on page 22 and following, one can be found liable for the tort of negligence if the person had a duty to act like a reasonable person, breached the duty to act like a reasonable person, and this breach caused damages.

In order to be found liable for an intentional act, you need to show that someone acted intentionally in a manner that caused harm in a specific way. It does not matter if the person desired or expected to cause any harm. We just ask if the person made an intentional act and whether or not this act met the definition of the specific offense.

For example, people can be found liable for trespassing if they 1) intentionally 2) enter the land of another person 3) without permission. Let us say that the room you are in right now is your land and the boundary line between your land and someone else's land is the line dividing your room from the room next to you. If I intentionally step across that line in to your room without permission, I could be liable for trespassing. I have intentionally entered the land of another (your land) without permission. That is all that is necessary to find me liable for trespassing. It does not matter if I intended to trespass. It does not matter if I know whether or not it is your land or whether or not I intended to trespass. We are just analyzing whether or not I entered your land intentionally and without permission.

Definition of Personal and Advertising Injury

The first step in determining whether or not there will be coverage for an offense under Coverage B, is to determine if there was an offense that meets the policy's definition of "Personal and Advertising Injury". The standard CGL Policy defines "Personal and Advertising Injury" as the following:

> "Personal and advertising injury" means injury, including consequential "bodily injury", arising out of one or more of the following offenses:
>
> **a.** False arrest, detention or imprisonment;
> **b.** Malicious prosecution;

c. The wrongful eviction from, wrongful entry into, or invasion of the right of private occupancy of a room, dwelling or premises that a person occupies, committed by or on behalf of its owner, landlord or lessor;

d. Oral or written publication, in any manner, of material that slanders or libels a person or organization or disparages a person's or organization's goods, products or services;

e. Oral or written publication, in any manner, of material that violates a person's right of privacy;

f. The use of another's advertising idea in your "advertisement"; or

g. Infringing upon another's copyright, trade dress or slogan in your "advertisement".

(CG 00 01 04 13, ISO Properties, Inc., 2012, Page 15; <u>Appendix Page 271</u>).

If an offense does not fit within one of the seven categories above, it does not meet the CGL Policy's definition of "personal and advertising injury". If it does meet one of the definitions above, then there is no coverage for the injuries caused by the offense. The coverage can be both for the personal injuries themselves as well as any consequential "bodily injury" arising out of the offense. It is important to note that Coverage B will pay for consequential bodily injury because sometimes people suggest that only Coverage A covers Bodily Injury and Property Damage to others, and that Coverage B only pays financial awards for the intangible frustrations or hurt feelings arising out of personal and advertising injuries like slander or invasion of privacy. Although it is correct to note that Coverage A provides coverage for Bodily Injury or Property Damage to others, it is also important to note that Coverage B also provides coverage for bodily injury if it arises out of a "personal and advertising injury". The possibility of bodily injury arising out of a personal or advertising injury offense could certainly exist in offenses such as false arrest, detention, or imprisonment.

As we saw in the example of trespassing on <u>page 143</u>, the offenses often have their own legal definition. Therefore, to understand what personal and advertising injuries are covered by the CGL Policy, we need to know both what the CGL Policy defines as "personal and advertising injury", AND how the law defines these specific offenses.

a. False arrest, detention, or imprisonment

False imprisonment is a specific intentional tort with a legal definition that has been developed over centuries in our common law tradition. A defendant may be found liable for the tort of false imprisonment if the defendant intentionally confines a plaintiff into a bounded area against the plaintiff's will, so long as the plaintiff is aware of the confinement, or is injured by the confinement. We can break this down into four elements: 1) Intent, 2) Confinement, 3) Against Plaintiff's Will, 4) Plaintiff knows of confinement or is injured by the confinement. Each of these elements also have their own meanings.

1) Intent: The defendant's actions will be considered intentional if the defendant wanted the confinement to happen or was substantially certain that confinement would occur. It does not matter if the defendant had a good or bad motive to confine someone. The question is only whether the defendant acted volitionally and intentionally to confine the plaintiff.

For example, imagine that you have a friend who is an alcoholic. Your friend has been sober for 147 days. Your friend's favorite team just won a championship and you know a bunch of people are going to a local bar to celebrate. You lock your friend in a room to prevent your friend from going to the bar. Locking your friend in the room was an intentional, volitional act to confine your friend. This satisfies the intent element of the tort of false imprisonment. If you accidently locked your friend in a room when you were closing your office for the night, you did not intend to confine your friend and therefore you would not be found liable for false imprisonment. The tort of false imprisonment requires the defendant's intent to confine a plaintiff.

2) Confinement: In order for someone to be found liable for the tort of false imprisonment, the plaintiff must have been confined into a bounded area. It does not matter how large or nice the bounded area may be. It could be the beautiful estate gardens within an ancient castle's walls. It just needs to be an identifiable area to which the plaintiff is confined without a reasonable means of escape. For example, if I lock you out of my office, you cannot say that I have confined you to the world outside of my office. However, if I lock you inside a huge office with a comfortable couch, nice view, and open bar, I could still be found liable for the tort of false imprisonment because I have confined you into a bounded—albeit nicely appointed—area.

3) Against the Plaintiff's Will: The defendant will *not* be found liable for false imprisonment if the confinement is not against the plaintiff's will. The idea of this tort is to honor the plaintiff's freedom of movement. Some parents send their small children to their rooms for a period of "time out" when the child needs to calm down or is making poor decisions. The children view this as punishment. A parent dealing with the busyness and noise of life with small children might be envious of such a "time out", longing to be sent to a room to experience such solitude and silence. Imagine that a tired parent asks a friend to lock the parent in a room for a restful period of "time out." If the friend agrees and locks the parent in a room, the parent locked in "time out" is *not* experiencing false imprisonment because it is not against the parent's will. One can only be found liable for false imprisonment if the confinement is against the plaintiff's will.

4) Plaintiff knows of the confinement or is injured by the confinement: This element reinforces the need for the confinement to be against the plaintiff's will. If a couple is sleeping in their room and you lock the door on them for a while and then unlock it before they awake, you will not be liable for false imprisonment because the plaintiffs did not know that they were confined. An exception to this is a situation where the plaintiff might not know of the confinement, but the plaintiff was injured by the confinement. This has been used in cases where infants may be locked in a room or car. The infant may not be aware of the confinement, but if the infant suffers dehydration or any harm, this harm will replace the requirement that the plaintiff must have knowledge of the confinement. If the plaintiff does not know about the confinement, and is not injured by the confinement, the confinement will not be considered false imprisonment.

How long does the confinement need to be for it to count as false imprisonment? There is no duration requirement. If the defendant intentionally confines the plaintiff into a bounded area against the plaintiff's will, and with the plaintiff's knowledge (or injury), there is false imprisonment.

In addition to false imprisonment, the first definition of "personal and advertising injury" also includes false arrest and false detention.

False Arrest: The tort of false arrest is a variation of false imprisonment. False arrest is essentially false imprisonment committed by someone asserting the legal authority to confine when the person confining really does not have the legal authority to confine. For example, in the example above, you might feel like you are experiencing "false imprisonment" if the police throw you in jail. After all, the police have intentionally confined you into a bounded area against your will, and you are aware of it. That sounds like false imprisonment, but there might not be anything false about it. Assuming your arrest is based on probable cause and the proper arrest warrant, the police will not be liable for false imprisonment because they have the legal authority to confine you.

Where the tort of false arrest is commonly used is against private security firms. Unlike the police, these private security firms might not understand the necessary probable cause and warrant requirements. This could lead to a security guard confining someone when the security guard did not have the legal right to confine the person. A defendant who commits false imprisonment while asserting the legal authority to confine could be liable for false arrest if it turns out that the defendant did not have the legal authority to confine.

False Detention: The tort of False Detention is similar to false imprisonment, but less severe. It exists where the plaintiff is not confined, but the defendant's actions still frustrate the plaintiff's freedom of movement. For example, instead of being confined, the plaintiff may be stopped for questioning against the plaintiff's will. If this was done intentionally, inappropriately, and without appropriate legal authority, someone could seek redress through the courts under the tort of False Detention.

Shopkeeper's Privilege

Coverage for "Personal and Advertising Injury" under false arrest, detention or imprisonment" often arises with litigation surrounding the improper execution of the Shopkeeper's Privilege. The shopkeeper's privilege typically allows a merchant to **reasonably detain** someone for a **reasonable amount of time** and in a **reasonable** manner, IF the merchant **reasonably believes that the person was shoplifting**. The idea of this privilege is that we should not expect shopkeepers to allow people to just walk into their stores, load up their pockets, not pay, and walk out of the store without interference. So long as the shopkeeper behaves reasonably in protecting their property, the shopkeeper will not be found liable for false arrest, detention, or imprisonment.

Reasonableness is obviously the key to the shopkeeper's privilege. If the amount of time or manner of detention was unreasonable, then the shopkeeper loses the privilege and could be liable for false arrest, detention, or imprisonment. If the shopkeeper was unreasonable in believing that the plaintiff was shoplifting, then the shopkeeper loses the privilege and could be liable for false arrest, detention, or imprisonment.

For example, imagine a large U.S. retailer that is always fighting customer theft has a store in Texas. It is August and it is hot. In walks a customer with a parka. The customer appears to be filling up the jacket with various items of merchandise. At one point it looks like the customer was able to fit a flat screen TV inside the huge jacket! The customer attempts to waddle out of the store only to have store security stop (detain) the person for questioning. The security officer may then choose to confine this person to a room until the police arrive. It seems like the store was reasonable in believing that the customer was shoplifting. So long as they detained the customer in a reasonable manner for a reasonable amount of time, the retailer would not be liable for false arrest, detention, or imprisonment.

On the other hand, imagine that a mother and child purchase goods from the same retailer and are stopped by store security officers. The security officers says that they think the child looks like a child who is not allowed back in the store because the child was caught shoplifting last week. The mother protests and offers to show identification for herself and the child to prove that the child was not the one caught shoplifting. The security personnel refuse to look at the identification. They point in the child's face and say, "You were caught shoplifting." The child cries. The security personnel then take the mother and child into a back room and say, "Wait here until the police arrive." The boy asks if he can go to the bathroom and the security personnel say, "No."

Does this sound like a reasonable detention of someone reasonably suspected of shoplifting? If so, then the merchant will not be found liable for false arrest, detention, or imprisonment. Now imagine that the security personnel forgot about the mother and child in the back room. Mother and child remain in the back room until they were discovered by the night shift six hours later? We might disagree on what length of time constitutes a *reasonable* detention, but my guess is that we would agree that an unreasonable amount of time to detain the mother and child begins some time short of six hours.

If the detention is unreasonable, then the merchant could be found liable for the tort of false imprisonment. If this offense took place in the coverage territory during the policy period, then the merchant's CGL Policy may pay for the merchant's legal defense under Coverage B, Personal and Advertising Injury. I provide extreme examples to help illustrate personal and advertising injuries. For a real example that evaluates the balance of when a merchant's conduct is or is not False Imprisonment, see *Debra McCann v. Wal-Mart Stores. 210 F.3d 51* (1st Cir. *2000*).

b. Malicious Prosecution

Malicious prosecution is included in the CGL Policy's definition of "personal and advertising injury". Many defendants who are dragged into court feel that there is no basis for them to be sued, and argue that this makes them the victim of "malicious prosecution." However, before policyholders get too excited about seeing coverage for malicious prosecution in the CGL Policy, they should understand that the tort of "malicious prosecution" has its own specific legal definition.

The tort of malicious prosecution exists when a plaintiff files a lawsuit 1) with malice, 2) without probable cause, 3) pursues legal proceedings to their termination, and 4) the defendant wins. (*Bertero v. National General Corp.* (1974) 13 Cal.3d 43, 50 [118 Cal.Rptr. 184, 529 P.2d 608]; *Drummond v. Desmarais* (2009) 176 Cal.App.4th 439, 450). Since the term "prosecution" usually refers to criminal law and this tort deals more with civil law, the Restatement on Torts refers to the tort of "malicious prosecution" instead as the "wrongful use of civil proceedings" (California Civil Jury Instructions, 1501. Wrongful Use of Civil Proceedings. 5 Witkin, Summary of California Law (10th ed. 2005) Torts, § 486).

1) With Malice: The term malice refers to intentionally committing an act out of ill will. It is moving beyond acting unreasonably, and instead acting in a way that is hurtful to others. A plaintiff acts with malice when the plaintiff "asserts a claim with knowledge of its falsity, because one who seeks to establish such a claim 'can only be motivated by an improper purpose.' A lack of probable cause will therefore support an inference of malice." (*Drummond, supra,* 176 Cal.App.4th at pp. 451—452).

Therefore, if someone files a lawsuit against another person or entity when the plaintiff knows the claims are false or without probable cause, the plaintiff may later be found liable for malicious prosecution. On the other hand, if a plaintiff does not know that the claims are false and has at least probable cause to file the claim, the plaintiff will not be found liable for malicious prosecution. This is true even if the plaintiff ends up losing the lawsuit. So long as the plaintiff did not have knowledge of the claims being false and as long as the plaintiff had probable cause to file the lawsuit, the plaintiff did not act with malice. If the plaintiff did not act with malice, then the plaintiff cannot be found liable for the tort of malicious prosecution.

2) Without Probable Cause: "A litigant will lack probable cause for his action either if he relies upon facts which he has no reasonable cause to believe to be true, or if he seeks recovery upon a legal theory which is untenable under the facts known to him." (*Soukup v. Law Offices of Herbert Hafif* (2006) 39 Cal.4th 260, 292 [46 Cal.Rptr.3d 638, 139 P.3d 30].) For example, let us say that I accuse you of throwing rocks at my car. There is a crack in my windshield that might have come from a rock hitting my windshield, and I accuse you of throwing the rock that cracked my windshield. It would demonstrate malice for me to say that it was you when I know that it was not you.

In this case, I do not know that it was *not* you. In theory, it could be you who threw a rock that cracked my car's windshield. I just do not have any facts to support that you threw the rock that cracked my windshield. In fact, I do not have any facts to suggest that anyone threw a rock at my car. I lack probable cause for accusing you of cracking my windshield because I am relying on facts for which I have no reasonable cause to believe to be true.

Even if I know some facts, I lack probable cause if I try to recover on a legal theory which is not supported by the facts that I know. For example, if I see that you like to juggle rocks on the side of the road, I would not have probable cause to accuse you of stealing my car. The fact that someone juggles rocks on the side of a road is not sufficient legal support to sue someone for theft. I lack probable cause if I rely on facts for which I have no reasonable cause to believe are true, or if I seek recovery upon a legal theory which is untenable under the facts I know.

3) Pursues Legal Proceedings to their termination: In order to find someone liable for the tort of malicious prosecution, the plaintiff must have pursued the lawsuit to its termination. This third element sharpens the fourth element where we will see that the original defendant has to win the case. That is, the original plaintiff who filed the malicious lawsuit has to lose. This element helps define what constitutes winning and losing when a case is settled before trial.

Addressing this concern, a court noted, "[W]hen a dismissal results from negotiation, settlement, or consent, a favorable termination is normally not recognized. Under these latter circumstances, the dismissal reflects ambiguously on the merits of the action." (*Weaver v. Superior Court* (1979) 95 Cal.App.3d 166, 184—185 [156 Cal.Rptr. 745], disapproved on other grounds in *Sheldon Appel Co., supra,* 47 Cal.3d at p. 882.). Therefore, in order for the defendant to be able to sue a plaintiff later for malicious prosecution, the defendant cannot settle or compromise in a way that reflects ambiguously on the merits of the action. The original defendant needs to win. In order to win, the original lawsuit must continue until there is a judgment clearly identifying the winner.

4) Defendant Wins: In order to succeed in a malicious prosecution lawsuit against the person or entity who maliciously sued an insured, the insured needs to win the case. This should make sense because it would be tough to prove that the plaintiff filed 1) maliciously or with 2) no probable cause if a judge ends up ruling in favor of the plaintiff. However, in addition to winning, the resolution needs to reflect that the defendant was not responsible for the misconduct alleged in the lawsuit. Commenting on a malicious prosecution lawsuit, a judge noted that "it is not enough that the present plaintiff (former defendant) prevailed in the [original] action. The termination must ' "reflect on the merits," ' and be such that it 'tended to indicate [the former defendant's] innocence of or lack of responsibility for the alleged misconduct.' " (*Drummond v. Desmarais* (2009) 176 Cal.App.4th 439, 450 [98 Cal.Rptr.3d 183], internal citations omitted.) This means that in order to sue someone for malicious prosecution, the insured has to do more than just win the original lawsuit in which the insured was sued. The insured must win the lawsuit in a way that shows that the insured lacked responsibility for the misconduct alleged in the original lawsuit.

Let us look at the tort of malicious prosecution by imagining that someone files a lawsuit against a store owner for false imprisonment. In this illustration, Jack and Jill are competing store owners. Jack alleges that Jill locked Jack in the back of a delivery truck for a few minutes. In response, Jack sues Jill for false imprisonment.

Recalling the elements of the tort of false imprisonment, Jack is alleging that Jill intentionally confined Jack into a bounded area against Jack's will. Jill does not think that she detained Jack in the back of a delivery truck. Jill says she never went near the delivery truck. Jill thinks Jack is filing the lawsuit out of ill will (malice) because the lawsuit will force Jill to spend money on legal fees. It may also make Jill look bad in the community, causing shoppers to go to Jack's store instead of Jill's. Jill thinks there is no probable cause to allege that she locked Jack in the back of the delivery van because Jill says that she was not in the area of the delivery truck when this event allegedly took place.

The good news for Jill is that she defends against Jack's false imprisonment lawsuit all the way until the final judgment, and Jill wins. The bad news is that this lawsuit caused Jill great financial and personal stress. As one judge more eloquently stated, Jack's lawsuit "compelled [Jill] to defend against a fabricated claim which not only subject[ed Jill] to the panoply of psychological pressures most civil defendants suffer, but also the additional stress of attempting to resist a suit commenced out of spite or ill will, often magnified by slanderous allegations in the pleadings." (*Merlet v. Rizzo* (1998) 64 Cal.App.4th 53, 59 [75 Cal.Rptr.2d 83].)

Now that Jill has won the case, Jill has probable cause to say that Jack filed the false imprisonment lawsuit against Jill 1) with malice, 2) without probable cause, that 3) Jill pursued the legal proceedings to their termination, and that 4) Jill won the case. Jill satisfies all of the elements to sue Jack for the tort of malicious prosecution.

When Jill sues Jack for malicious prosecution, Jill is now the plaintiff in the new lawsuit. Jack is now the defendant. In response to getting served with the malicious prosecution lawsuit, Jack could turn to his CGL Policy, turn to Coverage B, and find that malicious prosecution is a covered "personal and advertising injury offense". Jack could then file a claim with his insurance company seeking a defense against Jill's malicious prosecution claim.

For some of you, this is a frustrating point in the example. We are excited about getting a defense for claims against us, but we are not excited about Jack, who sued Jill with malice and no probable cause, getting a defense from an insurance company. Some states agreed with your frustration and passed laws eliminating insurance coverage for "a loss caused by the willful act of the insured" (*California Insurance Code* § 533).

> **Some States do not allow insurance for losses caused by the willful act of an insured.**

We can see the public policy at work with this law. For example, murder is also a malice crime. If you kill someone by accident, you will not be found guilty of murder. You might be found liable for negligent homicide, but you cannot be found guilty of murder unless your actions are rooted in malice. For murder, malice is often defined as intent to kill, intent to commit serious bodily harm, or depraved indifference to human life.

We do not like the idea that someone who committed murder could just pay a deductible and have the insurance company take over all responsibility. Similarly, with the tort of malicious prosecution, some states will not allow an insurance company to pay damages associated with the tort because of laws that prevent insurance coverage for a loss "caused by the willful act of the insured (*ibid*).

Even in states where insurance will not cover losses caused by the willful acts of the insured, the insurance company may have to defend the insured. This is because the insurance company's duty to defend the insured is viewed as an obligation separate from the insurance company's duty to make the insured whole. "As a result, the liability insurer may be obligated to defend, even if ultimately not to indemnify, malicious prosecution claims.... Notwithstanding *California Insurance Code* § 533, the court in *Downey Venture v. LMI Insurance Company* held an insurer that sold a liability insurance policy that expressly provided for indemnity and defense of any claims arising from the specified offense of malicious prosecution must provide a defense. The court reasoned that the duty to defend is a 'specific and distinct commitment' from that of indemnification" (3-19 New Appleman on Insurance Law Library Edition § 19.04).

Using the example of Jack suing Jill for false imprisonment and losing, let us imagine that Jill spent $50,000 in legal fees and frustration defending against the malicious lawsuit. Jill wins the suit and sues Jack for malicious prosecution. Jack gets a defense provided from his CGL Policy under Coverage B, Personal and Advertising Injury, Malicious Prosecution. Jill wins the malicious prosecution case. The jury awards Jill $50,000 for her legal fees and frustration, plus an extra $100,000 in punitive damages against the Jack. Punitive damages are designed to punish a wrong-doer.

Just as some states do not allow insurance coverage for the willful act of an insured, some states do not allow coverage for punitive damages. This is also a matter of public policy because wrong-doers may not really feel punished if insurance covers the damages. In a jurisdiction that allows insurance coverage for willful acts and punitive damages, Jack's CGL Policy should pay Jill $150,000. In a jurisdiction that does not allow coverage for punitive damages, but does allow coverage for an insured's willful acts, the insurance company would pay

Jill $50,000 for the damages arising out of the malicious prosecution, but not pay the $100,000 in punitive damages. In a jurisdiction that does not allow insurance to cover punitive damages, and does not allow insurance coverage for losses caused by the willful acts of the insured, the insurance company would pay nothing to Jill.

This does not mean that Jill would not be paid. Jill has a judgment from a court saying that Jack is responsible to pay Jill this amount. Maybe Jack will write a check or have to sell his store to come up with the money. The money just will not come from the insurance company in a jurisdiction that does not allow insurance coverage for the willful acts of the insured.

The jurisdiction will determine if the policy should pay defense costs only, or defense costs and damages. Whether or not punitive damages will be covered will also be determined by jurisdiction. To the extent allowed by law, the CGL Policy will provide coverage for claims of malicious prosecution under Coverage B of the CGL Policy because malicious prosecution is included in the CGL Policy's definition of "personal and advertising injury".

c. The wrongful eviction from, wrongful entry into, or invasion of the right of private occupancy of a room, dwelling or premises that a person occupies, committed by or on behalf of its owner, landlord or lessor

This section of the personal and advertising injury definition provides some coverage for offenses that may arise out interaction with property tenants. These include coverage for 1) wrongful eviction, and 2) wrongful entry and invasion of the right of private occupancy.

1) Wrongful Eviction
You will see that there is some coverage for wrongful eviction from, and wrongful entry into, a room, dwelling, or premises. In order to see what is covered under this section as "wrongful eviction" and "wrongful entry," it may be helpful to

---

understand what would be considered "rightful eviction" or "rightful entry."

Let us say that Lucy is a landlord who owns a large residential building and Tina is one of her tenants. The residential building is a gorgeous building in New York City. Lucy Landlord has an agreement with her tenants that says the tenants need to pay rent in exchange for using space in Lucy's building. If the tenants do not pay rent, Lucy may evict them. Tina Tenant feels like she has a deal, paying just $5,000 per month for her small apartment. Other tenants are paying $10,000 to $20,000 per month for their fancier residences. All tenants pay rent to Lucy Landlord's manager by the first of every month. Lucy realizes that some of her tenants have been a little slow to pay rent. Then Lucy realizes that several of her tenants have not paid at all for three months. Tina is one of those tenants.

Lucy Landlord moves all of Tina Tenant's furnishings to a storage shed and changes the lock on the door to "Tina's" apartment. Tina goes to visit Lucy to find out why Lucy evicted Tina. Lucy tells Tina that Lucy evicted Tina because Tina had not paid rent in the past three months. Lucy argues that Tina owes $15,000 for back rent and that Lucy *rightfully evicted* Tina because Lucy had not been paying rent.

Tina responds that she has been paying rent every month. She always pays by the first of the month. She always pays the manager. Lucy Landlord suddenly realizes that she has not seen her manager in the last week, or two. It turns out that no one in the building has seen the manager for a week, or two, or three.

Lucy may have "rightfully evicted" Tina if Tina had not been paying rent, but Tina was paying rent. Lucy now has a building full of empty apartments. All of her former tenants are scrambling through storage containers, searching for the things they need to get dressed, feed their families, and go to work today. If the situation above results in a claim (lawsuit) from tenants demanding payment for their damages, Lucy's CGL Policy would be available to defend her and pay damages, as

---

appropriate, under Coverage B, personal and advertising injury, definition c. Wrongful eviction.

2) Wrongful entry and invasion of the right of private occupancy.

Wrongful entry and invasion of the right of private occupancy are lesser variations of wrongful eviction. In these cases, instead of completely evicting a tenant, someone is wrongfully entering a private room or entering in a way that invades the occupant's right to private occupancy of a room.

For example, this time let us imagine that I am the landlord of the place where you currently live. You are my tenant. Laws vary by state, but you could imagine that it might be illegal, or at least in bad taste, for me to go over to your house without notifying you, see what food you have in the refrigerator, read your magazine subscriptions, make myself comfortable on your couch, and maybe enjoy some of your favorite television shows and movies. I did not evict you, but it sounds like we have a wrongful entry or invasion of the right of private occupancy of a room.

Similarly, if you go and rent a hotel room for a few days, you may take offense to the hotel trying to rent the room to someone else while you are out of the room for a few hours. You may really take offense to this when the second guest arrives in the room while you are dressed in your least appropriate attire. You would feel that this is an invasion of your right to private occupancy of a room. In response, you could file a claim for damages against the hotel's CGL Policy.

If individuals experience wrongful eviction, wrongful entry, or invasion of the right of private occupancy of a room, they might feel that they have suffered a personal injury for which they want compensation. If the occupants file a claim or lawsuit against a policyholder for these offenses, the CGL Policy may respond to defend and pay damages under Coverage B of the CGL Policy because these offenses are included in the CGL Policy's definition of "personal and advertising injury".

d. Oral or written publication, in any manner, of material that slanders or libels a person or organization or disparages a person's or organization's goods, products or services

Coverage B of the CGL Policy provides coverage for those sums that the insured becomes legally obligated to pay because of slander or libel against a person or organization or their goods, products, or services. (CG 00 01 04 13, ISO Properties, Inc., 2012, Page 15; <u>Appendix Page 271</u>). Slander and libel are both forms of the tort of defamation. Slander occurs when the defamation is oral. Libel occurs when the defamation is in writing. Defamation exists when one communicates a 1) false, 2) defamatory 3) statement of fact, of or concerning the plaintiff, and 4) publishes it to a third party.

1) Falsity: Notice that the first element of defamation is that the statement that was published has to be false. If what someone says is true, it is not defamation no matter how bad it is. I was volunteering in a legal clinic once when someone told me that this other person was saying some horrible things about her. These things were embarrassing, and she felt that they were hurting her reputation in the community. She wondered if she could sue the person. I mentioned that she could sue for defamation if the statements were false. She looked around, leaned toward me and asked with a quieter voice, and embarrassed smile, "What if it's true?"

I smiled back and said, "You can only sue for defamation if the statement is false." If the statement is false, it satisfies the first element for libel and slander. If what is said is true, it will not qualify as libel or slander. Since it will not qualify as libel or slander, it will not satisfy paragraph d. of the definition of a "personal or advertising injury". If it does not satisfy the definition of "personal and advertising injury", there will be no coverage from the offense from Coverage B, Personal and Advertising Injury, in the CGL Policy.

A true statement may still qualify for coverage under the CGL Policy as a violation of one's right to privacy. This is discussed under paragraph e. of the definition of "personal and advertising injury". Under paragraph e., there may be coverage for "oral or written publication, in any manner, of material that violates a person's right of privacy"*(ibid)*. An invasion of privacy does not have the same falsity requirement that we find in libel and slander.

2) Defamatory: You might not like people talking about you. This might be especially true if what people are saying is not true. However, people saying untrue things about you will only meet the definition of the tort defamation (libel/slander), if what the people are saying is considered defamatory. In order to be defamation, the statement would have to be one that would subject the plaintiff to scorn or ridicule, or lower the plaintiff's reputation in the eyes of a respectable minority of the community.

This means that if a news anchor tells people that they should read this book because it was written by Dwight Kealy who was a professional basketball player before becoming an attorney, I could not sue the news anchor for defamation. I was never a professional basketball player. What the news anchor is saying is false. However, this statement is not defamatory because it would not subject me to scorn or ridicule, or lower my reputation in the eyes of a respectable minority of the community.

The term "respectable minority of the community" is a term to qualify who might think less of me. For example, if a small group of lacrosse players think less of me after hearing that I was a professional basketball player, the news anchor's statement would still *not* be defamation. I could argue that the statement was false and that it subjected me to scorn, ridicule, or a lower reputation in the eyes of this small group of lacrosse players, but their group is probably not a "respectable minority of the community" sufficient to call the statement defamatory. If the statement made is not defamatory, then it will not be considered libel or slander.

3) Statement of fact, of or concerning the plaintiff: You might eat at a restaurant tonight, lean over to the table next to you and say, "This meat tastes like rat meat." I hope this is false, satisfying the first element of defamation. I think the restaurant owner would find this defamatory, satisfying the second element. But what you are saying will not be defamation because you are not communicating a statement of fact. You are offering your opinion. If, on the other hand, you lean over to the table next to you and say, "Don't order the meat sauce because this restaurant uses rat meat whenever it lists generic meat in the menu," now you have made a statement of fact of or concerning the restaurant. The requirement that the statement be a statement of fact eliminates statements that are opinions, exaggerations, and jokes. If the statement is not a statement of fact, it will not be considered defamation.

The requirement that the statement needs to be of or concerning the plaintiff also helps narrow who can sue for the tort of defamation. For example, imagine that you made a defamatory statement about my favorite restaurant. I am angry with you because you said something unkind about my favorite restaurant. I want to sue you for defamation. What you are saying may be a false and defamatory statement of fact, but you did not say it about me. You said it about my favorite restaurant. I would not be a proper plaintiff to sue you for defamation because you saying that the restaurant serves rat meat is not a statement of fact that is of or concerning me. If the restaurant wanted to sue, the restaurant could choose to do so, but only if all elements are satisfied.

4) Published it to a third party: In order for a statement to be libel or slander, the statement must be published to a third party. When we think of publishing, we often think of books and things that are printed. Remember, defamation can also be oral (slander), and so the publishing requirement does not refer to printing. A statement is published to a third party when the party committing the defamation causes a third party to see or hear the false defamatory statement of fact. The third party can be anyone other than the person or entity about which the statement is made. If you tell a restaurant owner that the restaurant owner is using rat meat, that is not defamation. You are not communicating the statement to a third party. You are communicating it directly to the restaurant owner. Maybe you are just trying to help the restaurant reform its kitchen practices. A statement is only defamation if it is communicated to a third party.

To help explain libel and slander, imagine that there are two main pizza restaurants near where you live. You own "Reader's Pizza." This is a nice restaurant near your home. I own "Author's Pizza." This is a shadier establishment on the other side of town. I put up a sign that says, "Do not eat at Reader's Pizza because they use rat meat for their pepperoni."

My statement about your restaurant is a false, defamatory statement, of or concerning you, that has been published to a third party. It is in writing, and so I could be found liable for libel. If, instead of writing the sign, I yell these same words to those driving by my restaurant, I could be found liable for slander because my statements were oral. In either case, if you sued me for the sign (libel) or yelling (slander), I could contact my CGL Policy and turn in a claim. The policy would see that I committed libel or slander or disparaged a person or organization's goods, products or services. This is covered under Coverage B, Personal and Advertising Injury, because it is included in paragraph d of the definition of "personal and advertising injury".

e. Oral or written publication, in any manner, of material that violates a person's right of privacy;

Coverage B of the CGL Policy provides coverage for oral or written publication, in any manner, of material that violates a person's right of privacy (CG 00 01 04 13, ISO Properties, Inc., 2012, Page 15; Appendix Page 271). This paragraph provides some protection for lawsuits arising out statements that invade another's privacy, but fall short of the tort of defamation (libel/slander). For example, someone may reveal a private fact about someone that is either true, or is not defamatory, but is still offensively personal. As we saw in paragraph d, if it is true or not defamatory, it will not qualify as defamation.

Imagine that you tell people that I have cancer. As a result, some people do not want to hire me to speak at different insurance coverage conferences because they feel sorry for me, or they do not think that I will be well-enough to speak at the event. If it is true that I have cancer—and thankfully at this moment it is not true—but if it is true, then your statement would not satisfy the tort of defamation because the first requirement for defamation is the falsity of the statement.

Furthermore, even if your statement about my cancer were true, saying that someone has cancer is not defamatory because it does not subject someone to scorn, ridicule, or lower the person's reputation in the eyes of a respectable minority of the community. However, just because it is not technically libel or slander, the statement could violate my right to privacy. Maybe you read this information from my personal medical records and I did not want the information shared. Coverage B, Personal and Advertising Injury, of the CGL Policy, provides coverage for those sums that the insured becomes legally obligated to pay because of oral or written publication, in any manner, of material that violates a person's right of privacy.

Before you start wondering how in the world some "news" organizations get away with disclosing all kinds of private issues about people, I should let you know that not everyone has the same rights when it comes to privacy. This applies both to defamation and violations of one's rights to privacy. For example, public figures and matters of public concern do not have the same level of privacy rights that we uphold for non-public persons, and matters that are not of public concern. Public persons include public officials as well as people who inject themselves into the public spotlight by the nature of their work or interests. Matters of public concern would be matters that are considered newsworthy. Matters are newsworthy when they are of interest to the general public beyond a simple morbid curiosity into the lives of private people.

For example, imagine that a news magazine publishes a story about a public person that is false. In order to sue the news organization for defamation, the public person would need to show not just that the information was false, but that the information was published with malice. (If the story was about a private person on a matter that is not newsworthy, we only require falsity). It will be considered published with malice if the publisher knew the information was false, or recklessly disregarded information concerning whether the information was true or false. If the magazine publishes a story about a private person, the private person does not need to prove that the magazine published the false information with malice. In order to sue for defamation for a private person on a matter that is not newsworthy, the private person just needs to show that the magazine published a false, defamatory, statement of fact about the private person.

Why do public people get reduced privacy protections? Imagine that an official of the U.S. Government wanted to sue the New York Times for defamation because the official alleged that the New York Times published an article that did not have all of the facts correct about a government operation. The newspaper may be afraid to publish stories because of the threat of litigation from government officials. If newspapers are afraid of publishing newsworthy, well-researched stories because of the possibility of getting sued by government officials, the media may be reluctant to publish any stories that are critical of the government. This, in turn, could have a chilling effect on the freedom of the press that we value.

One of the reasons why public (famous) persons have reduced privacy protections is because their status gives them access to the media. If there is a false statement, they have access to go to the media to correct the statement. Furthermore, there is also a question about what would be defamatory for a famous person today. Think of the things some famous people have done that have made them famous today, but would have subjected them to scorn, ridicule, or a lower reputation in generations past. If the statements are not defamatory, then the magazines that make these statements could not be found liable for defamation. In order for one to be liable for defamation against a public person or a newsworthy story, the plaintiff would have to show not only that the information was false and defamatory, but that it was published with either knowledge of the falsity, or by recklessly disregarding information concerning whether the information was true or false (malice). (See *New York Times Co. v. Sullivan*, 376 U.S. 254 (1964); *Gertz v. Robert Welch, Inc.*, 418 U.S. 323 (1974)).

In 2013, California passed an anti-paparazzi law to protect the privacy of the children of famous people. Famous people might get accustomed to being pursued and photographed wherever they go, but they took offense to the intrusive photographers taking photos of their young children. The law provides that:

(a) Any person who intentionally harasses the child or ward of any other person because of that person's employment shall be punished by imprisonment in a county jail not exceeding one year, or by a fine not exceeding ten thousand dollars ($10,000), or by both that fine and imprisonment. (California Penal Code § 11414(a))

Paragraph e. of the definition of "personal and advertising injury" provides important coverage for policyholders sued under the tort of Public Disclosure of Private Fact. The tort of Public Disclosure of a Private Fact consists of the 1) disclosure of 2) private facts that are 3) highly offensive to a reasonable person, and are 4) not newsworthy. Unlike defamation, the disclosed fact may be true. Going back to our restaurant example, imagine that you and I have competing pizza restaurants in the same town. I get a hold of your private medical records that show that you have a gross—but not contagious—disease. I make a sign that instructs patrons to eat at my restaurant and not eat at your restaurant because you have this gross disease. You cannot sue me for defamation because the information that I am publishing is true.

However, you could sue me for the tort of Public Disclosure of a Private Fact. I described the disease as "gross" to indicate that sharing this information would be highly offensive to a reasonable person. I describe the disease as "not contagious" because having a restaurant operated by someone with a highly contagious disease could be newsworthy because patrons would want to know if there is a restaurant that they need to avoid to prevent contracting a "gross" contagious disease. Since the disease is gross, but not contagious, I shared a private fact that was highly offensive and not newsworthy.

If you sue me because of this public disclosure of a private fact, I could contact my CGL Policy and turn in the claim. The policy should see that I made a "written publication...that violates a person's right of privacy" (CG 00 01 04 13, ISO Properties, Inc., 2012, Page 15; Appendix Page 271). This would be covered under Coverage B, Personal and Advertising Injury, paragraph e. of the definition of "personal and advertising injury".

f. The use of another's advertising idea in your "advertisement"

Coverage B of the CGL Policy provides coverage for damages arising out of the use of another's advertising idea in the insured's "advertisement". You will notice that "advertisement" is in quotation marks which means that it is specifically defined in the policy.

What is an advertisement?

The CGL Policy defines an advertisement as follows:

"Advertisement" means a notice that is broadcast or published to the general public or specific market segments about your goods, products or services for the purpose of attracting customers or supporters. For the purpose of this definition:

a. Notices that are published include material placed on the Internet or on similar electronic means of communication; and

b. Regarding websites, only that part of a website that is about your goods, products or services for the purposes of attracting customers or supporters is considered an advertisement.

(CG 00 01 04 13, ISO Properties, Inc., 2012, Page 13; Appendix Page 267).

Continuing the example of our pizza restaurants, imagine that you and I have competing pizza restaurants in the same city. I hear that you want to start giving free pizza coupons to the 10th person who walks in the door. This is your idea. I think it is a great idea and I start using this idea on flyers that I send out to the general public to attract customers. I also start using this idea on my website. If you sue me, I should get a defense from my CGL Policy under "personal and advertising injury" because you are alleging damages from me using your advertising idea in my advertisement.

However, imagine that instead of me using your advertising idea on a flyer, I use it on my website. I do not use your idea on the part of my website where I list my pizza information to attract customers. I use your idea on my blog page. My blog page is part of my website, but it is a separate page. The blog page has information about legal issues that affect pizza restaurants in St. Petersburg, Florida. I use the blog to show that I am involved with the pizza community. I hear that writing the blog will help my website become easier to find on search engines. I guess this means that I am using the blog to attract customers, but the blog is not about my "goods, products or services." Notice that if there are multiple pages on a website, the definition of "advertisement" only includes "that part of a website that is about your goods, products or services for the purposes of attracting customers...." (*ibid.*)

Personal and Advertising Injury under Coverage B of the CGL Policy will provide coverage for damages arising out "the use of another's advertising idea in your "advertisement". If I

---

can show that I used your idea in what my CGL Policy defines as my "advertisement", then my policy should provide me with a defense and pay you damages, as appropriate.

Personal and Advertising Injury under Coverage B of the CGL Policy will provide coverage for damages arising out of "the use of another's advertising idea in your "advertisement". If policyholders can show that they used another's advertising idea in what the CGL Policy defines as an "advertisement", their policy should provide them with a defense and pay damages, as appropriate.

g. Infringing upon another's copyright, patent, trade dress or slogan in your "advertisement".

Coverage B of the CGL Policy provides coverage for damages arising out of an insured infringing upon another's copyright, patent, trade dress, or slogan in the insured's "advertisement." Whereas paragraph f provided coverage for use of another's advertising *idea* in an "advertisement", paragraph g extends coverage beyond just another's *idea,* to infringing on another's copyright, trade dress or slogan in an "advertisement".

A **copyright** is a legal right granting the creator of a work the exclusive rights to use and distribute the item created. For example, this book is my creation. I have the exclusive rights to use and distribute it. If you decided that you want to print a bunch of copies of this book and sell them for a profit—without first making a deal with me—then you would be in violation of copyright law.

A client called once because he had received a cease and desist letter from a large company. The large company wanted him to stop using his own business name because the large company felt that this name infringed on their copyright. The client had just spent $5,000 for things like advertisements in the telephone book and flyers to send out to potential customers. My client was an electrician with no employees. Why would anyone care about his name?

The name he had picked was Intel Electric. Evidently, there was a larger company that used the name "Intel" that did not want anyone to confuse the small town electrician with the Silicon Valley semiconductor chip maker. If the client turned the cease and desist letter over to his insurance company, he should have received a defense. This is because the cease and desist letter accused the electrician of infringing on Intel's copyright in the electrician's advertisement. This should be covered under Paragraph G. of the definition of Personal and Advertising Injury in the CGL Policy.

Trade dress is a legal term referring to the visual appearance of a product or service. A company's trade dress may be protected if the trade dress is distinctive to the company, and infringing on the trade dress could be confusing for consumers. For example, McDonald's restaurants are identified by the large yellow "M" in front of their restaurants. These are sometimes called the "golden arches." If I open a hamburger restaurant called Michael's with a large "M" in front of my restaurant, I would be infringing on McDonalds' trade dress because their symbol is distinctive and my use of it could confuse consumers.

A **slogan** is a phrase that a company may use to identify itself. For example, the phrase, "Just Do It" became synonymous with "Nike" when the phrase was central to their marketing campaign. If another business started using the slogan, Nike could object. Nike would argue that the phrase is Nike's intellectual property and that someone else using the phrase could confuse consumers and violate Nike's rights.

When would there be coverage under paragraph g. of the definition of "Personal and Advertising Injury" for use of a slogan? Using our competing pizza restaurant example from earlier, imagine that Bert and Ernie have competing pizza restaurants in St. Petersburg, Florida. Bert uses the slogan, "Pepperoni Pizza Paradise of St. Petersburg." It is a catchy slogan accompanied by a little jingle heard on the radio. Ernie starts using this same slogan on flyers that he sends out to the general public to attract customers. Ernie also start using this slogan on his internet site. If Bert sues Ernie for infringing on Bert's slogan, Ernie should get a defense from Ernie's CGL Policy. The defense would come from Coverage B, "Personal and Advertising Injury", because Bert is alleging damages arising out of Ernie using Bert's slogan in Ernie's advertisement.

The infringement must be in an advertisement.

An important element of paragraph g Infringing upon another's copyright, patent, trade dress or slogan, is that in order for there to be coverage, the infringement has to be part of the insured's "advertisement". We discussed the CGL Policy's definition of "advertisement" in paragraph f The use of another's advertising idea in your "advertisement". If someone is sued for infringing on another's copyright, trade dress or slogan, there will only be coverage under the CGL Policy if the infringement arose out of the insured's "advertisement".

A business called an insurance agent once thinking that the business had a personal and advertising injury claim to file against their CGL Policy. They had received a demand letter from a company named Kelora Systems, LLC (Kelora). Kelora's demand letter said that the business was infringing on Kelora's patent. Kelora then offered to license the technology to the business for $70,000. If the business would not pay the $70,000, Kelora would add the business to a lawsuit already filed by Kelora against Ebay and Microsoft.

The business did not think they had infringed on Kelora's patent. They had never heard of Kelora. The business did not make any products themselves. They were a retail store that sold products made by others. They had a website that sold their products, but the website was not a particularly fancy website. They could not think of anything that they did that infringed on anyone else's patent.

What was the patent? It turns out that Kelora owned patent 821 entitled, "Method and System for Executing a Guided Parametric Search." You can see an example of what Kelora thought this patent protected by looking at cars on ebay.com. At ebay.com, you will find a display that looks something like this:

eBay Motors
Parts & Accessories (1,480,841)
Cars & Trucks (1,495)
Automotive Tools & Supplies (25,886)

The numbers in parenthesis tell you how many items are in that category. If you click on "Cars & Trucks (1,495)," you will get something like this:

Vehicle Mileage
Less than 20,000 (432)
Less than 36,000 miles (569)
Less than 50,000 miles (691)

Listing the category names as well as the number of items in that category is a convenient way to search for products. Kelora agreed that this was convenient. Kelora thought this was so convenient they wanted to make sure that the idea was patented. Kelora argued that the convenient way to organize data was protected under Kelora's patent for "Executing a Guided Parametric Search." If the business wanted to use the technology, they needed to pay Kelora $70,000 or face the lawsuit. The business forwarded the demand letter to the business's CGL Policy, thinking that the business would get its legal defense covered under Coverage B. Personal and Advertising Injury Liability of the CGL Policy.

The insurance company denied the claim, refusing to defend or pay damages arising out of the Kelora demand letter. Why did the CGL Policy deny coverage? It appears that this was a lawsuit arising out of infringing upon another's copyright, patent, trade dress or slogan...but it was not arising out of the business's "advertisement". The CGL Policy does not simply pay damages or defend whenever an insured infringes on a copyright, trade dress or slogan. Paragraph g. only provides this coverage when the infringement occurs in the insured's "advertisement". (For more information, look up Ebay Inc. v. Kelora Systems, LLC).

Personal and Advertising Injury under Coverage B of the CGL Policy will provide coverage for damages arising out of infringing upon another's copyright, trade dress or slogan in the policyholder's "advertisement". If you can show that someone infringed on your copyright, trade dress or slogan, and that the infringement occurred in what the CGL Policy defines as an "advertisement", then their policy should provide them with a defense and pay you damages, as appropriate.

Chapter 5: Coverage B, Personal and Advertising Injury, Exclusions

Remember that I described Coverage A of the CGL Policy as existing on a "covered unless excluded basis." That is, Coverage A has a broad insuring agreement that seems to cover all bodily injury and property damage, unless it is excluded. Coverage A did not give a list of only seven specific ways in which you could get injured to meet the definition of bodily injury. There is a broad insuring agreement that does not limit how creative a third party may be in getting injured. There are then specific exclusions that eliminate coverage in certain situations.

Unlike Coverage A, Coverage B does not start with a broad insuring agreement. Instead, Coverage B provides coverage for only seven specific "Personal and Advertising Injury" offenses. If an offense is not one of the seven named offenses, it will not be considered "Personal and Advertising Injury". If it is not considered "Personal and Advertising Injury", there will be no coverage for the offense under Coverage B of the CGL Policy.

Even though there are only seven offenses covered under Coverage B, the CGL Policy still provides a list of Coverage B exclusions. This ensures that coverage does not leak beyond the specific offenses the policy intends to cover. A common theme in these exclusions is that the insurance company's intent is to only provide coverage for the insured's mistakes. For example, there may be coverage for the intentional act of publishing defamatory material by mistake, but the insurance policy does not intend to provide coverage for publishing material that the insured knows is false. Similarly, although there is coverage if you wrongfully evict someone under Coverage B, the CGL Policy only intends to provide this coverage when the insured evicted the tenant by mistake. The CGL Policy excludes coverage in situations where the landlord knowingly violates the rights of a tenant.

a. Knowing Violation of Rights of Another

Under Coverage B of the standard CGL Policy, there is no coverage when the insured knowingly violates the rights of another. Notice that there was coverage under "Personal and Advertising Injury" for things like wrongful entry, wrongful eviction, and false arrest. These include the intentional acts of entering, evicting, or confining an individual in a manner that violates an individual's rights. There is no coverage for these offenses if the insured had the "knowledge that the act would violate the rights of another and would inflict 'personal and advertising injury'" (CG 00 01 04 13, ISO Properties, Inc., 2012, Page 6; Appendix Page 255).

When describing coverage for wrongful eviction, I gave an example where Lucy was the landlord of a nice residential building in New York and Tina was one of her tenants. Lucy evicted Tina because Lucy thought Tina had failed to pay rent. It turned out that Tina had been paying rent. Tina was paying Lucy's property manager who evidently fled the country before giving Lucy all of the money paid by tenants. If Lucy evicted Tina for not paying rent, then Lucy would have rightfully evicted Tina. Since Tina *had* paid, Lucy wrongfully evicted her. We found coverage for wrongful eviction under Coverage B "Personal and Advertising Injury", of the CGL Policy.

However, if Lucy knew that Tina had paid rent in full, then Lucy would have knowledge that her act of evicting Tina would violate Tina's rights to inhabit her apartment. This exclusion removes coverage for "Personal and Advertising Injury" when the policyholder knowingly violates the rights of another. If Lucy evicted Tina *with* knowledge that Tina had paid, this exclusion would remove any coverage for the personal and advertising injury Lucy committed when evicting Tina.

b. Material Published with Knowledge of Falsity

Under Coverage B of the standard CGL Policy, there is no coverage when an insured publishes material with knowledge that the material being published is false. It is important to note that the policy may provide coverage for false statements. This exclusion removes coverage only for those statements that the policyholder knew were false.

How do we know that the CGL Policy may provide coverage for false statements? We know that the CGL Policy may provide coverage for false statements because paragraph d of the definition of "Personal and Advertising Injury" provided coverage for libel and slander. Libel and slander are the written (libel) and oral (slander) expressions of the tort of defamation. Defamation exists when a plaintiff communicates a 1) false, 2) defamatory 3) statement of fact of or concerning the defendant and 4) publishes it to a third party. Although defamation only exists if there is a false statement, this exclusion removes coverage for statements that the insured knows are false.

At first glance, this may seem like a reasonable exclusion. You should not say or write false and defamatory things about other persons or entities. However, this exclusion makes an impact on whether or not there would *ever* be coverage for defamation of a public person or on a matter of public concern.

If we look back to the elements of defamation (see page 159ff), you will find that this exclusion makes it unlikely that the CGL Policy would defend or pay damages for an individual who would be found liable for defamation of a public person, or on a matter of public concern. This is based on the different level of privacy held by public persons and on matters of public concern. As we discussed in paragraph e. of the definition of "Personal and Advertising Injury", someone will only be found liable for defamation of a public person or on a matter of public concern if the person who made the false statement did so with malice. If someone made the statement with malice, it means that the person made the statement with knowledge of falsity or with reckless disregard to the truth.

This Coverage B exclusion removes any coverage for material published with knowledge of falsity. Since there is no coverage for material published with knowledge of falsity, and individuals will only be found liable for defamation of public persons or on matters of public concerns when the individual knew the information was false, this exclusion essentially removes coverage for defamation against public persons or on matters of public concern. If the plaintiff proves that the defendant policyholder made the statement with knowledge of the statement's falsity—which would be required in a defamation lawsuit alleging defamation of a public person or on a matter of public concern—then there would be no coverage for any associated damages because this exclusion removes any coverage for "Personal and Advertising Injury" for material that is published with the policyholder's knowledge of falsity.

c. Material Published Prior to Policy Period

The CGL Policy excludes Personal and Advertising Injury "arising out of oral or written publication of material whose first publication took place before the beginning of the policy period" (CG 00 01 04 13, ISO Properties, Inc., 2012, Page 6; Appendix Page 255). At first glance, this exclusion can look like the potentially dangerous "Prior Work Exclusion" added as a Coverage A exclusion in some non-standard CGL Policies (see discussion on page 130). With the "Prior Work Exclusion", there is the danger of a mason having no coverage for any walls built in the past that may fall during the current policy. The standard Coverage B exclusion of "Material Published Prior to the Policy Period" is different than the non-standard "Prior Work Exclusion" because of a basic difference between Coverage A and Coverage B.

Under Coverage A of the standard CGL Policy, we find coverage for occurrences that occur during a policy period. Under Coverage B, we do not discuss occurrences. We discuss offenses. With this in mind, we need to ask, "When does the offense of defamation take place?" Is it when someone is offended, or when the defamatory statement is made? If it is when someone is offended, then the "Material Published Prior to Policy Period Exclusion" can feel like the non-standard Coverage A "Prior Work Exclusion" because the work (in this case publication) might have been done in the past, and then there is no coverage for the occurrence (in this case offense) in the future.

In looking at the definition of the tort of defamation (libel/slander), we find that the offense takes place when someone *publishes* a false, defamatory, statement of fact about the defendant. Based on the elements of the tort, this offense takes place not when someone is offended by a statement, but when the false, defamatory, statement of fact about the defendant is *published.*

Coverage B applies "only if the offense was committed in the 'coverage territory' *during the policy period*" (CG 00 01 04 13, ISO Properties, Inc., 2012, Page 6; Appendix Page 254, emphasis added). Since the tort of defamation occurs at the point in time when a statement is published, and Coverage B only provides coverage for offenses committed during the policy period, then there would be no coverage for a statement published before a policy period because the offense would not have been committed during the policy period. This exclusion clarifies that there is only coverage for offenses made during the policy period. Any defamation arising out of material published before the policy period would need to seek coverage under prior policies when the material was published. This is because the offense occurs at the moment when the material is published.

d. Criminal Acts

Coverage B makes it clear that there is no coverage for "Personal and advertising injury" arising out of a criminal act committed by or at the direction of the insured (CG 00 01 04 13, ISO Properties, Inc., 2012, Page 6; Appendix Page 255). This may not be surprising on the surface, but it is important to recognize that sometimes the line between criminal law and civil law is blurred. For example, there is the famous case of the former U.S. Football player, O.J. Simpson, and his involvement with the death of his former wife, Nicole Brown Simpson, and her friend Ron Goldman. O.J. Simpson was found not guilty of murdering them in a criminal trial. He was later found liable for their wrongful deaths in a civil trial. How can someone be found not guilty in criminal court, and then be found liable for essentially the same deaths in civil court?

In criminal law, there is a defendant who is being prosecuted by the office of the district attorney. These attorneys are paid by tax payers and are said to represent the interest of "the people." You do not have to go out and sue someone who commits a crime against you. You call the police, and the district attorney's office decides whether or not to prosecute. If the accused defendant is convicted of a crime, we say that the defendant was found guilty of a crime. In order to be found guilty of a crime, the people need to prove *beyond a reasonable doubt* that the defendant committed every element of the crime. If the defendant is found guilty, he or she can be forced to go to jail or prison for an amount of time commensurate with the crime committed. The guilty party may also be forced to pay financial damages to the victim(s) of the criminal conduct. These financial damages are called restitution.

In civil law, there is a defendant who is being sued by a particular person or group with a grievance against the defendant. The party with the grievance against the defendant is called the plaintiff. Each party hires their own attorney. If the defendant loses the case, we do not say that the defendant is guilty. Instead, we say that the defendant is *liable*. In order to be found liable in civil court, the plaintiff needs to prove by a *preponderance of the evidence* that the defendant committed *all* of the elements of the civil wrong. This standard of proof only requires a finding that "it is more likely than not" that the defendant is liable for all of the elements of the civil wrong. This is a much lower standard than the criminal standard requiring "proof beyond a reasonable doubt." Finally, the resolution normally sought in civil court is for the defendant to pay financial damages. The unsuccessful defendant in civil court does not go to jail.

O.J. Simpson's criminal trial occurred prior to his civil trial. He was found not guilty of murder in criminal court because a jury determined that he could not be found guilty "beyond a reasonable doubt." However, a civil court jury determined that the preponderance of the evidence proved that O.J. Simpson was liable for the wrongful death of the victims.

How does O.J. Simpson's criminal and civil cases relate to the exclusion for Criminal Acts under Coverage B of the CGL

Policy?   O.J. Simpson had a business called Orenthal Enterprises. Orenthal Enterprises had an insurance policy that defended O.J. Simpson at Simpson's civil trial. The insurance policy excluded criminal acts, but by the time the civil trial began, O.J. Simpson had already been found not guilty of the criminal charges against him.   Since the criminal trial established that O.J. Simpson was not guilty of the criminal acts, his policy's exclusion for criminal acts was not activated. Since the criminal act exclusion was not activated, his policy was obligated to defend him in the civil trial in accordance with his policy's insuring agreement.

Applying the O.J. Simpson facts to "Personal and Advertising Injury" in the CGL Policy, imagine that O.J. Simpson was employed as a bouncer at a bar. While working as a bouncer, he tackles and detains an unruly patron. He then locks the patron in a closet until the police arrive. Coverage B provides coverage for false arrest, false detention, and false imprisonment. If the bouncer O.J. Simpson (or his employer) gets sued for the unruly patron's false detention or imprisonment, Coverage B of the CGL Policy should provide a defense.

However, making this more like the real O.J. Simpson case, imagine that the unruly patron dies in the closet before the police arrive. If O.J. Simpson is convicted of the *crime* of false imprisonment (or murder), the CGL Policy will *not* provide a defense in a later civil trial seeking additional financial damages. Coverage would be precluded by the Criminal Acts exclusion under Coverage B of the CGL Policy. However, if O.J. were found not guilty of this criminal conduct, then the bar's CGL insurance policy should provide a defense under Coverage B for damages arising out of the "Personal and Advertising Injury" of "false arrest, detention, or imprisonment."

e. Contractual Liability

Like Coverage A, Personal and Advertising Injury under Coverage B excludes Contractual Liability. Unlike Coverage A, Coverage B does not make an exception to provide coverage for an "Insured Contract". The only exception to the Coverage

B Contractual Liability Exclusion is "liability for damages that the insured would have in the absence of the contract or agreement". In other words, the CGL Policy will not extend Coverage B simply because there was a contract. The CGL Policy will also not deny coverage simply because there was a contract.

For example, imagine that you own a bar and want to hire me to be a bouncer. I am worried about potential liabilities, and so, before I work for you, I ask you to sign a contract with me. The contract states that that you will defend me in the event that I am sued for false arrest, detention, or imprisonment. You sign the agreement. You now have the contractual obligation to defend me if I get charged with one of these offenses.

Coverage B broadly excludes all Contractual Liability, but in the exclusion, it does not mean to exclude coverage for offenses the policy is designed to cover. In this case, "false arrest, detention, or imprisonment" are included in the CGL Policy's definition of "Personal and Advertising Injury". Coverage B of the CGL Policy provides coverage for these offenses. Since there would be coverage for these offenses in the absence of the contract or agreement, the CGL Policy would provide coverage for these offenses. If, however, our contract was to defend me for claims of personal injuries outside of those specifically defined under "Personal and Advertising Injury", then there would be no coverage. Contractual Liability will not extend coverage beyond the coverage already provided in Coverage B of the CGL Policy.

f. Breach of Contract

Contractual Liability (exclusion e., above) and Breach of Contract both involve an exchange of promises. As discussed in the previous exclusion, Contractual Liability is excluded unless the policy would have provided coverage absent the contract. Breach of contract deals with the consequences of breaking a promise. Breach of Contract is excluded unless it arises out of an implied contract to use another's advertising idea in the insured's "advertisement" (CG 00 01 04 13, ISO Properties, Inc., 2012, Page 6; Appendix Page 255).

For example, let us say that we form a contract. In order for us to form an enforceable contract, there must be an offer, acceptance, and consideration. I communicate to you that I would sell you this book for $10.00. You accept this offer. You may have accepted by silently giving me $10.00 or you might have yelled, "I accept." Either way, we have an offer and acceptance. Consideration exists because there is bargained for exchange. That is, you did not have to give me $10.00, and I did not have to sell you my book. We agree on the terms, and we have offer, acceptance, and consideration. At this moment, we have formed a contract. A breach of contract exists when a party to the contract breaks its promise. For example, in the above exchange, let us say that you gave me an envelope that contained a $5.00 bill instead of a $10.00 bill. We had a contract for $10.00. You broke your promise. It may have been an accident that can be corrected easily, but it is still a broken promise.

The starting point for Breach of Contract in Coverage B of the CGL Policy is that there is no coverage unless it is for an implied contract to use another's advertising idea in the insured's "advertisement" (ibid.). The difference between an expressed contract and an implied contract arises out of how the parties communicate with each other. An expressed contract is one where the terms are clearly spoken or written. For example, "I will sell you my book for $10.00" is an expressed contract. It is expressed because I have communicated the terms of the contract.

An implied contract is a contract where the terms were not expressly communicated. The terms were implied. An implied contract can be either an *implied in fact contract* or an *implied in law contract*. An implied in fact contract is a contract where one or both of the parties show agreement to the contract. For example, imagine that you walk into a book store, grab my book, walk the book to the checkout counter, and give the clerk money. Nothing was said or written. We do not have an expressed contract. Instead, your conduct suggests that you agree to the implied in fact contract that you will exchange money for my book.

An implied in law contract is an unwritten and unspoken law that is imposed by law to avoid unjust enrichment. For example, imagine that a physician operates on an unconscious patient in an emergency ward. The physician performs a service, the patient gets well, and the physician sends the former patient a bill. The patient never agreed to allow the physician to perform the service. There was no expressed offer or acceptance. However, it is implied that physicians should be paid for their services. Courts will hold that the patient and doctor formed an implied in law contract because it would not be fair for the patient to receive the benefit of the services without paying the doctor.

This exclusion states that there is no coverage for a breach of contract *unless* it is for "an implied contract to use another's advertising idea in your "advertisement" (CG 00 01 04 13, ISO Properties, Inc., 2012, Page 6; Appendix Page 255). When would there be a "Personal and advertising injury" arising out of an implied contract to use another's advertising idea in an insured's advertisement?

Imagine that you are working on an advertisement that you are going to print and distribute through the mail. You go online and look at a variety of professional-looking photographs on various websites. You pick a photograph that is perfect for your advertisement. You include it in your advertisement and send it out through the mail. As I mentioned before, it was implied in fact that you would pay for the book that you pick up off the shelf at the bookstore and take to the checkout counter. The owner of the photograph argues that it is also implied in fact that you would pay for the photograph that you picked up off the website and printed on your flyers. The owner of the photograph is arguing that you breached the implied in fact contract to pay for the use of the photograph.

Coverage B starts by excluding any breach of contract, but then allows an exception for breach of an implied contract to use another's advertising idea in the insured's "advertisement". If the owner of the website photo succeeds in showing that there was an implied contract for the insured to pay for the photo, then not paying for the photo would be a breach of contract. If this is a breach of an implied contract to use another's advertising idea in the insured's "advertisement", there should be coverage under Coverage B of the CGL Policy.

g. Quality or Performance of Goods- Failure to Conform to Statements

Coverage B, Personal and Advertising Injury excludes coverage for injuries "arising out of the failure of goods, products or services to conform with any statement of quality or performance made in your 'advertisement'" (CG 00 01 04 13, ISO Properties, Inc., 2012, Page 6; Appendix Page 255).

Sometimes you will hear an advertisement that makes crazy promises. Imagine an advertisement that offers a book that is not only good for satisfying your state's continuing education requirements, but can also be used as a cutting board, held over your head as an umbrellas when it rains, or, if you are ever falling from an airplane, you could hold the open book in both hands above your head as a parachute. If you attempt the latter, you—or your beneficiaries—might find that there could be injuries "arising out of the failure of the...[book]...to conform with any statement of...performance made in [the] 'advertisement'" (*ibid.*). This exclusion makes it clear that there will be no coverage "arising out of the failure of goods, products or services to conform with any statement of quality or performance made in your 'advertisement'" (*ibid.*).

It is tempting for a purchaser to view the advertisement as an *offer* that has been made by the seller of the book. However, under contract law, an advertisement is generally

NOT viewed as an offer made by a seller. Instead, an advertisement is viewed as an invitation to accept offers from the public. If the advertisement was an offer, then a buyer could walk into the store, say, "I accept," offer money (consideration), and suggest that a contract had been formed between the seller and buyer. Instead, when the customer comes in and offers to pay money for merchandise, the customer is making the offer. The merchant then has the power to accept the offer. When the offer is accepted (along with payment), the contract between buyer and seller is formed.

Although this may seem like a minor distinction, it is an important legal distinction for the analysis of Coverage B's exclusion of "Quality or Performance of Goods—Failure to Conform to Statements." The exclusion applies to statements made in an insured's advertisements, and statements in advertisements are generally *NOT* promises offered by the seller. Advertisements often include opinions and hyperbole to encourage buyers to make an offer to purchase the seller's goods.

In order for the term in the advertisement to be part of the contract, it must have been an identified, material term considered by the buyer. A material term is a term that is central to the decision to enter the contract. Some people who purchased automobiles from Hyundai and Kia between 2011 and 2013 argued that the advertised fuel efficiency of the vehicles was an identified, material term considered by the buyers. It was a material term because the buyers argued that the fuel efficiency was an essential element of their decision to purchase their vehicles. When the cars performed worse at the pump than advertised, customers felt that they were being financially harmed by the automakers' broken promise every time the customers filled up their tanks with fuel.

In November 2014, automakers Hyundai and Kia announced that they would pay a $360 million settlement for overstating gas mileage on 1.2 million vehicles produced between 2011 and 2013. This would be damages arising out of the failure of goods to conform with statements of quality in the automaker's advertisement. This is specifically excluded from Coverage B of the CGL Policy.

Even without the exclusion, it is difficult to find a place where coverage would be afforded for a similar offense under the seven definitions of Personal and Advertising Injury. Some people will read that there is a personal and advertising injury, and then look to the policy for coverage without first reviewing the seven definitions of Personal and Advertising Injury. Clearly in the above example there was no false arrest, malicious prosecution, or eviction. Someone alleging coverage out of failure of a product to conform with a statement in an advertisement would have to argue that the injury fits under either paragraph f. The use of another's advertising idea in the insured's "advertisement", or g. Infringing upon another's copyright, trade dress, or slogan in the insured's "advertisement". Even if a claimant could show that the fuel efficiency claims involves one of the car companies using another's advertising idea in an insured's advertisement, it would still be excluded under Coverage B's exclusion for "Personal and Advertising Injury" arising out of the failure of goods, products or services to conform with any statement of quality or performance made in the insured's "advertisement".

h. Wrong Description of Prices

Coverage B excludes coverage for "Personal and advertising injury" arising out of the wrong description of the price of goods, products or services stated in the insured's "advertisement" (CG 00 01 04 13, ISO Properties, Inc., 2012, Page 6; Appendix Page 255). This exclusion reinforces some principles of contract law.

A basic element of contract law is that you cannot sue for breach of contract if there is no contract. This means that before a consumer can sue a merchant for breaching a contract because the merchant advertised the wrong price of goods in the insured's advertisement, the consumer first needs to prove that the merchant and consumer formed a contract. As previously discussed under exclusion f. Breach of Contract, a contract is not formed unless there is an offer, acceptance, and consideration.

An advertisement is generally not viewed as an offer (see the discussion under exclusion g. Quality or Performance of Goods—Failure to Conform to Statements). Instead, an advertisement is viewed as an invitation that a merchant makes to encourage buyers to make offers. The buyer who reads the advertisement then has the ability to make an offer to purchase goods from the merchant. After the buyer makes the offer, the merchant has the power to accept or reject the buyer's offer.

Since the advertisement is not the offer, the consumer cannot walk into the store, accept the terms of the advertisement, and then sue the merchant for breach of contract because of wrong description of prices in the advertisement. The advertisement was not the offer. No contract is formed until the buyer makes the offer to purchase from the merchant, and the merchant accepts the offer.

Furthermore, the controlling law for the sale of goods holds that the price of goods is not an essential element to contract formation. The controlling law for the sale of goods is the Uniform Commercial Code (UCC). The essential element for contract formation under the UCC is not the price, but the quantity. So long as the parties agree on a quantity, a contract may be found to exist even if the price is omitted or incorrectly stated. A court can resolve the issue of a missing price by supplying a reasonable price if there is an adequate description of the goods and their quantity.

The exclusion for "Wrong Description of Prices" in an "advertisement" reinforces the contractual law principles holding that an advertisement is generally not an offer, there is no contract if there is not an offer, and one cannot sue for breach of contract if there is no contract. Even if there is a dispute over the price based on an advertisement that gets into court, the UCC holds that the price is not an essential element for contract formation.

All this is to say that the deck is stacked against someone trying to sue another based on the wrong description of prices in an advertisement because an advertisement is generally not an offer, and the UCC holds that price is not an essential element in a contract for the sale of goods. If, against these odds, a consumer still pursues legal action against a merchant based on the wrong description of prices in an advertisement, this exclusion makes it clear that the Coverage B will *not* provide coverage for Personal and advertising injury arising out of the wrong description of the price of goods, products, or services stated in [the policyholder's] "advertisement" (CG 00 01 04 13, ISO Properties, Inc., 2012, Page 6; Appendix Page 255).

i. Infringement of Copyright, Patent, Trademark or Trade Secret

Coverage B of the CGL Policy excludes any "'personal and advertising injury'" arising out of the infringement of copyright, patent, trademark, trade secret or other intellectual property rights" (CG 00 01 04 13, ISO Properties, Inc., 2012, Page 7; Appendix Page 255). This exclusion limits the extent of the "personal and advertising injury" definition that provides coverage for "infringing upon another's copyright, patent, trade dress or slogan in [an insured's] "advertisement" (See definition g. Infringing upon another's copyright, patent, trade dress, or slogan in your "advertisement" on page 168). Notice that the key distinction is that although there may be coverage for an infringement that takes place in an insured's "advertisement", this exclusion makes it clear that there is no coverage for infringement of copyright, patent, trademark, or trade secrets outside of an insured's advertisement.

Under paragraph g. "Infringing upon another's copyright, trade dress or slogan in your 'advertisement'" of the Personal and advertising definition, we addressed a situation where a client was sued for infringing upon another company's proprietary information. When the client turned in the claim to the client's insurance company, the insurance company denied coverage for the claim. Although there was a claim that the client had infringed upon someone's copyright, there were no facts to suggest that this was done in the insured's "advertisement". The CGL Policy specifically excludes any infringement of copyright, patent, trademark, or trade secret unless the infringement is in the insured's "advertisement". The exclusion does not apply to infringements of copyright, patent, trade dress or slogan in the insured's "advertisement".

j. Insureds in Media and Internet Type Businesses

The CGL Policy excludes "'personal and advertising injury' committed by an insured who is a media and internet type business" (CG 00 01 04 13, ISO Properties, Inc., 2012, Page 7; Appendix Page 256). Since "personal and advertising injury" is excluded for media and internet type businesses, every business may want to ask, "Are we a media or internet business?" For example, my law office has a website: www.DwightKealy.com. I seek to attract customers through this website. I started the website www.GoGetCE.com as a site where insurance agents can receive insurance continuing education credit by going online, downloading an insurance book, and then answering a series of questions. The only way anyone has ever purchased the test to get CE credit has been on the internet. Do I have an internet type business? If the answer is yes, then my CGL Policy would exclude all "personal and advertising injury".

To remove some of the doubts as to what businesses are eliminated by this exclusion, the policy exclusion specifically lists those businesses for which this exclusion applies.

"Personal and advertising injury" [is excluded when it is] committed by an insured whose business is:

1) Advertising, broadcasting, publishing or telecasting;
2) Designing or determining content of websites for others; or
3) An Internet search, access, content or service provider.
(CG 00 01 04 13, ISO Properties, Inc., 2012, Page 7; Appendix Page 256).

Doubts may remain even after reading these three categories. For example, if enough people visit my websites, other businesses may want to pay me to include an advertisement for their business on my website. Although I did not think that I was in the advertising business, now someone might be considering to pay me to include their advertisement on my website. It may look like I am in the business of advertising.

To make the murky waters of what constitutes a media or internet business a little less murky, this exclusion clarifies that the "placing of frames, borders or links, or advertising, for you or others anywhere on the internet, is not *by itself*, considered the business of advertising, broadcasting, publishing or telecasting" (*ibid.*). Unfortunately, the policy does not provide any clarity to tell us what they mean when they say that this conduct "by itself" will not exclude a business from Personal and Advertising Injury. That is, the policy does not tell us what more would need to be done in addition to placing frames, borders, links, or advertising of others on the internet to activate this exclusion.

At first glance, this exclusion looks like it applies to ALL of the defined personal and advertising injuries—from False Arrest to infringing upon another's copyright. However, the exclusion clarifies that the exclusion does not apply to "paragraphs 14a., b., and c. of "personal and advertising injury" under the definitions section" (CG 00 01 04 13, Insurance Services Office, Inc., 2012). Paragraphs 14 a., b., and c. include: a. False arrest, detention, or imprisonment; b. Malicious prosecution; and c. Wrongful eviction and wrongful entry. This clarifies that this exclusion is focused on excluding only those personal and advertising injuries that may be more common for media and internet type businesses. If a business's stated purpose falls under—or close to—the three definitions above, they should consider an insurance policy specifically designed for media and internet businesses.

k. Electronic Chatrooms or Bulletin Boards

The CGL Policy excludes "'personal and advertising injury' arising out of an electronic chatroom or bulletin board the insured hosts, owns, or over which the insured exercises control" (CG 00 01 04 13, Insurance Services Office, Inc., 2012,

Page 7; <u>Appendix Page 256</u>). Unlike the previous exclusion, this exclusion does NOT make any exceptions for the personal and advertising injuries found in paragraphs 14a., b., and c. in the definition of "personal and advertising injury". This exclusion applies to ALL of the defined personal and advertising injuries—from False Arrest to infringing upon another's copyright.

> **The CGL Policy excludes personal and advertising injury arising out of Electronic Chatrooms or Bulletin Boards.**

If there is a claim arising out of electronic chatrooms or bulletin boards, and you want to look to the CGL Policy for coverage, imagine that Coverage B has been physically ripped out of the CGL Policy and thrown into a shredder. This exclusion states that there is no coverage for claims arising out of electronic chatrooms or bulletin boards.

Why would the exclusion be so broad for electronic chatrooms and bulletin boards when there were exceptions that provided some coverage for media and internet type businesses (see paragraph j. above)? In 2008, Lori Drew was indicted for crimes stemming from her role in the 2006 death of her 13 year old neighbor Megan Meier.   Megan Meier committed suicide. How could Lori Drew be implicated in the suicide death of a 13 year old girl, and what does this have to do with electronic chatrooms or bulletin boards?

Megan and Lori's daughter had been friends. As it sometimes happens among 13 year olds, after they were friends, they were definitely *not* friends. Lori did not like some mean things that Megan was saying about Lori's daughter. In response, Lori created a MySpace page for a fake boy named "Josh." "Josh" and Megan became "friends" online. Then Lori had this "Josh" breakup with Megan.

According to Megan's mother, "Josh" told Megan, "'I don't know if I want to be friends with you any longer because I hear you're not nice to your friends." According to The Associated Press, "The person using Josh's account was sending cruel messages.... Megan called her mother, saying electronic bulletins were being posted about her, saying things like, "Megan Meier is a slut. Megan Meier is fat." (http://abcnews.go.com/GMA/story?id=3929774).

Megan received a final message from "Josh" on October 16 2006. It told her that "the world would be a better place without you" and urged her to "have a [lousy] rest of your life". Megan responded, "You are the kind of boy a girl would kill herself over." Shortly afterwards, Megan hanged herself. (http://www.theguardian.com/technology/2008/nov/27/myspace -usa).

The story is tragic. What started as something that Lori Drew thought might be an interesting joke, became a criminal trial for which she needed a defense. Even if the offense could trigger coverage under the CGL's policy's "personal and advertising injury" offenses of libel, this exclusion makes it clear that there will be no coverage for offenses arising out of an electronic chatroom or bulletin board the insured hosts, owns, or over which the insured exercises control (CG 00 01 04 13, Insurance Service Office, Inc., 2012, page 7; <u>Appendix Page 256</u>).

I. Unathorized Use of Another's Name or Product

The CGL Policy excludes "'personal and advertising injury' arising out of the unauthorized use of another's name or product in your e-mail address, domain name or metatag, or any other similar tactics to mislead another's potential customers" (CG 00 01 04 13, Insurance Service Office, Inc., 2012, page 7; <u>Appendix Page 256</u>). This exclusion serves to corral some overly aggressive entrepreneurs who may have wanted to misuse Coverage B's coverage for "another's advertising idea" or "infringing upon another's copyright, trade dress or slogan" (CG 00 01 04 13, page 15; <u>Appendix Page 271</u>).

Imagine that a small company that sells shoes would like to attract business by looking like the much larger shoe company named "Nike." The small company sends emails to potential clients using an email address that looks like it will go to Nike, but the emails will really go to the small shoe company. The small shoe company has a domain name and internal code on a website that makes consumers and search engines think that they are going to Nike, but they are really going to the small shoe company. This could result in significant increased business for the small shoe company.

This could also result in litigation from the much larger shoe company that does not want its name misrepresented and its clients pilfered. If the small shoe company's legal strategy is to turn over any potential claims for this conduct to their CGL Policy, they may be disappointed. The CGL Policy clearly excludes "'personal and advertising injury' arising out of the unauthorized use of another's name or product in your e-mail address, domain name or metatag, or any other similar tactics to mislead another's potential customers" (CG 00 01 04 13, Insurance Service Office, Inc., 2012, page 7; Appendix Page 256).

m. Pollution

The CGL Policy Excludes "'personal and advertising injury' arising out of the actual, alleged, or threatened discharge, dispersal, seepage, migration, release or escape of 'pollutants' at any time" (CG 00 01 04 13, Insurance Service Office, Inc., 2012, page 7; Appendix Page 256). Coverage A, Bodily Injury and Property Damage to others, also had a pollution exclusion. However, the pollution exclusion in Coverage A contained notable exceptions to provide coverage for events like a hostile fire, that new carpet smell, or smoke or fumes dispersed through a building's heating, ventilation, or air conditioning vents. Coverage B does not provide any exceptions to the pollution exclusion. If the only place an insured can find coverage for pollution is under Coverage B, this exclusion will remove any possibility of pollution coverage.

For example, imagine that a landlord wrongfully evicts a manufacturing business tenant. Wrongful eviction is included in the definition of "personal and advertising injury" in the CGL Policy. As a result of the eviction, no one is on the premises to handle the regular maintenance and cleanup associated with the manufacturing business. As a few days turns into a few weeks, various lubricants and toxins begin leaking from equipment, out of the premises, and into the neighboring stream. We now have a pollution exposure. Even though the landlord could argue that the damage to the stream was the result of a "personal and advertising injury" exposure (wrongful eviction), there will be no coverage because of coverage B's complete exclusion for pollution.

n. Pollution-Related

In case the Pollution exclusion was not broad enough to prevent coverage for pollution, Coverage B of the CGL Policy provides an additional exclusion that removes coverage for pollution-related exposures. This exclusions makes it explicit that there will be no coverage for any loss, cost or expense arising out of any:

> 1) Request , demand, order or statutory or regulatory requirement that any insured or others test for, monitor, clean up, remove, contain, treat, detoxify or neutralize, or in any way respond to, or assess the effects of, "pollutants"; or
> 2) Claim or suit by or on behalf of a governmental authority for damages because of testing for, monitoring, cleaning up, removing, containing, treating, detoxifying or neutralizing, or in any way responding to, or assessing the effects of, "pollutants" (CG 00 01 04 13, ISO, 2012, page 7; Appendix Page 256).

Remember the "neighboring stream" used as an example for Coverage B's paragraph m. pollution exclusion? I mentioned that there would be no coverage for the pollution exposure to the "neighboring stream" because it arose out of a "personal and advertising injury" and that the paragraph m. exclusion for pollution removes all pollution coverage without any exceptions. Coverage B's paragraph n. pollution-related exclusion builds on the pollution exclusion in paragraph m.. If a state law says that the stream needs to be tested, monitored, cleaned up, treated, or detoxified, this exclusion will make it clear that there will be no coverage for these items under Coverage B.

This exclusion also makes it clear that there will be no clean-up of the stream, even if there is a claim or suit by a governmental authority. When discussing Coverage A's pollution exclusion, I mentioned the pipeline that burst in 2013, dumping 233,000 gallons of molasses into Honolulu Harbor. The U.S. Attorney in Hawaii pursued the company responsible until the company paid a total penalty of $1 million along with pleading guilty to two counts of violating the Rivers and Harbors Act of 1899. This is an example of a governmental authority filing a claim or suit against a business due to a pollution exposure. Even if there is a lawsuit filed by the government like the one filed against the Hawaiian pipeline company, this exclusion makes it clear that there will be no coverage for monitoring, cleaning up, containing, treating, detoxifying, or neutralizing, or in any way responding to, or [even just] assessing the effects of pollutants (CG 00 01 04 13, ISO, 2012, page 7; Appendix Page 256).

o. War

Coverage B of the CGL excludes coverage for "'personal and advertising injury', however caused, arising, directly or indirectly out of War...warlike action...or [any] insurrection, rebellion, [or] revolution" (CG 00 01 04 13, ISO, 2012, page 7; Appendix Page 257). The Coverage B exclusion uses the exact words used for excluding war under Coverage A. Please refer to Coverage A, exclusion i. War, for a general discussion on the war exclusion. The difference between the Coverage A and Coverage B war exclusions, is not rooted in the exclusion, but in the difference in coverage granted. Coverage A provides coverage for bodily injury or property damages to others so long as the coverage is not excluded. Coverage B only provides coverage for the seven named "Personal and Advertising Injury" offenses, unless excluded.

It is not difficult to imagine the possibility of war causing a Coverage A bodily injury or property damage occurrence. At first glance, it may be more difficult to imagine war causing a Coverage B personal and advertising injury offense. However, as warfare changes, a hostile act might include cyber-attacks against the government or financial institutions. Imagine that during war, a business's computers are hijacked and this causes financial or governmental records to change. This could lead to prisoners not being released when they should be released (false detention), people being evicted for not paying rent when they had paid rent (wrongful eviction), or a variety of libel or invasion of privacy claims against an insured. These are all personal and advertising injuries that could be covered under Coverage B of the CGL Policy, except for the war exclusion. The war exclusion makes it clear that there will be no coverage for 'personal and advertising injury', however caused, arising, directly or indirectly out of War...warlike action...or [any] insurrection, rebellion, [or] revolution" (ibid.).

p. Distribution of Material in Violation Of Statutes

Coverage B excludes "personal and advertising injury" arising directly or indirectly out of any action or omission that violates one of a handful of specifically identified consumer protection statutes. The specific statutes addressed are: 1) The Telephone Consumer Protection Act (TCPA), 2) the CAN-SPAM Act of 2003, and 3) The Fair Credit Reporting Act (FCRA) / Fair and Accurate Credit Transactions Act (FACTA). The name CAN-SPAM is an abbreviation for the legislative act's full name: **Controlling the Assault of Non-Solicited Pornography And Marketing Act of 2003**. Together, TCPA and CAN-SPAM are designed to protect consumers from unwanted solicitations through phone, fax, and email. FCRA and FACTA are federal laws designed to regulate and protect consumers from the misuse of their personal consumer information.

This exclusion uses the same wording as Exclusion q. Distribution of Materials in Violation of Statutes found under Coverage A of the CGL Policy. Please see the discussion for

Coverage A's exclusion q. Distribution of Materials in Violation of Statutes for a broader discussion on the exclusion. Since the two exclusions use the same words, the difference between the exclusions lies not in their words, but in the types of offenses covered by Coverage A and Coverage B. Coverage A provides coverage for bodily injury or property damages to others so long as the coverage is not excluded. Coverage B only provides coverage for the seven named "Personal and Advertising Injury" offenses, unless excluded.

It is possible that one's mistake with a marketing plan or mistake with client information could "violate a person's right of privacy". This is covered under paragraph e. of the definition of "personal and advertising injury". However, this mistake may also violate TCPA, CAN-SPAM, FCRA, or FACTA. This exclusion makes it clear that there will be no coverage for "personal and advertising injury" arising directly or indirectly out of any action or omission that violates or is alleged to violate" TCPA, CAN-SPAM, FCRA, or FACTA (CG 00 01 04 13, Insurance Services Offices, In., 2012, Page 7; Appendix Page 257).

Chapter 6: Coverage C – Medical Payments

The standard CGL Policy contains a section called Coverage C – Medical Payments. The title, "Medical Payments", is confusing to some policyholders who mistaken think that the place where you would find coverage for any needed medical treatment would be in the section entitled "Medical Payments." This can be especially frustrating when policyholders look at their insurance limits and find that they have limits of $1 Million (or more) for Coverage A and Coverage B, but a limit of only $5,000 for Medical Payments. If policyholders think that any payment for medical bills has to come from the section entitled "Medical Payments", and they see that there is a limit of only $5,000 for "Medical Payments," they may panic and insist that they have their Medical Payment limit increased to $1 Million.

Sample Policy Limits	
Coverage	**Limit**
Each Occurrence:	$1 Million
Personal and Advertising Injury	$1 Million
General Aggregate	$2 Million
Products Completed Operations Aggregate	$2 Million
Medical Payments (Any one person)	$ 5,000

Although the above reaction from a panicked policyholder is understandable because the limit does say "Medical Payments," you have to remember that Coverage A provided coverage for **bodily injury** and property damage to others. A bodily injury occurrence is likely to result in some medical bills. Such a bodily injury occurrence would have access to the full $1 million occurrence limit.

Similarly, remember that Coverage B provided coverage for "Personal and Advertising Injury", and that this was defined in the policy as "injury, *including consequential 'bodily injury'*, arising out of one or more of the [seven named personal and advertising injury] offenses" (CG 00 01 04 13, ISO, 2012, Page 6; Appendix Page 254). With both Coverage A and Coverage B designed to cover bodily injury, the fact that the $5,000 limit for "Medical Payments" is so small suggests that "Medical Payments" under Coverage C must cover something different than the medical bills covered under Coverage A and Coverage B. Indeed, it does.

Insuring Agreement

The CGL Policy's Coverage C, Medical Payments, has its own insuring agreement and its own reduced limit. Whereas the insuring agreement for Coverage A and B stated that the policy will pay "those sums that the insured becomes legally obligated to pay as damages," Coverage C does not require the insured to be legally obligated to pay damages. Instead, Coverage C's insurance agreement goes right into saying that it will pay those "medical expenses as described below" (CG 00 01 04 13, ISO, 2012, Page 8; Appendix Page 257).

What Type of Medical Expenses Will be Paid under Coverage C?

Unlike the broad coverage for "damages" considered in the insuring agreements for Coverage A and Coverage B, Coverage C will only pay specific types of medical bills. The insuring agreement states that it will only pay "medical expenses *as described* for "bodily injury". The medical payments it describes are limited to:

1) First aid administered at the time of an accident;
2) Necessary medical, surgical, X-ray and dental services, including prosthetic devices; and
3) Necessary ambulance, hospital, professional nursing and funeral services.

When you consider these three categories of medical expenses covered by Coverage C, remember that the amount paid is capped at a greatly reduced per person limit. As an example, think of someone injured at a store. The injured person might need first aid or ambulance services. The reduced limit could provide these services. Depending on the extent of the injuries, the necessary medical and surgical services could be significant, but the amount paid under Coverage C medical payments will be capped. If the injured party needs more money from the policy, the injured party would need to seek damages for bodily injury under either Coverage A or Coverage B.

What Type of Accidents Are Covered under Coverage C?

Coverage C will only pay for medical payments caused by an accident when it occurs in one of the following situations:

1) On premises the insured owns or rents;
2) On ways next to premises the insured owns or rents; or
3) Because of the insured's operations

These three limitations explain what Coverage C intends to cover. For example, imagine that I have a store where I sell trees. You can buy the trees at my store and take them home to plant yourself. I also plant trees. You could hire me to take the trees to your yard and plant them for you. It is possible that a tree could fall on a customer and cause bodily injury at my store during the tree selection process. It is also possible that a customer could be injured during my business operations which would include my work in moving and planting the trees. Coverage C would provide medical payments for a customer injured at my store (#1 above), on the sidewalk next to my store (#2 above), or because of my operations (#3 above). Conversely, Coverage C would not provide coverage for any medical payments that occur for any reason other than for bodily injury caused by an accident on the insured's premises (#1 above), next to the insured's premises (#2 above), or because of the insured's operations (#3 above).

Conditions of location, reporting time, and claimant cooperation

In addition to requiring that the bodily injury be caused by an accident on the insured's premises, next to the insured's premises, or because of the insured's operations, Coverage C will only provide coverage for accidents that happen at certain locations, are reported within a certain amount of time, and with certain cooperation by the claimant. The insuring agreement states that medical payments will only be paid in the following situations:

Location	a) The accident takes place in the "coverage territory" and during the policy period;
Reporting Time	b) The expenses are incurred and reported to [the insurance company] within one year of the date of the accident; and
Claimant Cooperation	c) The injured person submits to examination, at [the insurance company's] expenses, by physicians of [the insurance company's] choice as often as [the insurance company] reasonably requires.

(CG 00 01 04 13, ISO, 2012, Page 8; Appendix Page 257ff)

You may recall that under Coverage A, the insurance company only required that the occurrence that caused the bodily injury took place during the policy period. It did not require that the occurrence be reported within one year. It certainly did not require that the claimant submit to examination by the insurance company's physicians. You can see in the above limitations that the insurance company is trying to limit payments under Coverage C to situations where specific conditions have been met.

No Finding of Fault

At this point, it may sound like the insurance company is being unusually stingy with Coverage C. It will only pay three kinds of medical payments. It will only pay for three kinds of accidents. It adds three conditions. Plus, the dollar amount available to pay the claims is only a fraction of the limit in Coverage A and B. The reason the insurance company provides these limiting guidelines for Coverage C is because of how quickly and generously the insurance company will provide Coverage C benefits. *The insurance company pays Coverage C regardless of whether or not the insured is at fault for the medical payments.*

Coverage A and B only provided coverage for damages for which the insured was legally obligated to pay. When Coverage C states that it "will make…payments regardless of fault," it is saying that Coverage C is available to pay for medical expenses even when the insured is *not* legally obligated to pay the medical expenses.

The most common way to find out if an insured is legally obligated to pay damages is for a court to find the insured liable for the tort of negligence. A tort is a civil wrong for which a lawsuit may be filed in civil court. One can be found liable for the tort of negligence if the person had a duty to act like a reasonable person, breached the duty to act like a reasonable person, and this breach caused damages.

For example, reasonable tree planters do not plant trees that will immediately fall on houses. If I plant a tree and it immediately falls and causes damages, then I could be liable for paying damages under the tort of negligence. If I plant a tree and then it falls along with half of the other trees in a city when a powerful storm passes through, I would not be liable for negligence because my failure to act like a reasonable tree planter (my breach) did not cause the damages. The storm caused the damage. In order to be found liable for the tort of negligence, a plaintiff needs to show that the defendant owed the plaintiff a duty, breached the duty, and that breaching the duty caused the plaintiff damages. If my actions or omissions did not cause the tree to fall, I cannot be found liable for the damages caused by the tree falling.

Using the tree installation example, imagine that I am planting a large tree for a customer. I have a hydraulic lift that I use to offload the tree. I went to a special class to get certified on how to use the lift to offload trees. I use yellow tape to cordon off the area around where I am working so that everyone is safe. Everyone within 50 feet of where I work has to wear a safety helmet. In short, I am incredibly safe and the most reasonable tree installer imaginable. However, while I am planting a tree, an unexpected tornado arises immediately, grabs the tree I am planting, and then tosses the tree at my customer. My customer is injured and requires some minor first aid and a trip in an ambulance to the hospital.

In order for Coverage A or B to compensate the customer, the customer (plaintiff) would have to show that I, the insured, was legally liable for the customer's bodily injury. This would be difficult to prove. I cordoned off the area, required everyone to wear safety helmets, and I am certified on how to use the equipment. You cannot say that I was unreasonable for planting during a storm because the tornado was sudden and unexpected. Since I did not breach the duty of providing reasonable care, I cannot be found liable for the tort of negligence. Assuming that there are no other legal theories to make me liable for the bodily injury to the customer, Coverage A and B will not pay any damages associated with the accident.

Unlike Coverage A and B, Coverage C *would* be likely to pay its reduced limit to assist the customer with medical expenses. This is because with Coverage C, we do not ask if the insured is legally liable to pay the damages. We ask if the bodily injury was caused by an accident: 1) On premises the insured owns or rents; 2) On ways next to premises the insured owns or rents; or 3) Because of the insured's operations. This bodily injury accident happened because of my (the insured's) operations.

Although we could not prove that I was negligent in causing the customer's injuries and get coverage under Coverage A or B, the customer can prove that the customer was injured because of my operations. After all, my operations brought the tree that injured the customer to the customer's house. Since the bodily injury fits into one of the three situations where Coverage C is offered, Coverage C will be available to the injured customer even though the insured was not at fault for the customer's injuries.

What is the purpose of Coverage C Medical Payments?

In reading the example above, you might have wondered why in the world the insurance company would have a coverage section that provides coverage for accidents for which the insured is not at fault. The purpose of Coverage C, Medical Payments, is to reduce lawsuits and promote goodwill between claimants and the insurance company. Depending on your sense of humor, some people have called Medical Payments, the insurance company's "petty cash fund" or "hush money." By this, people mean that it is small amounts of money that the insurance company can access quickly to resolve potential claims quietly. The insurance company is authorized to pay Medical Payments to promote good will and to reduce the possibility that the injured party will file a more significant claim against the insured for bodily injury.

For example, imagine that a customer slips and falls in a store. This hurts, but sometimes the pain comes more out of the embarrassment from the indignity of slipping and crashing in the middle of a crowded room than any actual physical pain associated with hitting the floor. From experience, businesses and insurance companies understand that the people who sue are not just the people who are injured, but the people who are injured and felt that the business or insurance company was unhelpful, unsympathetic, or just plain rude. Stores and insurance companies have developed ways to reduce claims by showing that they care about customers. For example, some stores train their staff to quickly assist fallen customers, make sure they feel taken care of, and even offer some coupons for free meals or merchandise. The purpose of these gestures is to show the customer that the store cares about the customer and wants to help.

Just as the store sought to help the fallen customer quickly to avoid litigation, the insurance company created Coverage C as a way to resolve minor medical bills quickly. If the customer requires first aid, the insurance company is there with the reduced medical payments limit to provide necessary first aid. Because Coverage C, Medical Payments, does not require a finding of fault, the insurance company can process and settle the claims quickly and cheaply.

If someone wants to file a claim for bodily injury beyond what is available under Coverage C, the individual can still file a claim for bodily injury under Coverage A or, if applicable, Coverage B. However, with Coverage A and B comes the requirement of proving that the insured is legally obligated to pay the damages. Depending on the level of damages, attorneys for both the defendant and plaintiff may have to get involved to file and defend lawsuits on the matter.

I recently saw a case where there was a dispute over how much a business should have to pay an injured customer. Both parties agreed that the customer was injured. The parties just disagreed on the amount. The store thought the injuries were around $60. The customer thought the injuries were closer to $3,000. Plus, the customer thought the store's employees were rude and unsympathetic.

In response, the customer sued the store. The store then spent tens of thousands of dollars in legal fees to defend itself from the lawsuit. If this disagreement fell under Coverage C, it could have been resolved with no finding of fault and no attorneys.

You have heard the saying that "the customer is always right." This, of course, is not always true, but with no finding of fault required for Medical Payments, it does not matter who is "right." For Medical Payments, you can imagine that the insurance company is agreeing that the "customer is always right" in an effort to resolve some minor medical bills as quickly and inexpensively as possible. The insurance company can resolve the matter without litigation, and without even knowing if their policyholder is at fault. The medical payments coverage and reduced limit exists to resolve minor disputes quickly without the need to fully investigate or litigate which party might be responsible for the medical payments, pain and suffering, lost wages, etc..

When would someone NOT want Coverage C, Medical Payments

Even after hearing that Coverage C is different than Coverage A and B, some insured's still insist on seeing a full $1 million limit for Medical Payments. They see the $5,000 Medical Payments limit, and it just looks insufficient next to the $1 million per occurrence limit. They want to see $1 Million next to the Medical Payments limit to match the $1 Million per occurrence limit. In response, it may be helpful to point out that *some businesses prefer to eliminate any coverage for Coverage C. Medical Payments*.

For example, between the bustling towns of Los Angeles and San Diego sits a quieter city, my hometown: Temecula, California. Temecula has a little historic Old Town and rolling hills. On the rolling hills are grapes. Where there are grapes, you often find wineries. As a result, Temecula has become a destination for people who want to visit wineries in Southern California. Imagine that you are an entrepreneurial Temecula resident who decides to start a service that will help ferry patrons to the various wineries using an old-fashioned horse drawn carriage.

Although your marketing flyers talk about transporting patrons in luxury to various scenic wineries, privately you might admit that your job is to transport intoxicated people to various alcoholic drinking establishments. Locals appreciate your service because you keep drunk drivers off the roads. Patrons appreciate it because it is a beautiful way to see the wineries without having to worry about driving. You have a great business and your customers love you, but for the sake of us analyzing Coverage C, let us focus on what could go wrong when you are in the business of transporting intoxicated people.

You are aware of the risks associated with your business, so you take extra precautions to protect your customers from each other and themselves. The place where you drop off and pick up customers is well-lighted and swept clean. You have a non-slip red carpet that you put out to ensure customers have a safe and elegant entrance and exit to the carriage. Under the red carpet are modified gymnastic mats to provide a soft landing for any customers who might lose their balance on the way to or from the carriage. What am I suggesting with these details? I am showing that you are incredibly safe and go beyond what a reasonable person would do to provide the extraordinarily safe and relaxing experience that you provide.

You purchase a CGL insurance policy to help pay for damages and defense costs that could arise from your business's operations. Your CGL insurance policy has a $1 million per occurrence limit that means it will pay up to $1 million for any one occurrence. Your CGL insurance policy has a $1 million general aggregate limit. Once the general aggregate limit is paid, there is no more money in the general aggregate to pay for any additional claims. Your CGL insurance policy has a $5,000 per person limit for Coverage C, Medical Payments.

Your Winery Carriage Business CGL Policy:

General Aggregate Limit: $ 1,000,000
Per Occurrence Limit: $ 1,000,000
Medical Payments Limit: $ 5,000

On your very first day in business, the first person to step out of your carriage slips and twists an ankle. First aid and an ambulance are necessary. First aid and an ambulance fit within the type of medical bills covered by Medical Payments. An accident that happens "because of the insured's operations" fits within the type of accident that is covered by Medical Payments. Finally, the accident happened in the coverage territory, and we will assume that the claimant reported the accident within one year and cooperated with your insurance company. In response, your insurance company pays up to the $5,000 limit for the accident, regardless of fault.

Reading this, you might feel that this is how insurance is supposed to work. You are right, but I did not tell you the rest of the story. After the first customer twisted an ankle getting out of the carriage, a second person stepped out, tripped over the fallen first customer, and twisted an ankle. Then a third person stepped out, tripped, and twisted an ankle. You had 10 people in the back of your carriage and now you have a pile of ten people with twisted ankles needing first aid. The insurance company pays the $5,000 per person Medical Payments limit for each of the ten customers. All totaled, your insurance company paid $50,000 for your first day in business. This money comes out of your policy's general aggregate limit. This means that your $1 million general aggregate limit has now been reduced by $50,000 to $950,000.

You thought you were just unlucky on your first day of business, but it turns out that the same thing happens on day two and day three. This continues for your first 20 days in business. Every day you end up with ten people making a medical payments claim. The insurance company has an abbreviated claims process without any regard to fault, paying the $5,000 limit to every injured customer. Your insurance company is paying $50,000 per day in claims without any regard to fault. Multiply this by 20 days and you see that the insurance company has now paid out $1 million without any regard to fault. The $1 Million General Aggregate has been drained down to zero. There is no more money in the General Aggregate to pay for damages for which you might be legally liable.

```
Possible Claims Paid With No Finding of Fault:

$      5,000        Medical Payments paid per person
       x 10         Claims per day
$     50,000        Medical Payments paid per day.
       x 20         Days
$1,000,000          Medical Payments paid in 20 days
```

```
Impact of Medical Payment Claims on General Aggregate:

 $1,000,000         General Aggregate
- $1,000,000        Medical Payment Claim
 $         0        General Aggregate
```

In light of the scenario above, some businesses that deal regularly with the public might prefer to eliminate Coverage C entirely from the policy. They do this not because they do not want to help people with medical expenses. They do this because they only want their insurance policy to pay medical payments when their business is legally liable to pay.

for which the insured is legally liable to pay. If the carriage business is at fault in causing the injuries to the passengers exiting the carriage, the customers can always file a claim against Coverage A of the carriage business's CGL Policy. Coverage A would be available to pay damages for bodily injury or property damage to others caused by the insured's operations. The customers would just have to prove that the carriage business was at fault. Eliminating Coverage C eliminates the abbreviated claims process available to reduce costs and promote goodwill. The coverage does not serve its purpose if it does not reduce costs.

If the example of wineries and carriage drivers seems too far-fetched, think of exposures that could arise on the insured's premises or "on ways next to premises the insured owns or rents." You own a business downtown. You work during the day, and are home at night. You hear that your office is centrally located between one of the best bars, and one of the best places to dance. The most convenient way to walk between the best bar and the best place to dance, is to take the sidewalk next to your office. You have heard this on the news because it seems that this walkway is also the city's most popular place to trip or get robbed. When tripping or getting robbed results in "medical expenses...for bodily injury caused by an accident...on ways next to the premises you own or rent," you have a Coverage C Medical Payments exposure. Remember, the insuring agreement states that the insurance company "make these payments regardless of fault." Rather than insisting that the limit for Medical Payments should be increased to match the occurrence limit, some businesses that understand Coverage C prefer to have the limit either kept low or eliminated entirely.

Coverage C – Medical Payments

Coverage C – Medical Payments, Exclusions

Even though Coverage C makes payments without regard to fault, it still provides some exclusions to insure that coverage does not extend beyond the accidents for which it intends to pay. Many of these exclusions are designed to emphasize that the purpose of the CGL Policy is to pay for bodily injury, property damage, or personal and advertising injury to others; not to the insured. Other exclusions, like Injury on Normally Occupied Premises, Athletic Activities, and Products-Completed Operations Hazard, eliminate coverage that could be too broad without requiring a finding of fault on the part of the insured.

a. Any Insured

Coverage C will not provide medical payments to any insured unless the insured is a "volunteer workers". This leaves us with two questions: 1) Who is an insured, and 2) Who are "volunteer workers".

1) Who is an insured?

All CGL policies have a Section called, "Who is an Insured." The first paragraph in the section discusses the **Named Insureds**. The second paragraph discusses the **Automatic Insureds**. Named Insureds are individuals or entities that are named on the declarations page of a policy. Automatic Insureds are granted insured status because of their close relationship with the named insured. Automatic Insureds include employees and "volunteer workers" of the named insured, real estate managers, legal representatives when the named insured dies, and newly acquired organizations. In addition to the Named and Automatic Insureds, there are also Additional Insureds. Additional Insures are individuals or entities that are added as insureds to a policy by a special endorsement to the policy. The additional insured endorsement changes the definition of "Who is an Insured" to include an individual or entity that otherwise may not be insured by the policy. (See *Understanding Named, Automatic, and Additional Insureds in the CGL Policy*, Dwight M. Kealy, Pages

---

1, 11). Coverage C is excluded for any insureds unless the insured is a volunteer worker.

2) Who are "volunteer workers"?

Although technically an insured, Coverage C makes an exception to the exclusion to provide coverage for "volunteer workers".   You will notice that "volunteer workers" is in quotation marks which means that it is defined in the policy. The CGL Policy defines "volunteer workers" as "a person who is not your 'employee', and who donates his or her work and acts at the direction of and within the scope of duties determined by you, and is not paid a fee, salary or other compensation by you or anyone else for their work performed for you" (CG 00 01 04 13, Insurance Services Office, Inc., 2013, Page 16; Appendix Page 273). If an insured satisfies the definition of a "volunteer worker", then Coverage C will not be excluded for the "volunteer worker".   Coverage C is excluded for all other insureds.

This first exclusion to Coverage C makes sense when you remember that liability insurance is primarily designed to provide coverage for bodily injury or property damage to **_others._** If you are an insured, then you are not an _other_ and the CGL Policy does not intend to provide coverage for your bodily injuries. For example, an employee is an insured. If an employee is injured on the job, then the insured's worker's compensation insurance policy should pay for the applicable medical bills; not the CGL Policy. The CGL Policy makes an exception for the volunteer who is donating time without pay because this person would not have the compensation—or worker's compensation—available to provide for the volunteer's injuries.

Furthermore, in some businesses, the line between who is a helpful, regular customer, and who is a "volunteer worker" can get blurry. If the insurance policy did not make an exception for "volunteer workers", then excluding Coverage C for _all insureds_ could exclude the helpful, regular customer who might fall within the definition of a "volunteer worker," making the helpful regular customer an insured.   Coverage C is designed to provide for medical payments to these customers and volunteers without a finding of fault. However, this exclusion will eliminate coverage for any insureds other than volunteer workers.

b. Hired Person

Although a hired person is not defined in the CGL Policy, this exclusion makes it clear that there will be no Coverage C-Medical Payments for "a person hired to do work for or on behalf of any insured or a tenant of any insured" (CG 00 01 04 13, Insurance Services Office, Inc., 2012, Page 8; Appendix Page 258). A person hired to do work for an insured or tenant of an insured could be an employee. Employees who suffer bodily injury on a job look to their employer's Worker's Compensation Insurance for medical expense coverage. They cannot go around, or supplement, their employer's Worker's Compensation Insurance by seeking compensation (with no finding of fault!) from Coverage C of the CGL Policy. If someone is hired by any insured or a tenant of any insured, the hired person cannot collect medical payments from Coverage C of the CGL Policy.

If the hired worker is not an employee of any insured or tenant of any insured, then the worker could be an employee of a third party or an independent contractor. For example, if a tenant or insured hires a plumber to come to a premises to fix a pipe, there is a chance that the plumber could get injured. If the plumber is an employee of a larger plumbing company, the plumber could seek compensation for bodily injury from his/her employer's workers' compensation insurance. If the plumber is a sole proprietor or independent contractor who is working directly for the insured or tenant of an insured, then the plumber is exchanging financial compensation for the risk of getting injured on the premises. The sole proprietor or independent contractor can purchase health, life, and disability insurance policies, or a worker's compensation insurance policy, to cover bodily injury suffered while working. There will be no coverage for Medical Payments under Coverage C of a CGL Policy for someone hired to work on behalf of any insured or a tenant of any insured.

c. Injury On Normally Occupied Premises

Coverage C excludes coverage "to a person injured on that part of premises you own or rent that the person normally occupies" (CG 00 01 04 13, Insurance Services Office, Inc., 2012, Page 8; Appendix Page 258). This creates a two part test: 1) Did the injury occur on premises that the insured owns or rents, and 2) Was the injured person injured on that part of the premises the injured person normally occupies. If the answer to both questions is yes, then Coverage C Medical Payments will be excluded.

This exclusions clarifies that the medical expense coverage that Coverage C intends to provide is for customers and guests at a particular location, or as a result of the insured's operations. It is not intended for those who normally occupy an insured's premises. To understand the importance of this exclusion, we can think back to the purpose of Coverage C-Medical Payments. There is no finding of fault. Payments are made to promote goodwill and reduce claim exposures that could arise when people like customers need first aid for something arising out of an insured's operations, or for an accident that occurred on or next to an insured's premises.

Imagine that you own a large apartment building. Now think of all of the people in your apartment building who may need to go to the hospital this year because of some activity that takes place on the premises. A few people will make late night hospital visits for touching things that are too sharp or too hot in the kitchen. A few children will suffer cuts, bruises, and broken bones for whatever bad adventure they pursued after telling their friends, "Hey, watch this!" There could be some heart attacks and even deaths. Does the insured—or the insurance company—want to provide coverage for all of the medical payments that could happen on normally occupied premises *without regard to fault*? Of course not. To make this clear, Coverage C, Medical Payments excludes injuries to persons who are injured on that part of the premises that the injured party normally occupies. If the insurance company is going to provide coverage for these types of injuries, the claimants will have to prove that the insured is legally obligated to pay the damages. If there is legal liability, then the CGL Policy could pay from Coverage A or Coverage B, as appropriate. An injury on normally occupied premises is excluded under Coverage C.

d. Workers' Compensation and Similar Laws

Coverage C excludes coverage for any person, whether or not an "employee" of any "insured", for whom "benefits for the 'bodily injury' are payable or must be provided under a workers' compensation or disability benefits law or a similar law" (CG 00 01 04 13, ISO, 2012, Page 8; Appendix Page 258).

This exclusion reinforces Coverage C's exclusion of medical payments for insureds and hired persons (See Coverage C, Exclusions a. and b.). That is, in all of these exclusions, you see that if someone is compensated to be at the place where they are injured, there will be no coverage under Coverage C, Medical Payments. One of the ways people are compensated to be at a location is to be employees of a business that pays people to work at a location. This exclusion makes it clear that if individuals are injured during the course of their employment, they need to look to their employer's worker's compensation insurance—not Coverage C of the premises-holder's CGL Policy.

Medical Payments for employees should be paid under worker's compensation or disability benefits law. All states except New Jersey and Texas have mandatory worker's compensation laws. Even New Jersey and Texas make it mandatory for certain occupations. This Coverage C exclusion makes it clear that if the state says that the medical payments should be paid by worker's compensation insurance, then you need to look to the worker's compensation insurance policy for payment. If businesses want coverage to satisfy Worker's Compensation Laws, they need to purchase a Worker's Compensation policy. Coverage C, Medical Payments is not available to pay for medical expenses with no finding of fault for bodily injury that is payable, or should be provided, in accordance with state workers' compensation laws.

e. Athletic Activities

Coverage C excludes coverage when a person is "injured while practicing, instructing or participating in any physical exercises or games, sports, or athletic contests" (*ibid*). Can you imagine if coverage C paid for injuries during these kinds of athletic activities? Remember, Coverage C will pay, with no finding of fault, when the injury occurs in the following locations:

1) on premises the insured owns or rents, and
2) on ways next to premises the insured owns or rents.

Regarding injuries on premises the insured owns or rents, what if the premises the insured owns or rents is a football field or hockey rink? Regarding injuries on the ways next to the premises the insured owns or rents, what if the way next to the insured's premises is a skateboard park? If a policy was going to provide coverage for bodily injury in these situations with no finding of fault, it seems that the insurance company would pretty much have to post somebody at the field, rink, and skateboard park to pass out money to all the people injured throughout the day. Instead, the insurance policy clarifies that there will be no coverage under Coverage C for a person "injured while practicing, instructing or participating in any physical exercises or games, sports, or athletic contests" (CG 00 01 04 13, ISO, 2012, Page 8; Appendix Page 258).

f. Products-Completed Operations Hazard

Coverage C, Medical Payments does not provide coverage when the bodily injury is "included within the 'products-completed operations hazard'"(*ibid*). Remember that one of the reasons for Coverage C is to offer goodwill to claimants and to reduce claims exposure. For example, paying up to $5,000 for first aid for someone who slips at a restaurant could help eliminate the larger potential legal expenses associated with defending the restaurant owner against a lawsuit from the injured customer. Would providing up to $5,000 to someone injured by an insured's product or completed operations hazard have the same effect of reducing legal expenses? This exclusion indicates that the insurance companies have responded to this question by stating, "No, providing Coverage C, Medical Payments for products and completed operations exposures would NOT reduce the insurance company's legal expenses."

To understand why the insurance company has decided to exclude this coverage, imagine that you make a product. Maybe you make something potentially dangerous—like knives. Maybe you make something that does not seem dangerous at all—like play dough or silly putty. Whatever you choose to make for this example, imagine you have millions of customers using your product.

Customer number one turns in a medical payment claim because of your product. At this point, all you know is that someone was injured by your product and that there are millions of other customers out there using the product. Do you want your insurance company to start paying out up to the limits ($5,000) with no finding of fault to all customers who could say that they are injured by your product? (1 million customers x $5,000 = $5 Billion). Or, from the insurance company's perspective, will paying the $5,000 with no finding of fault show the goodwill that will help prevent claims? Again, I suggest that with this exclusion, the insurance company has answered this question with a clear, "No."

What if it turns out that your knives were recommended by the knife juggling association as the best knife for juggling? What if someone learns that you can smoke your play dough recipe and it ends up being the latest dangerous drug craze? There is nothing wrong with your product, but every night someone gets rushed to the hospital for juggling your knives or smoking your play dough. Coverage C provides bodily injury coverage without regard to fault. Coverage A also provides coverage for bodily injury, but only for damages for which the insured is legally obligated to pay. This exclusion makes it clear that if someone wants to file a claim for bodily injury relating to an insured's product, the claimant needs to look to Coverage A and prove that the insured is at fault. Coverage C excludes any coverage for bodily injury arising out of the "products-completed operations hazard".

g. Coverage A Exclusions

The final Coverage C, Medical Payments exclusion is a catchall that applies every exclusion that was in Coverage A, to Coverage C. You can skim through the Coverage A exclusions discussed previously and realize that if coverage is excluded for Coverage A, it will also be excluded for Coverage C.

Coverage A Exclusions

You could imagine that there could be some bodily injury relating to Coverage A exclusions like liquor liability, worker's compensation, pollution, aircraft, auto, or watercraft, mobile equipment, and war. These items are excluded under Coverage A. You cannot avoid these Coverage A exclusion by rushing to Coverage C to try to get coverage under Coverage C with no finding of fault. If coverage is excluded under Coverage A or B, there will be no coverage for the bodily injury under Coverage C.

Chapter 7: Supplementary Payments – Coverage A and B

The Supplementary Payments section contains six additional benefits that are paid in addition to the policy limits. If you have ever seen a television game show or infomercial, you understand the basic concept of Supplementary Payments. On television, you hear that there is a set of knives for only $19.99. It sounds like a good deal, and then the advertiser says, "But wait. There's more."

You then hear that for no additional cost, you get a second set of knives for free. "But wait," you hear again, "There's more." You learn that for a limited time you will also get a knife sharpener. Finally, if you call now, you will get a free cutting board and matching apron to go with your knives. Does this sound familiar? The Supplementary Payments section of the CGL Policy is the "Wait. There's more" section of the CGL Policy.

Just as the infomercial provided extra items at no additional cost, the Supplementary Payments Section of the CGL Policy provides additional coverage for no additional cost. This coverage is free not only in that the insurance company does not charge a premium for the coverage, but coverage is also free in that _payments from the Supplementary Payments Section of the CGL Policy do not reduce the limits of insurance available to the insured._

If a policyholder has $1 million limits and the insurance company pays $1 million under Supplementary Payments, the policyholder still has the full $1 million limits available. The last line of the section on Supplementary Payments makes this clear: "[Supplementary] Payments will not reduce the limits of insurance" (CG 00 01 04 13, Insurance Services Office, Inc., 2012, Page 9; Appendix Page 259). Supplementary Payments – Coverages A and B will pay for the items listed in paragraphs A-G without any additional costs to the insured. Any payments made out of these paragraphs will not reduce the limits of insurance available to the insured.

Supplementary Payments will pay:

a. All expenses we incur

The first paragraph of supplementary payments is the shortest in words and broadest in coverage. "All expenses we incur" is not just the heading of paragraph A--it is the entire paragraph. It is from this paragraph where we get the support to say that *the standard CGL Policy pays for defense costs in addition to the policy limits.* This paragraph is stating that the insurance company will pay, "with respect to any claim [it] investigate[s] or settle[s], or any 'suit' against an insured [it] defend[s]...ALL EXPENSES [IT] INCUR[S]" (CG 00 01 04 13, Insurance Services Office, Inc., 2012, Page 8; Appendix Page 259, emphasis added).

> **IMPORTANT:** If an insurance policy is using its own policy wording instead of the standard ISO policy wording, you should look under the Supplementary Payments Section to make sure that the policy has not removed the standard ISO wording that states, "These payments will not reduce the limits of insurance." This is the sentence that ensures that defense costs are paid in addition to the policy limits. Without this sentence, defense costs would reduce policy limits.

Where this gets tricky for some policyholders and insurance professionals is that people often look to exclusions to find out what is not covered by the insurance policy. However, exclusions are only necessary to remove coverage that was offered in the policy. If a non-standard insurance policy never promised that "All expenses the insurance company incurs will not reduce the limits of insurance," it does not need an exclusion to take away the promise. The policy does not need an exclusion to take away a promise that it never made.

One of the best ways to understand the impact of having defense costs paid as a supplementary payment instead of within the policy limits, is to compare the standard policy with a policy that does not pay defense costs as a supplementary payment. Imagine that you own a business and you have a CGL Policy with limits of $1 million. Now imagine that you are sued for $10 million in damages arising out of your operations. You give the lawsuit to your insurance company and they hand it over to a law firm to defend you. It is a complex lawsuit. The law firm assigns a team of attorneys to work on the lawsuit. They work on it for many years. The law firm does a great job, reducing your damages down from $10 million to $1 million.

Here is the potentially bad news: it cost the law firm $1 Million to defend and resolve your law suit. If you have a standard CGL Policy, this is not bad news at all. The standard ISO CGL Policy pays defense costs *IN ADDITION* to damages. We see this here in paragraph A of Supplementary Payments – Coverage A and B, where "all expenses we incur" is paid in addition to the policy limits. This means that when your standard CGL insurance policy paid $1 million—or $10 million(!)—in defense costs, you still have the $1 million policy limit available to pay the remaining $1 million in damages.

If, however, you have a policy where the defense costs are not a supplementary payment, then the law firm already spent the $1 million limit that you had for coverage. When the law firm spent the one millionth dollar from the policy, it spent the last dollar you had available for coverage. The good news is that your policy paid for the attorneys to get your damages reduced from $10 million to $1 million. The bad news is that you purchased a policy where defense costs were included in the limit, and the law firm used up your policy limits defending you. You now owe the $1 million in damages, and you do not have any more policy limits to pay for these damages. The standard CGL Policy will pay for "All expenses [the insurance company] incurs" in addition to the policy limits.

b. Up to $250 for bail bonds

The standard CGL Policy will pay up to $250 for bail bonds "required because of accidents or traffic law violations arising out of the use of any vehicle to which the Bodily Injury Liability Coverage applies" (CG 00 01 04 13, Insurance Services Office, Inc., 2012). When you are thinking of the millions of dollars in defense costs that the insured may get because of Paragraph A's "all expenses we incur," Paragraph's B's $250 for a bail bond may not seem very exciting. Even still, if you ever need it, it is nice to know that the CGL Policy will provide it.

One of the ways bail bonds are used is to help ensure that someone who has been arrested will appear at trial. For example, imagine that I am in a car accident, I say obnoxious things to a police officer, get arrested, and get thrown in jail. The next day I appear before a judge who sets a court date for next month. The judge orders me to post $10,000 as bail. If I write a check for $10,000 to the court, I get to walk out of jail. I get the $10,000 back when I appear for the court date next month. The bond is used to ensure that I appear. The judge picks an amount sufficient to get me to want to appear and get my money back.

What do I do if I do not have $10,000? If I do not have the money to post bond myself, I can purchase a bail bond. Different states allow bond rates of different amounts. In California and several other states, the cost of a bail bond is set at 10% of the total amount. This means that if I need to post $10,000 bail and I do not have $10,000, I can go to the corner bail bond shop and pay $1,000—10% of the total bond amount—to purchase a bail bond. The bail bond company will then post the $10,000 bail and get the $10,000 back when I show up for trial. If I do not show up for trial, the bond company will not get their $10,000 back.

With this in mind, you can see that there is often crossover between bail bondsmen and bounty hunters. Bond companies have an interest in finding people to get them to appear in court so that the bond company can get the money back that they posted as bond. The more dangerous or likely for a person to flee, the higher the bond. The higher bond amount gives a greater incentive for the bail bondsman to find the accused and bring the accused to trial so that the bail bondsman can collect the amount posted as bail.

Supplementary Payments of the CGL Policy provides for up to $250 for the cost of bail bonds. What does a $250 bail bond purchase? In 2014, 19-year old Justin Bieber was arrested after arguing with police, smelling like alcohol, and trying to race a yellow Lamborghini against a red Ferrari in a residential area of Miami Beach. After an hour in jail, a Miami judge released Bieber with a "'standard' $2,500 bond" (Alan Duke, CNN, *Justin Bieber Arrested on Drunken Driving, Resisting Arrest Charges.* January 24, 2014. http://www.cnn.com/2014/01/23/showbiz/justin-bieber-arrest/). If this bond was set in California where the bond amount is set at 10%, then the $250 available for Supplementary Payments would have been sufficient to cover the cost of the bond to release Justin Bieber from jail.

Now that you understand how bonds work and what you can get for $250, there is still a question of when a CGL Policy would pay for a bond. The $250 is for "bail bonds required because of accidents or traffic law violations arising out of the use of any vehicle to which the Bodily Injury Liability Coverage applies" (CG 00 01 04 13, ISO, 2012, Page 8; <u>Appendix Page 259</u>). Coverage A of the CGL Policy excludes Aircraft, Auto, or Watercraft. When would there be Bodily Injury relating to a traffic law violation arising out of the use of a vehicle that would not be excluded by the aircraft, auto, or watercraft exclusion?

To answer this, you need to remember the difference between an auto and mobile equipment. Autos are not covered under the CGL Policy. Autos are covered under auto policies. Mobile Equipment, on the other hand, is covered by the CGL Policy, and Mobile Equipment is *not* covered under auto policies. Both Autos and Mobile Equipment are considered vehicles. Therefore, going back to Justin Bieber in 2014, imagine that instead of racing a yellow Lamborghini, he was racing a yellow forklift. If there was an accident or traffic law violation triggering coverage, then supplementary payments could be available to pay up to $250 for the cost of the bond required to provide the bail he needed to post to stay out of jail. Using the example above, the $250 would likely be enough to pay for a similar $2500 bond that Justin Bieber had to post in 2014.

In offering payment for the bonds, the insurance policy makes it clear that the insurance company does not need to furnish the bonds. That is, they do not need to pay the $2500 to the court. The supplementary payment is only for the $250 necessary to purchase the bond from a bond company.

c. Cost of bonds to release attachments

The CGL Policy's Supplementary Payments Section states that it will pay for "the cost of bonds to release attachments, but only for bond amounts within the applicable limit of insurance" (CG 00 01 04 13, Insurance Services Office, Inc., 2012, Page 8; Appendix Page 259). An attachment is a legal process to seize property through the courts. It can be an action to take back property that was wrongfully taken, or it can be an action to take property to satisfy a debt that is owed.

To understand how bonds work with the attachment process, imagine that I accuse you of stealing my baseball card collection. You say that you did not steal my baseball card collection and that the baseball cards that you have are your cards. The legal claim to return wrongfully disposed personal property to the rightful owner is called replevin. In order to get back my baseball card collection, I file a replevin lawsuit against you. I am the plaintiff. You are the defendant.

Historically in the common law tradition, the plaintiff (in this case, me) was entitled to the immediate return of the personal property when the replevin lawsuit was initiated. If the plaintiff won the lawsuit, the plaintiff got to keep the personal property and recover damages for the wrongful detention of the personal property. If the plaintiff lost the lawsuit, the plaintiff had to return the property. This means that in the common law tradition, I would get the baseball cards back when I file the lawsuit. I would get to keep the cards if I ended up winning the replevin lawsuit. If I lose the lawsuit, you would get your baseball cards back.

Plaintiff Bonds: In the majority of jurisdictions today, the plaintiff has to post a security bond when initiating a lawsuit for replevin. The bond is to cover damages (plus interest) suffered by the defendant as a result of being without the property in the event that the plaintiff loses the replevin lawsuit. For example, what if people visit your store because of your baseball card collection, and you lose business as a result of being without your baseball cards. If you win the replevin lawsuit, you would be entitled to get your cards back as well as financial damages. The financial damages could be any lost business that you suffered as a result of being without the baseball card collection. The plaintiff bond that I, the plaintiff, had to purchase when initiating the lawsuit is designed to cover the financial damages you might suffer while being without your baseball cards.

Defendant Bonds: Imagine that you were really attached to your baseball cards and did not like the idea that you had to turn them over to me just because I called them "mine" and sued you for the cards. Or, imagine that the personal property is something more personal, like your pet dog, or something crucial for your business operations, like all of the coin laundry machines in your coin laundry machine business. You probably are not excited about giving me your dog even if I post a bond along with my lawsuit. You want to keep your property. To address this issue, the defendant can purchase a defendant bond that enables the defendant to keep the property during the lawsuit. The amount of the defendant bond is sufficient to pay damages (plus interest) to the plaintiff if the plaintiff wins the lawsuit. With the bond, the defendant gets to keep the personal property during the lawsuit. If the plaintiff wins the lawsuit, the plaintiff gets the property as well as the amount of the defendant bond

Supplementary Payments provide for the "cost of bonds to release attachments." Now you know that an attachment is a legal process to seize property through the courts, and you know how bonds work in a legal action to seize property, but what is a bond to release attachments? To explain this, imagine that you own a coin laundry machine business, and you owe me $20,000. Your laundry machines are worth $20,000. I go to court to start the attachment process so that I can get your laundry machines. I plan to sell the machines to satisfy the $20,000 debt that you owe me. You make about $10,000 per month from these laundry machines and this is your only income. If I take the laundry machines and sell them to pay off your debt, you will no longer make anything from the machines.

As we saw with the defendant who wanted to keep the baseball cards (or dog, etc.) in the replevin action, you could get a bond to release the attachment. The bond to release the attachment would allow you to keep the property (laundry machines) during the litigation process. It would cover the $20,000 owed plus any interest that might accrue during the litigation process.

The Supplementary Payments section of the CGL Policy pays for "the cost of bonds to release attachments." Therefore, assuming a one year trial with an annual interest rate of 10%, the bond necessary to release the $20,000 attachment would be at least $22,000. In a state that charges 10% for such a bond, the cost of the bond would be $2,200. The insurance policy would pay this amount for the bond to release the attachment.

An important caveat with this supplementary payment is that the policy states that it will only pay for "bond amounts within the applicable limit of insurance" (CG 00 01 04 13, Insurance Service Office, Inc., 2012, Page 8; Appendix Page 259). This does not seem consistent with the Supplementary Payments statement that "these payments will not reduce the limits of insurance." Indeed, in *Graf v. Hospitality Mutual Insurance Company*, No. 13-2167 (1st Circuit, 2014), a court ruled that an insurance company was not required to pay for the cost of an attachment bond after the insurance company had exhausted its limits.

The most the insurance company was obligated to pay in that case was the $500,000 policy limit for damages. The policy paid this amount, but this was not enough to pay for the damages caused to the plaintiff. In response, the plaintiff secured an attachment on the defendant's liquor license as a way to collect revenue from the business to satisfy the outstanding amount owed to the plaintiff. The insurance company had already paid the full policy limits and refused to pay for the cost of the attachment bond because it was not "within the applicable limit of insurance." The court agreed.

The supplementary payment for the cost of bonds to release attachments is paid in addition to any damages paid under coverage A and B. However, since the payment for these bonds has to be "within the applicable limit of insurance," there will be no payment for the cost of these bonds once a policy's limits are exhausted.

d. Reasonable expenses incurred by the insured

The CGL Policy's Supplementary Payments section paragraph d. states that it will pay for "all reasonable expenses incurred by the insured." Before an insured gets too excited about this, the insured should understand that these reasonable expenses are what the insurance company thinks are reasonable—not what the insured thinks are reasonable. These expenses are only paid when they are incurred by the insured at the request of the insurance company "to assist [the insurance company] in the investigation or defense of the claim or 'suit', including actual loss of earnings up to $250 a day because of time off from work" (*Ibid.*).

Using a previous example, imagine that I am in a mobile equipment accident in Florida while in a forklift race against Justin Bieber. (See Supplementary Payment B for background on this example). The forklift is mobile equipment, and bodily injury and property damage to others caused by mobile equipment is covered by my CGL Policy. I do not live in Florida. I live in California. The insurance company requests that I fly out to Florida to assist the insurance company in investigating the lawsuit against me or my business. I read the heading that the insurance company would pay for my reasonable expenses, and I decide that it would be reasonable for me to spend a week at The Breakers Hotel in Palm Beach. What I think is reasonable might cost $500 per night *more* than what the insurance company thinks is reasonable. The insurance company is only going to pay what it thinks are my reasonable expenses.

In addition, the insurance company is not going to pay me for all of the lost business that I say that I lost because I was missing work while in Florida. The insurance company is only going to reimburse actual lost earnings, and these lost earnings will be capped at a maximum of $250 per day.

e. All court costs taxed against the insured

The Supplementary Payments section provides payments for "all court costs taxed against the insured...[but] these payments do not include attorneys' fees or attorneys' expenses taxed against the insured" (CG 00 01 04 13, Insurance Services Office, Inc., 2012, Page 8; Appendix Page 259). In the U.S., most attorney fees from litigation are paid using the American Rule. The American Rule requires that each side pay for its own attorneys. However, there are exceptions made by contract or by law. For example, parties can sign a contract where they could agree that the prevailing party in a lawsuit is entitled to compensation for legal fees. States and the Federal Government can also pass laws providing legal fees to the prevailing plaintiff's attorneys. The government may do this in certain areas to encourage attorneys to represent groups of people who could not otherwise pay for the legal services. For example, California allows plaintiff attorneys to recover attorney fees in elder abuse cases. Even though a contract or law could require a losing defendant to pay the legal fees of a plaintiff, this provision in the CGL Policy makes it clear that Supplementary Payments will *not* pay for "attorneys' fees or attorneys' expenses taxed against the insured" (*Ibid*).

If this provision does not pay for attorney fees, what court costs taxed against the insured will it cover? You can do an internet search for the court costs in your county. You will find that there is a cost to file a lawsuit. There is also a cost to file the answer that is required when one receives a lawsuit. For example, the cost to file a lawsuit or initial answer to a lawsuit is currently $450 in the Superior Court of Riverside County, California. There are also costs for serving summons, subpoenas, depositions, transcripts, etc. If these court costs are taxed against the insured in a lawsuit, Supplementary Payments of the CGL Policy should pick up the cost. However, there will be no payment for "attorneys fees or attorneys' expenses taxed against the insured" (*Ibid.*).

f. Pre-judgment interest and g. Post-judgment interest

The Supplementary Payments section of the CGL Policy provides payment for both pre-judgment and post-judgment interest. For prejudgment awards, the insurance company will not pay any prejudgment interest based on the period of time after the insurance company makes an offer to pay the applicable limit.

To explain pre and post judgment interest, imagine that I am a tree trimmer with a CGL Policy. I go outside of your office to trim a tree and I find what I think is the perfect branch. Unfortunately, it is not a branch. It is a power cable. I cut through cable. The good news is that I am still okay. The bad news is that when I cut the cable, somehow I started a fire that burned your office building to the ground. I remind you that the good news is that no one is injured. You point out that the bad news is that your business suffered $1 million in damage as a result of the fire that I caused. You demand that I pay $1 million. I turn the claim over to my CGL Policy.

Instead of paying the $1 million, my insurance company thinks that it is unlikely that my cutting the power cable burned down your building. They refuse to pay the $1 Million you demand. In response, you sue me. A year goes by as we prepare for trial. We pay for experts who can tell us whether or not cutting a power cable can burn down a building. At trial, we find that a jury agrees with you and your experts. The court enters a $1 million judgment against me to you.

The problem is this: you wanted $1 million a year ago. Maybe you found a loan or you paid the $1 million out of your own pocket last year when I should have paid it. Or, maybe your business has been closed all year waiting for the $1 million you need to reopen your business. Whatever happened, you just know that you want interest on the money that you think I have owed you for the past year. A court could determine that a reasonable annual rate of interest for borrowing money is 10%. With this in mind, the court could order me to pay you a total of $1.1 million. That is the $1 million that I owe you for damages plus the $100,000 (10%) that I owe you for interest on the $1 million that I kept from you last year. Supplementary Payments provides for the prejudgment interest awarded against an insured and these payments do not reduce the limits of insurance.

The CGL Policy, however, makes it clear that it will only pay the prejudgment interest on the part of the judgment it would have paid. For example, let us say that instead of causing $1 million in damage to your building, I cause $10 million in damage. My CGL Policy only has limits of $1 Million. A judgment could come down saying that I owe you $10 Million plus 10% in prejudgment interest. 10% of $10 million is $1 million in interest! The insurance company is not going to pay $1 million in interest in addition to the $1 million in damages. The policy makes it clear that the insurance company will only pay the interest on that part of the judgment the insurance company would have paid.

Assuming policy limits of $1 million, the insurance company would only pay a judgment up to $1 million. Therefore, the insurance company would only pay the prejudgment interest on the $1 million judgment it would have paid. This would limit the prejudgment interest in this case to $100,000 which is 10% of the total judgment. Please note, a court can determine a different percentage to use as a reasonable rate of interest. I chose 10% for easy math. Furthermore, please remember that the interest rate that I provided is an annual rate of interest. If it takes two years to reach a judgment, then the prejudgment interest owed would be 10% per year for two years. If the amount of time is less than a full year, then the interest rate can be prorated for the appropriate amount of time.

If an insurance company makes an offer to pay the applicable limit of insurance, the insurance company "will not pay any prejudgment interest based on that period of time after the [insurance company makes the] offer" (CG 20 01 04 13, Insurance Services Office, Inc., 2012, Page 8; Appendix Page 259). Using the example above, imagine that my insurance company immediately recognized that they should pay $1 million and they offered to pay the full $1 million limits to you. For whatever reason, you refused this offer. In the event that an insurance company makes an offer to pay the full limits, it will not pay any prejudgment interest for the time after the offer was made. This makes sense when you think of prejudgment interest as something that someone should pay because the other person should have had the money earlier. If I paid you immediately and you were satisfied, I should not owe you any prejudgment interest for you being without the $1 million for a year because you were never without the money. Prejudgment interest is an attempt to compensate a claimant for the reasonable interest on money that an insured owes for the time between when damages were demanded, and when damages were awarded.

In addition to paying prejudgment interest, Supplementary Payments also provides payment for post judgment interest. Let us say that we go to court and a judge orders me to pay you $1 million. You and your attorneys give each other high fives. Then you notice my attorney file something with the judge's clerk. They give your attorneys a copy. It is a notice of an appeal. Instead of just paying the $1 million ordered by the court, my attorneys think there was a legal error that was made at our trial. My attorneys have decided to seek an appeal on the decision with the appellate court. The insurance policy states that it will pay "all interest on the full amount of any judgment that accrues after entry of the judgment and before [the insurance company has] paid, offered to pay, or deposited in court the part of the judgment that is within the applicable limit of insurance" (CG 00 01 04 13, Insurance Services Office, Inc., 2012, Page 9; Appendix Page 259).

It takes a year before we can get to the appellate court for a hearing. At the appellate court hearing, you win again. If you wanted $1 Million a year earlier when you won the first case, now you probably want the $1 Million plus reasonable interest. Assuming a court determines that a reasonable rate of interest is 10%, the insurance company would pay $1 million for the judgment, plus $100,000 for the interest on the full amount of the judgment that accrued after the initial entry of judgment. Supplementary Payments – Coverage A and B will pay both prejudgment and post judgment interest, and these payments will not reduce the policy limits.

Chapter 8: Limits of Insurance

Throughout this book, I have written about the coverage provided by the CGL Policy. We saw that Coverage A provides coverage for bodily injury or property damage to others, unless excluded. Coverage B pays for seven specifically defined personal and advertising injuries. Coverage C provides coverage for medical payments in specific situations without regard to fault. However, even when the insurance company is obligated to pay, it is not obligated to give the policyholder a blank check. Instead, the CGL Policy identifies the maximum amount that it will pay for certain types of claims. It identifies these amounts as segregated buckets of money that the policy calls "limits."

The CGL Policy's limits are commonly divided into the following limits:

```
+------------------------------------------------------------------+
|                    SAMPLE POLICY LIMITS                          |
|                                                                  |
| General Aggregate Limit.....................................$2,000,000 |
| Product/Completed Operations Aggregate Limit...$2,000,000        |
| Each Occurrence Limit.......................................$1,000,000 |
| Personal & Advertising Injury Limit                              |
|        (any one person or organization).............$1,000,000   |
| Damage to Premises Rented to You Limit                           |
|        (any one premises).................................$  100,000 |
| Medical Expense Limit (any one person)...........$    5,000      |
+------------------------------------------------------------------+
```

The **occurrence limit** is the most that the insurance policy will pay for any one occurrence. The **aggregate limit** is the most that an insurance policy will pay regardless of the number of occurrences.

For our purposes, you can imagine that the aggregate limit is like a 2 gallon tank of water. Assuming most of you enjoy what seems like an endless supply of water, imagine that your municipal water has been shut off. The only water you have is this 2 gallon tank of water. The occurrence limit is a 1 gallon bucket. If there is an occurrence, you can take your 1 gallon occurrence bucket and fill it up using the water in the 2 gallon aggregate tanks.

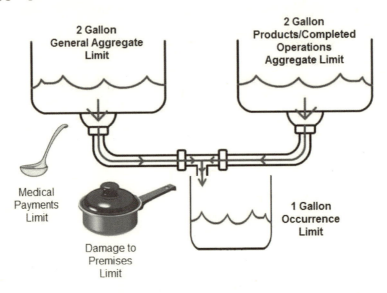

An occurrence in this situation could be anything that requires you to get water. Maybe you need to cook, get a drink, take a bath, or put out a fire. When there is an occurrence, you walk your 1 gallon occurrence bucket over to the 2 gallon aggregate tank to get as much water as you need to address the occurrence. Maybe you only need a little bit of water from the 2 gallon aggregate tank for a drink of water. Maybe you need to fill the 1 gallon occurrence bucket to the brim to try to put out a fire. Whatever amount you need, the most water that you can get at any one time is the 1 gallon bucket's occurrence limit. If you are fighting a fire and get two full, 1 gallon buckets of water from the 2 gallon aggregate tank, you have taken all of the water from the 2 gallon aggregate tank. There is no more water in the aggregate tank. You may have more occurrences and run to the 2 gallon aggregate for more water, but the aggregate tank is dry. Once the aggregate limit is exhausted, there is no more money to pay for occurrences.

There are two separate aggregate tanks: The Products and Completed Operations Aggregate and the General Aggregate. The Product and Completed Operations Aggregate Limit is available to pay for any occurrences arising out of the insured's product or completed operations. The General Aggregate is available to pay for any occurrences arising out of anything other than the insured's products or completed operations.

Products and Completed Operations Aggregate

An insured's products are tangible items—other than real property—that the insured makes, sells, or distributes to others. (CG 00 01 04 13, Insurance Services Office, Inc., 2012, Page 16; Appendix Page 273). An insured's completed operation is work that the insured has completed or "put to its intended use" (CG 00 01 04 13, Insurance Services Office, Inc., 2012, Page 15; Appendix Page 271). If there is a bodily injury or property damage occurrence arising out of an insured's product or completed operations, the policy will pay for the damages out of the Products and Completed Operations Aggregate.

Occurrences from Ongoing Operations are paid out of the General Aggregate. The difference between operations and completed operations is that a completed operation involves work that is finished. An ongoing operation involves work that is not finished. For example, imagine that I am a mason. While I am building a wall, it is an ongoing operation exposure. If a partially completed wall falls on a car while I am building the wall, we have an ongoing operations exposure. If someone is injured, we have a bodily injury occurrence arising out of my ongoing operations. If just the car is damaged, then we have a property damage occurrence arising out of my ongoing operations. This occurrence will be paid out of the General Aggregate because it is an ongoing operations exposure. It would only get paid out of the products/completed operations aggregate if it was a completed operation exposure.

Fast forward into the future. It is three weeks after I complete the wall. The wall falls on a car. It causes bodily injury to the person in the car and property damage to the car. Payment for this occurrence will come out of the

Product/Completed Operations Aggregate because the occurrence involved my completed operation—the wall. If somehow there is an occurrence that involves both the general aggregate and completed operations aggregate, the most that will be paid is the occurrence limit. Using the 2 gallon aggregate tank and 1 gallon occurrence bucket example, you can take the occurrence bucket to one or both aggregate tanks, but the most that the bucket can hold is the occurrence limit.

When talking about the Products/Completed Operations Aggregate, a question often arises about which insurance policy should pay for the occurrence when the policyholder has held multiple annual CGL Policies since the wall was completed. To address this, we have to first remember that the Occurrence Form Policy pays for occurrences that take place during the policy period. If this year there is an occurrence arising out of the policyholder's completed operations, this year's CGL Policy should pay for the occurrence.

Limits do not change the insuring agreement. If the insuring agreement says that it will pay for bodily injury or property damage that occurs during the policy period, then the policy should only pay for occurrences that take place during the policy period. The Product/Completed Operations Limit does not extend coverage into the future for Products/Completed Operations. The limits are simply the buckets of money available from which the policy will get the funds to pay for damages that the insuring agreement says the insurance company should pay. If there is an occurrence arising out of Products or Completed Operations, then the Products/Completed Operations Aggregate should pay. If there is an occurrence arising out of anything else that the insurance company is obligated to pay, then the money will come out of the General Aggregate.

For example, imagine that a contractor has a CGL occurrence policy for the year 2014. If there is an occurrence after 2014 arising out of work that the contractor completed in 2014, the first question that the 2014 insurance company will ask is whether the occurrence took place during 2014. The insurance company is not asking when the contractor did the work. The insurance company is asking when the occurrence that caused the bodily injury or property damage took place. If there is no occurrence during the policy period in which the work was completed, then the policy in place when the work was completed has no duty to pay or defend.

To help explain occurrences in construction, let us go back to the situation where I built a wall. Imagine that I am a mason who built a wall in 2013. In 2014, the wall fell down and injured a person. They will be okay in a few months, but the injured person had to spend a few nights in the hospital and the bill is going to come in over $100,000. I had an Occurrence Form CGL Policy in 2013 and a separate Occurrence Form CGL Policy in 2014. Which policy pays? Remember, the policyholder has the duty of proving that an occurrence took place during the policy period. Can the policyholder prove that bodily injury took place in 2014? Yes. Can the policyholder prove that bodily injury took place in 2013? No. The bodily injury was in 2014. The only way to get coverage out of the 2013 policy is to show that an occurrence took place during 2013, and it seems clear that there was no bodily injury that took place in 2013. In this situation, the 2014 policy should pay for the occurrence that took place in 2014 out of the 2014 policy's products/completed operations aggregate. The 2014 pays because there was an occurrence during its policy period. It pays out of the products/completed operations aggregate because the occurrence arose out the policyholder's completed operations. The product/completed operations aggregate provides the money to pay for occurrences arising out of products and completed operations exposures. The existence of the limit does not change the insuring agreement's requirement that an occurrence take place during the policy period.

General Aggregate

When I suggested that the general aggregate is the bucket of money available to pay for everything other than products and completed operations exposures, I meant everything. A customer could suffer bodily injury slipping on an office floor.

An insured's operations could start a fire causing property damage to others. There could also be personal and advertising injury, medical payments, or damage to premises leased to the insured. All of these payments come out of the general aggregate. If a CGL Policy has to pay damages for something that is not a products/completed operations exposure, the CGL Policy will pay for the damages out of the general aggregate.

Damage to Premises Rented to You Limit (any one premises)

The CGL Policy provides a reduced limit that can pay damages to premises rented to the insured. It is important to think about this policy limit within the context of the CGL Policy's Coverage A exclusion j. Damage to Property.

Remember, the Damage to Property exclusion makes it clear that the CGL Policy is designed to cover bodily injury and property damage *to others*—not to the insured. Exclusion j. Damage to Property removes coverage for property that the insured owns, rents, or occupies. The starting point with this exclusion is realizing that there is no coverage for damage to property that the insured owns. However, the CGL Policy does provide a reduced limit to provide funds for occurrences that result in "Damage to Premises Rented to You." This reduced limit provides coverage for:

"...'property damage' to any one premises, while rented to [the insured], or in the case of damage by fire, while rented to [the insured] or temporarily occupied by [the insured] with permission of the owner" (CG 00 01 04 13, Insurance Services Office, 2012).

While a standard CGL occurrence limit might be $1 Million, the reduced "Damage to Premises Rented to You" limit is often only $100,000 or $50,000. Notice that the limit does not say that it will pay for the insured's personal property, inventory, or furniture. It is only paying for damage to one premises while it is rented to the insured. The individual or entity that benefits

Limits of Insurance

from this coverage is not the insured. The one who benefits from the coverage is the owner of the premises.

In this sense, the coverage is still providing coverage to *others* and not to the insured. However, although the exclusion begins by stating that there is no coverage for damage to property that the insured owns, rents, or occupies, this limit provides limited coverage for damage to property rented by the insured. Payments made out of the Damage to Premises Rented to You Limit come out of the General Aggregate.

Medical Payments (any one person)

Coverage C, Medical Payments provides coverage for medical payments in specific situations without regard to fault. The insurance company provides these first aid type payments in an abbreviated claims process to promote goodwill—and reduce litigation—between claimants and the insurance company. Since payment is made without regard to the insured's fault, the insurance company limits the amount that will be paid by providing a reduced Medical Payments Limit. Whereas it may be common for a policy to have a $1 Million per occurrence limit, a common medical payment limit is often only $5,000. The insurance company is offering payment without regard to fault, but only a limited amount to try to resolve the matter without litigation.

The medical payment limit is paid on a per-person basis. This does not mean that only one person in a policy year can receive this limit. It means that this is the limit for every individual person who has a medical payments claim. For example, imagine that I have an office on the second floor with a nice window overlooking a busy street. There is a parade going down the street and the sidewalk below is crowded. I stand up against my glass windows, watching the parade. The patrons become unruly and at some point they start throwing some rocks at windows. My window breaks. We are not sure if it is from me leaning against the window or because rocks were thrown, or both. What we do know is that shards of glass from my broken window fell like rain on the crowded sidewalk below. Twenty people below my window suffer minor injuries. They all require first aid and my policy agrees to pay the $5,000 Medical Payment limit for each of the 20 people who received first aid. 20 x $5,000 = $100,000. In this example, my insurance policy would pay $100,000 out of my CGL Policy's General Aggregate to pay the $5,000 Medical Payments limit for each of the 20 individuals who had a valid Medical Payments claim.

Limits Illustrated

As a way to explain how the CGL Policy limits work, let us walk through an unfortunate year for a policyholder—and the insurance company. For this example, imagine that I have a tree trimmer/plant nursery business with the following limits:

SAMPLE POLICY LIMITS

General Aggregate Limit $2,000,000
Product/Completed Operations Aggregate Limit ... $2,000,000
Each Occurrence Limit $1,000,000
Personal & Advertising Injury Limit
    (any one person or organization) $1,000,000
Damage to Premises Rented to You Limit
    (any one premises) .... $ 100,000
Medical Expense Limit (any one person) .... $ 5,000

    Policy Term: January 1st – December 31st
    Business Description: Tree Trimmer/Nursery

March 1: Property Damage from Operations.

Occurrence Limit:	$1,000,000
Amount of Loss:	$ 600,000
Amount Paid:	$ 600,000
General Aggregate Before Payment:	$2,000,000
General Aggregate After Payment:	$1,400,000

On March 1, I was cutting through what I thought was a perfectly good branch that turned out not to be a branch. It was a power cable. Cutting the power cable caused a city block to be without power. My CGL Policy pays for property damage for which I am legally obligated to pay and defines property damage as "physical injury to tangible property, including all resulting loss of use of that property" (CG 00 01 04 13, Insurance Services Office, Inc., 2012, Page 15; Appendix Page 272). I am responsible for the property damage, and so my policy should pay. It is not a product/completed operations exposure, so the policy would not pay out of the Products and Completed Operations Aggregate. Instead, the policy should pay out of the General Aggregate. The amount owed is under my occurrence limit and I have sufficient funds in my general aggregate limit to pay for the claim. Therefore, my CGL Policy pays $600,000 for the occurrence out of my policy's General Aggregate.

April 1: Bodily Injury and Medical Payments from Operations.

Occurrence Limit: $ 1,000,000

	Amount of Loss	Amount Paid
Medical Payments, Child	$ 10,000	$ 5,000
Medical Payments, Adult	$ 5,000	$ 5,000
Bodily Injury, Coverage A	$ 1,300,000	$ 990,000
Total Occurrence:	$ 1,315,000	$ 1,000,000

General Aggregate Before Payment: $ 1,400,000
General Aggregate After Payment: $ 400,000

On April 1, I cut a similar branch with similar results. This time, unfortunately, there were some people near the tree where I cut what turned out to be a power cable. A child filed a claim for $10,000 of medical payments. An adult filed a claim for $5,000 in medical payments. Thirteen other people were injured with claims of $100,000 each.

The insurance company is likely to resolve the medical payment claims quickly because it is an abbreviated claims process with no finding of fault and a reduced limit. However, the most that they will pay is the Medical Expense limit. The child and adult could each get a maximum of $5,000 for medical payments through Coverage C, Medical Payments. The child wanted $10,000, but will only get $5,000 through the Medical Expense limit. The child can file a claim under Coverage A for bodily injury to get the full $10,000, but this will not be as fast and the child will have to prove that I, the policyholder, was at fault. In our example, a total of $10,000 was paid for the two $5,000 medical payment claims. Payments for Medical Payments reduce the General Aggregate Limit. This $10,000 also reduced the occurrence limit from $1,000,000 to $990,000 for any damages arising out of the same occurrence. And there were other damages.

Thirteen additional people each claim $100,000 in damages for a combined total of $1,300,000 in damages. The maximum occurrence limit is $1,000,000. The policy has already paid $10,000 in medical payments for the same occurrence. This means that there is only $990,000 remaining to pay for the $1,300,000 in damages.

Sometimes people who have insurance will say that they do not want their insurance to pay a claim because they are afraid that this may drive up the cost of their future policy premiums. People should be careful what they wish for. Imagine that you are one of the thirteen people in line who has a $100,000 medical bill because of my negligent tree trimming. Imagine that after paying for the Medical Payments, the insurance company puts the remaining 13 claimants in a single file line and starts paying each claimant $100,000. The first nine people get their $100,000. The tenth person gets $90,000. The insurance company has now paid out all of the money it had for the occurrence. You are one of the last three people in line. You have a $100,000 medical bill caused by my negligence, but there is no more money in the occurrence limit for you. Do you feel that everything is fine because the insurance company tried to pay, but the limits were insufficient to pay for your medical bills? Even the person who received $90,000 instead of $100,000 has an outstanding bill of $10,000 that should be paid by the negligent party. I mention this to remind readers that an insurance policy provision that limits the insurance company's duty to pay does not limit the insured's obligation to pay damages caused by the insured's negligent acts. I caused damages that are $310,000 greater than my CGL Policy limits. Hopefully I have an excess/umbrella policy over my CGL Policy to cover this $310,000. If I do not have coverage, then the attorneys for the injured parties will look to my business assets and bank accounts to find the remaining $310,000 I should have to pay for the damages I caused.

May 1: Bodily Injury from Premises.

Occurrence Limit:	$1,000,000
Amount of Loss:	$ 500,000
Amount Paid:	$ 400,000
General Aggregate Before Payment:	$ 400,000
General Aggregate After Payment:	$ 0

By May, I have learned my lesson: Do not cut branches. I decide to stay at my nursery office where I coordinate to have others go out and trim or plant trees for me. A customer comes to my office and somehow a branch on one of my trees breaks and falls on the customer. The customer suffers bodily injury of $500,000. My insurance policy has a $1,000,000 occurrence limit. My policy would pay the $500,000 if there were $500,000 still in the policy. This is not a products/completed operations exposure and so my policy would pay out of the General Aggregate. I started the year with a $2 Million General Aggregate. Unfortunately, my policy has already paid out $1,600,000 for the occurrences listed above. There is only $400,000 remaining in my General Aggregate. The most my policy will pay is the occurrence limit, subject to the amount remaining in the aggregate limit.   Since there is only $400,000 left in my General Aggregate, my CGL Policy will only pay $400,000 of the $500,000 in damages that I caused. Hopefully I have an excess/umbrella policy to pay for the remaining $100,000 in damages that I caused. If not, the claimant may look to my assets and bank accounts to pay for any remaining damages not paid by my insurance policy.

June 1: Bodily Injury from Product

Occurrence Limit:	$1,000,000
Amount of Loss:	$ 500,000
Amount Paid:	$ 500,000

Aggregates Before Payment:

General Aggregate	$ 0
Products/Completed Operations Aggregate	$2,000,000

Aggregates After Payment:

General Aggregate	$ 0
Products/Completed Operations Aggregate	$1,500,000

By June, you can imagine that I do not think it is safe to trim trees or have people come to my office. The phone rings, and I think it is still safe to answer the phone. It is someone calling about the product that I make that helps move heavy trees. It turns out that the product was defective. It caused a tree to fall, injuring people and property. The damages are $500,000. $500,000 is under my occurrence limit. Although there is no more money left in my General Aggregate, my Product/Completed Operations Aggregate has not been touched. My insurance policy will pay the $500,000 products/completed operations claim because it falls within the occurrence limit and there is money to pay for the claim out of the Products and Completed Operations Aggregate Limit.

Appendix A: Sample Occurrence Form Commercial General Liability Policy

COMMERCIAL GENERAL LIABILITY COVERAGE FORM

Various provisions in this policy restrict coverage. Read the entire policy carefully to determine rights, duties and what is and is not covered.

Throughout this policy the words "you" and "your" refer to the Named Insured shown in the Declarations, and any other person or organization qualifying as a Named Insured under this policy. The words "we", "us" and "our" refer to the company providing this insurance.

The word "insured" means any person or organization qualifying as such under Section **II** – Who Is An Insured.

Other words and phrases that appear in quotation marks have special meaning. Refer to Section **V** –Definitions.

SECTION I – COVERAGES

COVERAGE A – BODILY INJURY AND PROPERTY DAMAGE LIABILITY

1. Insuring Agreement

   a. We will pay those sums that the insured becomes legally obligated to pay as damages because of "bodily injury" or "property damage" to which this insurance applies. We will have the right and duty to defend the insured against any "suit" seeking those damages. However, we will have no duty to defend the insured against any "suit" seeking damages for "bodily injury" or "property damage" to which this insurance does not apply. We may, at our discretion, investigate any "occurrence" and settle any claim or "suit" that may result. But:

      (1) The amount we will pay for damages is limited as described in Section **III** – Limits Of Insurance; and

      (2) Our right and duty to defend ends when we have used up the applicable limit of insurance in the payment of judgments or settlements under Coverages **A** or **B** or medical expenses under Coverage **C**.

   No other obligation or liability to pay sums or perform acts or services is covered unless explicitly provided for under Supplementary Payments – Coverages **A** and **B**.

   b. This insurance applies to "bodily injury" and "property damage" only if:

APPENDIX A

(1) The "bodily injury" or "property damage" is caused by an "occurrence" that takes place in the "coverage territory";

(2) The "bodily injury" or "property damage" occurs during the policy period; and

(3) Prior to the policy period, no insured listed under Paragraph **1.** of Section II – Who Is An Insured and no "employee" authorized by you to give or receive notice of an "occurrence" or claim, knew that the "bodily injury" or "property damage" had occurred, in whole or in part. If such a listed insured or authorized "employee" knew, prior to the policy period, that the "bodily injury" or "property damage" occurred, then any continuation, change or resumption of such "bodily injury" or "property damage" during or after the policy period will be deemed to have been known prior to the policy period.

c. "Bodily injury" or "property damage" which occurs during the policy period and was not, prior to the policy period, known to have occurred by any insured listed under Paragraph **1.** of Section II – Who Is An Insured or any "employee" authorized by you to give or receive notice of an "occurrence" or claim, includes any continuation, change or resumption of that "bodily injury" or "property damage" after the end of the policy period.

d. "Bodily injury" or "property damage" will be deemed to have been known to have occurred at the earliest time when any insured listed under Paragraph **1.** of Section II – Who Is An Insured or any "employee" authorized by you to give or receive notice of an "occurrence" or claim:

(1) Reports all, or any part, of the "bodily injury" or "property damage" to us or any other insurer;

(2) Receives a written or verbal demand or claim for damages because of the "bodily injury" or "property damage"; or

(3) Becomes aware by any other means that "bodily injury" or "property damage" has occurred or has begun to occur.

e. Damages because of "bodily injury" include damages claimed by any person or organization for care, loss of services or death resulting at any time from the "bodily injury".

2.Exclusions

This insurance does not apply to:

APPENDIX A

a. **Expected Or Intended Injury**

"Bodily injury" or "property damage" expected or intended from the standpoint of the insured. This exclusion does not apply to "bodily injury" resulting from the use of reasonable force to protect persons or property.

b. **Contractual Liability**

"Bodily injury" or "property damage" for which the insured is obligated to pay damages by reason of the assumption of liability in a contract or agreement. This exclusion does not apply to liability for damages:

(1) That the insured would have in the absence of the contract or agreement; or

(2) Assumed in a contract or agreement that is an "insured contract", provided the "bodily injury" or "property damage" occurs subsequent to the execution of the contract or agreement. Solely for the purposes of liability assumed in an "insured contract", reasonable attorneys' fees and necessary litigation expenses incurred by or for a party other than an insured are deemed to be damages because of "bodily injury" or "property damage", provided:

(a) Liability to such party for, or for the cost of, that party's defense has also been assumed in the same "insured contract"; and

(b) Such attorneys' fees and litigation expenses are for defense of that party against a civil or alternative dispute resolution proceeding in which damages to which this insurance applies are alleged.

c. **Liquor Liability**

"Bodily injury" or "property damage" for which any insured may be held liable by reason of:

(1) Causing or contributing to the intoxication of any person;

(2) The furnishing of alcoholic beverages to a person under the legal drinking age or under the influence of alcohol; or

(3) Any statute, ordinance or regulation relating to the sale, gift, distribution or use of alcoholic beverages.

This exclusion applies even if the claims against any insured allege negligence or other wrongdoing in:

(a) The supervision, hiring, employment, training or monitoring of others by that insured; or

(b) Providing or failing to provide transportation with respect to any person that may be under the influence of alcohol;

APPENDIX A

if the "occurrence" which caused the "bodily injury" or "property damage", involved that which is described in Paragraph **(1)**, **(2)** or **(3)** above.

However, this exclusion applies only if you are in the business of manufacturing, distributing, selling, serving or furnishing alcoholic beverages. For the purposes of this exclusion, permitting a person to bring alcoholic beverages on your premises, for consumption on your premises, whether or not a fee is charged or a license is required for such activity, is not by itself considered the business of selling, serving or furnishing alcoholic beverages.

d. Workers' Compensation And Similar Laws

Any obligation of the insured under a workers' compensation, disability benefits or unemployment compensation law or any similar law.

e. Employer's Liability

"Bodily injury" to:

(1) An "employee" of the insured arising out of and in the course of:

    (a) Employment by the insured; or

    (b) Performing duties related to the conduct of the insured's business; or

(2) The spouse, child, parent, brother or sister of that "employee" as a consequence of Paragraph **(1)** above.

This exclusion applies whether the insured may be liable as an employer or in any other capacity and to any obligation to share damages with or repay someone else who must pay damages because of the injury.

This exclusion does not apply to liability assumed by the insured under an "insured contract".

f. Pollution

(1) "Bodily injury" or "property damage" arising out of the actual, alleged or threatened discharge, dispersal, seepage, migration, release or escape of "pollutants":

    (a) At or from any premises, site or location which is or was at any time owned or occupied by, or rented or loaned to, any insured. However, this subparagraph does not apply to:

        (i) "Bodily injury" if sustained within a building and caused by smoke, fumes, vapor or soot produced by or originating from equipment that is used to heat, cool or dehumidify the building, or equipment that is used to heat water for personal use, by the building's occupants or their guests;

APPENDIX A

(ii) "Bodily injury" or "property damage" for which you may be held liable, if you are a contractor and the owner or lessee of such premises, site or location has been added to your policy as an additional insured with respect to your ongoing operations performed for that additional insured at that premises, site or location and such premises, site or location is not and never was owned or occupied by, or rented or loaned to, any insured, other than that additional insured; or

(iii) "Bodily injury" or "property damage" arising out of heat, smoke or fumes from a "hostile fire";

(b) At or from any premises, site or location which is or was at any time used by or for any insured or others for the handling, storage, disposal, processing or treatment of waste;

(c) Which are or were at any time transported, handled, stored, treated, disposed of, or processed as waste by or for:

(i) Any insured; or

(ii) Any person or organization for whom you may be legally responsible; or

(d) At or from any premises, site or location on which any insured or any contractors or subcontractors working directly or indirectly on any insured's behalf are performing operations if the "pollutants" are brought on or to the premises, site or location in connection with such operations by such insured, contractor or subcontractor. However, this subparagraph does not apply to:

(i) "Bodily injury" or "property damage" arising out of the escape of fuels, lubricants or other operating fluids which are needed to perform the normal electrical, hydraulic or mechanical functions necessary for the operation of "mobile equipment" or its parts, if such fuels, lubricants or other operating fluids escape from a vehicle part designed to hold, store or receive them. This exception does not apply if the "bodily injury" or "property damage" arises out of the intentional discharge, dispersal or release of the fuels, lubricants or other operating fluids, or if such fuels, lubricants or other operating fluids are brought on or to the premises, site or location with the intent that they be discharged, dispersed or released as part of the operations being performed by such insured, contractor or subcontractor;

APPENDIX A

(ii) "Bodily injury" or "property damage" sustained within a building and caused by the release of gases, fumes or vapors from materials brought into that building in connection with operations being performed by you or on your behalf by a contractor or subcontractor; or

(iii) "Bodily injury" or "property damage" arising out of heat, smoke or fumes from a "hostile fire".

(e) At or from any premises, site or location on which any insured or any contractors or subcontractors working directly or indirectly on any insured's behalf are performing operations if the operations are to test for, monitor, clean up, remove, contain, treat, detoxify or neutralize, or in any way respond to, or assess the effects of, "pollutants".

(2) Any loss, cost or expense arising out of any:

(a) Request, demand, order or statutory or regulatory requirement that any insured or others test for, monitor, clean up, remove, contain, treat, detoxify or neutralize, or in any way respond to, or assess the effects of, "pollutants"; or

(b) Claim or suit by or on behalf of a governmental authority for damages because of testing for, monitoring, cleaning up, removing, containing, treating, detoxifying or neutralizing, or in any way responding to, or assessing the effects of, "pollutants".

However, this paragraph does not apply to liability for damages because of "property damage" that the insured would have in the absence of such request, demand, order or statutory or regulatory requirement, or such claim or "suit" by or on behalf of a governmental authority.

g. Aircraft, Auto Or Watercraft

"Bodily injury" or "property damage" arising out of the ownership, maintenance, use or entrustment to others of any aircraft, "auto" or watercraft owned or operated by or rented or loaned to any insured. Use includes operation and "loading or unloading".

This exclusion applies even if the claims against any insured allege negligence or other wrongdoing in the supervision, hiring, employment, training or monitoring of others by that insured, if the "occurrence" which caused the "bodily injury" or "property damage" involved the ownership, maintenance, use or entrustment to others of any aircraft, "auto" or watercraft that is owned or operated by or rented or loaned to any insured.

This exclusion does not apply to:

APPENDIX A

(1) A watercraft while ashore on premises you own or rent;

(2) A watercraft you do not own that is:

    (a) Less than 26 feet long; and

    (b) Not being used to carry persons or property for a charge;

(3) Parking an "auto" on, or on the ways next to, premises you own or rent, provided the "auto" is not owned by or rented or loaned to you or the insured;

(4) Liability assumed under any "insured contract" for the ownership, maintenance or use of aircraft or watercraft; or

(5) "Bodily injury" or "property damage" arising out of:

    (a) The operation of machinery or equipment that is attached to, or part of, a land vehicle that would qualify under the definition of "mobile equipment" if it were not subject to a compulsory or financial responsibility law or other motor vehicle insurance law where it is licensed or principally garaged; or

    (b) The operation of any of the machinery or equipment listed in Paragraph **f.(2)** or **f.(3)** of the definition of "mobile equipment".

h. Mobile Equipment

"Bodily injury" or "property damage" arising out of:

(1) The transportation of "mobile equipment" by an "auto" owned or operated by or rented or loaned to any insured; or

(2) The use of "mobile equipment" in, or while in practice for, or while being prepared for, any prearranged racing, speed, demolition, or stunting activity.

i. War

"Bodily injury" or "property damage", however caused, arising, directly or indirectly, out of:

(1) War, including undeclared or civil war;

(2) Warlike action by a military force, including action in hindering or defending against an actual or expected attack, by any government, sovereign or other authority using military personnel or other agents; or

(3) Insurrection, rebellion, revolution, usurped power, or action taken by governmental authority in hindering or defending against any of these.

j. Damage To Property

"Property damage" to:

APPENDIX A

(1) Property you own, rent, or occupy, including any costs or expenses incurred by you, or any other person, organization or entity, for repair, replacement, enhancement, restoration or maintenance of such property for any reason, including prevention of injury to a person or damage to another's property;

(2) Premises you sell, give away or abandon, if the "property damage" arises out of any part of those premises;

(3) Property loaned to you;

(4) Personal property in the care, custody or control of the insured;

(5) That particular part of real property on which you or any contractors or subcontractors working directly or indirectly on your behalf are performing operations, if the "property damage" arises out of those operations; or

(6) That particular part of any property that must be restored, repaired or replaced because "your work" was incorrectly performed on it.

Paragraphs **(1)**, **(3)** and **(4)** of this exclusion do not apply to "property damage" (other than damage by fire) to premises, including the contents of such premises, rented to you for a period of seven or fewer consecutive days. A separate limit of insurance applies to Damage To Premises Rented To You as described in Section **III** – Limits Of Insurance.

Paragraph **(2)** of this exclusion does not apply if the premises are "your work" and were never occupied, rented or held for rental by you.

Paragraphs **(3)**, **(4)**, **(5)** and **(6)** of this exclusion do not apply to liability assumed under a sidetrack agreement.

Paragraph **(6)** of this exclusion does not apply to "property damage" included in the "products-completed operations hazard".

k. Damage To Your Product

"Property damage" to "your product" arising out of it or any part of it.

l. Damage To Your Work

"Property damage" to "your work" arising out of it or any part of it and included in the "products-completed operations hazard".

This exclusion does not apply if the damaged work or the work out of which the damage arises was performed on your behalf by a subcontractor.

m. Damage To Impaired Property Or Property Not Physically Injured

"Property damage" to "impaired property" or property that has not been physically injured, arising out of:

(1) A defect, deficiency, inadequacy or dangerous condition in "your product" or "your work"; or

(2) A delay or failure by you or anyone acting on your behalf to perform a contract or agreement in accordance with its terms.

This exclusion does not apply to the loss of use of other property arising out of sudden and accidental physical injury to "your product" or "your work" after it has been put to its intended use.

n. Recall Of Products, Work Or Impaired Property

Damages claimed for any loss, cost or expense incurred by you or others for the loss of use, withdrawal, recall, inspection, repair, replacement, adjustment, removal or disposal of:

(1) "Your product";

(2) "Your work"; or

(3) "Impaired property";

if such product, work, or property is withdrawn or recalled from the market or from use by any person or organization because of a known or suspected defect, deficiency, inadequacy or dangerous condition in it.

o. Personal And Advertising Injury

"Bodily injury" arising out of "personal and advertising injury".

p. Electronic Data

Damages arising out of the loss of, loss of use of, damage to, corruption of, inability to access, or inability to manipulate electronic data.

However, this exclusion does not apply to liability for damages because of "bodily injury".

As used in this exclusion, electronic data means information, facts or programs stored as or on, created or used on, or transmitted to or from computer software, including systems and applications software, hard or floppy disks, CD-ROMs, tapes, drives, cells, data processing devices or any other media which are used with electronically controlled equipment.

q. Recording And Distribution Of Material Or Information In Violation Of Law

"Bodily injury" or "property damage" arising directly or indirectly out of any action or omission that violates or is alleged to violate:

(1) The Telephone Consumer Protection Act (TCPA), including any amendment of or addition to such law;

APPENDIX A

(2) The CAN-SPAM Act of 2003, including any amendment of or addition to such law;

(3) The Fair Credit Reporting Act (FCRA), and any amendment of or addition to such law, including the Fair and Accurate Credit Transactions Act (FACTA); or

(4) Any federal, state or local statute, ordinance or regulation, other than the TCPA, CAN-SPAM Act of 2003 or FCRA and their amendments and additions, that addresses, prohibits, or limits the printing, dissemination, disposal, collecting, recording, sending, transmitting, communicating or distribution of material or information.

Exclusions **c.** through **n.** do not apply to damage by fire to premises while rented to you or temporarily occupied by you with permission of the owner. A separate limit of insurance applies to this coverage as described in Section **III** – Limits Of Insurance.

COVERAGE B – PERSONAL AND ADVERTISING INJURY LIABILITY

1. **Insuring Agreement**

   a. We will pay those sums that the insured becomes legally obligated to pay as damages because of "personal and advertising injury" to which this insurance applies. We will have the right and duty to defend the insured against any "suit" seeking those damages. However, we will have no duty to defend the insured against any "suit" seeking damages for "personal and advertising injury" to which this insurance does not apply. We may, at our discretion, investigate any offense and settle any claim or "suit" that may result. But:

      (1) The amount we will pay for damages is limited as described in Section **III** – Limits Of Insurance; and

      (2) Our right and duty to defend end when we have used up the applicable limit of insurance in the payment of judgments or settlements under Coverages **A** or **B** or medical expenses under Coverage **C.**

      No other obligation or liability to pay sums or perform acts or services is covered unless explicitly provided for under Supplementary Payments – Coverages **A** and **B.**

   b. This insurance applies to "personal and advertising injury" caused by an offense arising out of your business but only if the offense was committed in the "coverage territory" during the policy period.

2. **Exclusions**

   This insurance does not apply to:

APPENDIX A

a. Knowing Violation Of Rights Of Another

"Personal and advertising injury" caused by or at the direction of the insured with the knowledge that the act would violate the rights of another and would inflict "personal and advertising injury".

b. Material Published With Knowledge Of Falsity

"Personal and advertising injury" arising out of oral or written publication, in any manner, of material, if done by or at the direction of the insured with knowledge of its falsity.

c. Material Published Prior To Policy Period

"Personal and advertising injury" arising out of oral or written publication, in any manner, of material whose first publication took place before the beginning of the policy period.

d. Criminal Acts

"Personal and advertising injury" arising out of a criminal act committed by or at the direction of the insured.

e. Contractual Liability

"Personal and advertising injury" for which the insured has assumed liability in a contract or agreement. This exclusion does not apply to liability for damages that the insured would have in the absence of the contract or agreement.

f. Breach Of Contract

"Personal and advertising injury" arising out of a breach of contract, except an implied contract to use another's advertising idea in your "advertisement".

g. Quality Or Performance Of Goods – Failure To Conform To Statements

"Personal and advertising injury" arising out of the failure of goods, products or services to conform with any statement of quality or performance made in your "advertisement".

h. Wrong Description Of Prices

"Personal and advertising injury" arising out of the wrong description of the price of goods, products or services stated in your "advertisement".

i. Infringement Of Copyright, Patent, Trademark Or Trade Secret

"Personal and advertising injury" arising out of the infringement of copyright, patent, trademark, trade secret or other intellectual property rights. Under this exclusion, such other intellectual property rights do not include the use of another's advertising idea in your "advertisement".

APPENDIX A

However, this exclusion does not apply to infringement, in your "advertisement", of copyright, trade dress or slogan.

j. Insureds In Media And Internet Type Businesses

"Personal and advertising injury" committed by an insured whose business is:

(1) Advertising, broadcasting, publishing or telecasting;

(2) Designing or determining content of web sites for others; or

(3) An Internet search, access, content or service provider.

However, this exclusion does not apply to Paragraphs **14.a., b.** and **c.** of "personal and advertising injury" under the Definitions section.

For the purposes of this exclusion, the placing of frames, borders or links, or advertising, for you or others anywhere on the Internet, is not by itself, considered the business of advertising, broadcasting, publishing or telecasting.

k. Electronic Chatrooms Or Bulletin Boards

"Personal and advertising injury" arising out of an electronic chatroom or bulletin board the insured hosts, owns, or over which the insured exercises control.

l. Unauthorized Use Of Another's Name Or Product

"Personal and advertising injury" arising out of the unauthorized use of another's name or product in your e-mail address, domain name or metatag, or any other similar tactics to mislead another's potential customers.

m. Pollution

"Personal and advertising injury" arising out of the actual, alleged or threatened discharge, dispersal, seepage, migration, release or escape of "pollutants" at any time.

n. Pollution-related

Any loss, cost or expense arising out of any:

(1) Request, demand, order or statutory or regulatory requirement that any insured or others test for, monitor, clean up, remove, contain, treat, detoxify or neutralize, or in any way respond to, or assess the effects of, "pollutants"; or

(2) Claim or suit by or on behalf of a governmental authority for damages because of testing for, monitoring, cleaning up, removing, containing, treating, detoxifying or neutralizing, or in any way responding to, or assessing the effects of, "pollutants".

APPENDIX A

o. War

"Personal and advertising injury", however caused, arising, directly or indirectly, out of:

(1) War, including undeclared or civil war;

(2) Warlike action by a military force, including action in hindering or defending against an actual or expected attack, by any government, sovereign or other authority using military personnel or other agents; or

(3) Insurrection, rebellion, revolution, usurped power, or action taken by governmental authority in hindering or defending against any of these.

p. Recording And Distribution Of Material Or Information In Violation Of Law

"Personal and advertising injury" arising directly or indirectly out of any action or omission that violates or is alleged to violate:

(1) The Telephone Consumer Protection Act (TCPA), including any amendment of or addition to such law;

(2) The CAN-SPAM Act of 2003, including any amendment of or addition to such law;

(3) The Fair Credit Reporting Act (FCRA), and any amendment of or addition to such law, including the Fair and Accurate Credit Transactions Act (FACTA); or

(4) Any federal, state or local statute, ordinance or regulation, other than the TCPA, CAN-SPAM Act of 2003 or FCRA and their amendments and additions, that addresses, prohibits, or limits the printing, dissemination, disposal, collecting, recording, sending, transmitting, communicating or distribution of material or information.

COVERAGE C – MEDICAL PAYMENTS

1. Insuring Agreement

a. We will pay medical expenses as described below for "bodily injury" caused by an accident:

(1) On premises you own or rent;

(2) On ways next to premises you own or rent; or

(3) Because of your operations;

provided that:

(a) The accident takes place in the "coverage territory" and during the policy period;

APPENDIX A

    (b) The expenses are incurred and reported to us within one year of the date of the accident; and

    (c) The injured person submits to examination, at our expense, by physicians of our choice as often as we reasonably require.

b. We will make these payments regardless of fault. These payments will not exceed the applicable limit of insurance. We will pay reasonable expenses for:

    (1) First aid administered at the time of an accident;

    (2) Necessary medical, surgical, X-ray and dental services, including prosthetic devices; and

    (3) Necessary ambulance, hospital, professional nursing and funeral services.

2. Exclusions

We will not pay expenses for "bodily injury":

a. Any Insured

To any insured, except "volunteer workers".

b. Hired Person

To a person hired to do work for or on behalf of any insured or a tenant of any insured.

c. Injury On Normally Occupied Premises

To a person injured on that part of premises you own or rent that the person normally occupies.

d. Workers' Compensation And Similar Laws

To a person, whether or not an "employee" of any insured, if benefits for the "bodily injury" are payable or must be provided under a workers' compensation or disability benefits law or a similar law.

e. Athletics Activities

To a person injured while practicing, instructing or participating in any physical exercises or games, sports, or athletic contests.

f. Products-Completed Operations Hazard

Included within the "products-completed operations hazard".

g. Coverage A Exclusions

Excluded under Coverage **A.**

SUPPLEMENTARY PAYMENTS – COVERAGES A AND B

1. We will pay, with respect to any claim we investigate or settle, or any "suit" against an insured we defend:

APPENDIX A

a. All expenses we incur.

b. Up to $250 for cost of bail bonds required because of accidents or traffic law violations arising out of the use of any vehicle to which the Bodily Injury Liability Coverage applies. We do not have to furnish these bonds.

c. The cost of bonds to release attachments, but only for bond amounts within the applicable limit of insurance. We do not have to furnish these bonds.

d. All reasonable expenses incurred by the insured at our request to assist us in the investigation or defense of the claim or "suit", including actual loss of earnings up to $250 a day because of time off from work.

e. All court costs taxed against the insured in the "suit". However, these payments do not include attorneys' fees or attorneys' expenses taxed against the insured.

f. Prejudgment interest awarded against the insured on that part of the judgment we pay. If we make an offer to pay the applicable limit of insurance, we will not pay any prejudgment interest based on that period of time after the offer.

g. All interest on the full amount of any judgment that accrues after entry of the judgment and before we have paid, offered to pay, or deposited in court the part of the judgment that is within the applicable limit of insurance.

These payments will not reduce the limits of insurance.

2. If we defend an insured against a "suit" and an indemnitee of the insured is also named as a party to the "suit", we will defend that indemnitee if all of the following conditions are met:

a. The "suit" against the indemnitee seeks damages for which the insured has assumed the liability of the indemnitee in a contract or agreement that is an "insured contract";

b. This insurance applies to such liability assumed by the insured;

c. The obligation to defend, or the cost of the defense of, that indemnitee, has also been assumed by the insured in the same "insured contract";

d. The allegations in the "suit" and the information we know about the "occurrence" are such that no conflict appears to exist between the interests of the insured and the interests of the indemnitee;

APPENDIX A

e. The indemnitee and the insured ask us to conduct and control the defense of that indemnitee against such "suit" and agree that we can assign the same counsel to defend the insured and the indemnitee; and

f. The indemnitee:

(1) Agrees in writing to:

(a) Cooperate with us in the investigation, settlement or defense of the "suit";

(b) Immediately send us copies of any demands, notices, summonses or legal papers received in connection with the "suit";

(c) Notify any other insurer whose coverage is available to the indemnitee; and

(d) Cooperate with us with respect to coordinating other applicable insurance available to the indemnitee; and

(2) Provides us with written authorization to:

(a) Obtain records and other information related to the "suit"; and

(b) Conduct and control the defense of the indemnitee in such "suit".

So long as the above conditions are met, attorneys' fees incurred by us in the defense of that indemnitee, necessary litigation expenses incurred by us and necessary litigation expenses incurred by the indemnitee at our request will be paid as Supplementary Payments. Notwithstanding the provisions of Paragraph **2.b.(2)** of Section **I** – Coverage **A** – Bodily Injury And Property Damage Liability, such payments will not be deemed to be damages for "bodily injury" and "property damage" and will not reduce the limits of insurance.

Our obligation to defend an insured's indemnitee and to pay for attorneys' fees and necessary litigation expenses as Supplementary Payments ends when we have used up the applicable limit of insurance in the payment of judgments or settlements or the conditions set forth above, or the terms of the agreement described in Paragraph **f.** above, are no longer met.

SECTION II – WHO IS AN INSURED

1. If you are designated in the Declarations as:

a. An individual, you and your spouse are insureds, but only with respect to the conduct of a business of which you are the sole owner.

b. A partnership or joint venture, you are an insured. Your members, your partners, and their spouses are also insureds, but only with respect to the conduct of your business.

APPENDIX A

c. A limited liability company, you are an insured. Your members are also insureds, but only with respect to the conduct of your business. Your managers are insureds, but only with respect to their duties as your managers.

d. An organization other than a partnership, joint venture or limited liability company, you are an insured. Your "executive officers" and directors are insureds, but only with respect to their duties as your officers or directors. Your stockholders are also insureds, but only with respect to their liability as stockholders.

e. A trust, you are an insured. Your trustees are also insureds, but only with respect to their duties as trustees.

2. Each of the following is also an insured:

a. Your "volunteer workers" only while performing duties related to the conduct of your business, or your "employees", other than either your "executive officers" (if you are an organization other than a partnership, joint venture or limited liability company) or your managers (if you are a limited liability company), but only for acts within the scope of their employment by you or while performing duties related to the conduct of your business. However, none of these "employees" or "volunteer workers" are insureds for:

   (1) "Bodily injury" or "personal and advertising injury":

   (a) To you, to your partners or members (if you are a partnership or joint venture), to your members (if you are a limited liability company), to a co-"employee" while in the course of his or her employment or performing duties related to the conduct of your business, or to your other "volunteer workers" while performing duties related to the conduct of your business;

   (b) To the spouse, child, parent, brother or sister of that co-"employee" or "volunteer worker" as a consequence of Paragraph **(1)(a)** above;

   (c) For which there is any obligation to share damages with or repay someone else who must pay damages because of the injury described in Paragraph **(1)(a)** or **(b)** above; or

   (d) Arising out of his or her providing or failing to provide professional health care services.

   (2) "Property damage" to property:

   (a) Owned, occupied or used by;

   (b) Rented to, in the care, custody or control of, or over which physical control is being exercised for any purpose by;

APPENDIX A

you, any of your "employees", "volunteer workers", any partner or member (if you are a partnership or joint venture), or any member (if you are a limited liability company).

b. Any person (other than your "employee" or "volunteer worker"), or any organization while acting as your real estate manager.

c. Any person or organization having proper temporary custody of your property if you die, but only:

   (1) With respect to liability arising out of the maintenance or use of that property; and

   (2) Until your legal representative has been appointed.

d. Your legal representative if you die, but only with respect to duties as such. That representative will have all your rights and duties under this Coverage Part.

3. Any organization you newly acquire or form, other than a partnership, joint venture or limited liability company, and over which you maintain ownership or majority interest, will qualify as a Named Insured if there is no other similar insurance available to that organization. However:

   a. Coverage under this provision is afforded only until the 90th day after you acquire or form the organization or the end of the policy period, whichever is earlier;

   b. Coverage **A** does not apply to "bodily injury" or "property damage" that occurred before you acquired or formed the organization; and

   c. Coverage **B** does not apply to "personal and advertising injury" arising out of an offense committed before you acquired or formed the organization.

No person or organization is an insured with respect to the conduct of any current or past partnership, joint venture or limited liability company that is not shown as a Named Insured in the Declarations.

SECTION III – LIMITS OF INSURANCE

1. The Limits of Insurance shown in the Declarations and the rules below fix the most we will pay regardless of the number of:

   a. Insureds;

   b. Claims made or "suits" brought; or

   c. Persons or organizations making claims or bringing "suits".

2. The General Aggregate Limit is the most we will pay for the sum of:

   a. Medical expenses under Coverage **C**;

b. Damages under Coverage **A,** except damages because of "bodily injury" or "property damage" included in the "products-completed operations hazard"; and

c. Damages under Coverage **B.**

3. The Products-Completed Operations Aggregate Limit is the most we will pay under Coverage **A** for damages because of "bodily injury" and "property damage" included in the "products-completed operations hazard".

4. Subject to Paragraph **2.** above, the Personal And Advertising Injury Limit is the most we will pay under Coverage **B** for the sum of all damages because of all "personal and advertising injury" sustained by any one person or organization.

5. Subject to Paragraph **2.** or **3.** above, whichever applies, the Each Occurrence Limit is the most we will pay for the sum of:

a. Damages under Coverage **A;** and

b. Medical expenses under Coverage **C**

because of all "bodily injury" and "property damage" arising out of any one "occurrence".

6. Subject to Paragraph **5.** above, the Damage To Premises Rented To You Limit is the most we will pay under Coverage **A** for damages because of "property damage" to any one premises, while rented to you, or in the case of damage by fire, while rented to you or temporarily occupied by you with permission of the owner.

7. Subject to Paragraph **5.** above, the Medical Expense Limit is the most we will pay under Coverage **C** for all medical expenses because of "bodily injury" sustained by any one person.

The Limits of Insurance of this Coverage Part apply separately to each consecutive annual period and to any remaining period of less than 12 months, starting with the beginning of the policy period shown in the Declarations, unless the policy period is extended after issuance for an additional period of less than 12 months. In that case, the additional period will be deemed part of the last preceding period for purposes of determining the Limits of Insurance.

SECTION IV – COMMERCIAL GENERAL LIABILITY CONDITIONS

1. Bankruptcy

Bankruptcy or insolvency of the insured or of the insured's estate will not relieve us of our obligations under this Coverage Part.

APPENDIX A

2. Duties In The Event Of Occurrence, Offense, Claim Or Suit

   a. You must see to it that we are notified as soon as practicable of an "occurrence" or an offense which may result in a claim. To the extent possible, notice should include:

      (1) How, when and where the "occurrence" or offense took place;

      (2) The names and addresses of any injured persons and witnesses; and

      (3) The nature and location of any injury or damage arising out of the "occurrence" or offense.

   b. If a claim is made or "suit" is brought against any insured, you must:

      (1) Immediately record the specifics of the claim or "suit" and the date received; and

      (2) Notify us as soon as practicable.

     You must see to it that we receive written notice of the claim or "suit" as soon as practicable.

   c. You and any other involved insured must:

      (1) Immediately send us copies of any demands, notices, summonses or legal papers received in connection with the claim or "suit";

      (2) Authorize us to obtain records and other information;

      (3) Cooperate with us in the investigation or settlement of the claim or defense against the "suit"; and

      (4) Assist us, upon our request, in the enforcement of any right against any person or organization which may be liable to the insured because of injury or damage to which this insurance may also apply.

   d. No insured will, except at that insured's own cost, voluntarily make a payment, assume any obligation, or incur any expense, other than for first aid, without our consent.

3. Legal Action Against Us

No person or organization has a right under this Coverage Part:

   a. To join us as a party or otherwise bring us into a "suit" asking for damages from an insured; or

   b. To sue us on this Coverage Part unless all of its terms have been fully complied with.

APPENDIX A

A person or organization may sue us to recover on an agreed settlement or on a final judgment against an insured; but we will not be liable for damages that are not payable under the terms of this Coverage Part or that are in excess of the applicable limit of insurance. An agreed settlement means a settlement and release of liability signed by us, the insured and the claimant or the claimant's legal representative.

4. Other Insurance

If other valid and collectible insurance is available to the insured for a loss we cover under Coverages **A** or **B** of this Coverage Part, our obligations are limited as follows:

a. Primary Insurance

This insurance is primary except when Paragraph **b.** below applies. If this insurance is primary, our obligations are not affected unless any of the other insurance is also primary. Then, we will share with all that other insurance by the method described in Paragraph **c.** below.

b. Excess Insurance

(1) This insurance is excess over:

(a) Any of the other insurance, whether primary, excess, contingent or on any other basis:

(i) That is Fire, Extended Coverage, Builder's Risk, Installation Risk or similar coverage for "your work";

(ii) That is Fire insurance for premises rented to you or temporarily occupied by you with permission of the owner;

(iii) That is insurance purchased by you to cover your liability as a tenant for "property damage" to premises rented to you or temporarily occupied by you with permission of the owner; or

(iv) If the loss arises out of the maintenance or use of aircraft, "autos" or watercraft to the extent not subject to Exclusion **g.** of Section I – Coverage **A** – Bodily Injury And Property Damage Liability.

(b) Any other primary insurance available to you covering liability for damages arising out of the premises or operations, or the products and completed operations, for which you have been added as an additional insured.

(2) When this insurance is excess, we will have no duty under Coverages **A** or **B** to defend the insured against any "suit" if any other insurer has a duty to defend the insured against that "suit". If no other insurer defends, we will undertake to do so, but we will be entitled to the insured's rights against all those other insurers.

APPENDIX A

(3) When this insurance is excess over other insurance, we will pay only our share of the amount of the loss, if any, that exceeds the sum of:

   (a) The total amount that all such other insurance would pay for the loss in the absence of this insurance; and

   (b) The total of all deductible and self-insured amounts under all that other insurance.

(4) We will share the remaining loss, if any, with any other insurance that is not described in this Excess Insurance provision and was not bought specifically to apply in excess of the Limits of Insurance shown in the Declarations of this Coverage Part.

c. Method Of Sharing

If all of the other insurance permits contribution by equal shares, we will follow this method also. Under this approach each insurer contributes equal amounts until it has paid its applicable limit of insurance or none of the loss remains, whichever comes first.

If any of the other insurance does not permit contribution by equal shares, we will contribute by limits. Under this method, each insurer's share is based on the ratio of its applicable limit of insurance to the total applicable limits of insurance of all insurers.

5. Premium Audit

a. We will compute all premiums for this Coverage Part in accordance with our rules and rates.

b. Premium shown in this Coverage Part as advance premium is a deposit premium only. At the close of each audit period we will compute the earned premium for that period and send notice to the first Named Insured. The due date for audit and retrospective premiums is the date shown as the due date on the bill. If the sum of the advance and audit premiums paid for the policy period is greater than the earned premium, we will return the excess to the first Named Insured.

c. The first Named Insured must keep records of the information we need for premium computation, and send us copies at such times as we may request.

6. Representations

By accepting this policy, you agree:

a. The statements in the Declarations are accurate and complete;

b. Those statements are based upon representations you made to us; and

c. We have issued this policy in reliance upon your representations.

APPENDIX A

7. Separation Of Insureds

Except with respect to the Limits of Insurance, and any rights or duties specifically assigned in this Coverage Part to the first Named Insured, this insurance applies:

a. As if each Named Insured were the only Named Insured; and

b. Separately to each insured against whom claim is made or "suit" is brought.

8. Transfer Of Rights Of Recovery Against Others To Us

If the insured has rights to recover all or part of any payment we have made under this Coverage Part, those rights are transferred to us. The insured must do nothing after loss to impair them. At our request, the insured will bring "suit" or transfer those rights to us and help us enforce them.

9. When We Do Not Renew

If we decide not to renew this Coverage Part, we will mail or deliver to the first Named Insured shown in the Declarations written notice of the nonrenewal not less than 30 days before the expiration date.

If notice is mailed, proof of mailing will be sufficient proof of notice.

SECTION V – DEFINITIONS

1. "Advertisement" means a notice that is broadcast or published to the general public or specific market segments about your goods, products or services for the purpose of attracting customers or supporters. For the purposes of this definition:

a. Notices that are published include material placed on the Internet or on similar electronic means of communication; and

b. Regarding web sites, only that part of a web site that is about your goods, products or services for the purposes of attracting customers or supporters is considered an advertisement.

2. "Auto" means:

a. A land motor vehicle, trailer or semitrailer designed for travel on public roads, including any attached machinery or equipment; or

b. Any other land vehicle that is subject to a compulsory or financial responsibility law or other motor vehicle insurance law where it is licensed or principally garaged.

However, "auto" does not include "mobile equipment".

3. "Bodily injury" means bodily injury, sickness or disease sustained by a person, including death resulting from any of these at any time.

4. "Coverage territory" means:

APPENDIX A

---

a. The United States of America (including its territories and possessions), Puerto Rico and Canada;

b. International waters or airspace, but only if the injury or damage occurs in the course of travel or transportation between any places included in Paragraph **a.** above; or

c. All other parts of the world if the injury or damage arises out of:

   (1) Goods or products made or sold by you in the territory described in Paragraph **a.** above;

   (2) The activities of a person whose home is in the territory described in Paragraph **a.** above, but is away for a short time on your business; or

   (3) "Personal and advertising injury" offenses that take place through the Internet or similar electronic means of communication;

provided the insured's responsibility to pay damages is determined in a "suit" on the merits, in the territory described in Paragraph **a.** above or in a settlement we agree to.

5. "Employee" includes a "leased worker". "Employee" does not include a "temporary worker".

6. "Executive officer" means a person holding any of the officer positions created by your charter, constitution, bylaws or any other similar governing document.

7. "Hostile fire" means one which becomes uncontrollable or breaks out from where it was intended to be.

8. "Impaired property" means tangible property, other than "your product" or "your work", that cannot be used or is less useful because:

   a. It incorporates "your product" or "your work" that is known or thought to be defective, deficient, inadequate or dangerous; or

   b. You have failed to fulfill the terms of a contract or agreement;

   if such property can be restored to use by the repair, replacement, adjustment or removal of "your product" or "your work" or your fulfilling the terms of the contract or agreement.

9. "Insured contract" means:

   a. A contract for a lease of premises. However, that portion of the contract for a lease of premises that indemnifies any person or organization for damage by fire to premises while rented to you or temporarily occupied by you with permission of the owner is not an "insured contract";

   b. A sidetrack agreement;

APPENDIX A

c. Any easement or license agreement, except in connection with construction or demolition operations on or within 50 feet of a railroad;

d. An obligation, as required by ordinance, to indemnify a municipality, except in connection with work for a municipality;

e. An elevator maintenance agreement;

f. That part of any other contract or agreement pertaining to your business (including an indemnification of a municipality in connection with work performed for a municipality) under which you assume the tort liability of another party to pay for "bodily injury" or "property damage" to a third person or organization. Tort liability means a liability that would be imposed by law in the absence of any contract or agreement.

Paragraph f. does not include that part of any contract or agreement:

(1) That indemnifies a railroad for "bodily injury" or "property damage" arising out of construction or demolition operations, within 50 feet of any railroad property and affecting any railroad bridge or trestle, tracks, road-beds, tunnel, underpass or crossing;

(2) That indemnifies an architect, engineer or surveyor for injury or damage arising out of:

    (a) Preparing, approving, or failing to prepare or approve, maps, shop drawings, opinions, reports, surveys, field orders, change orders or drawings and specifications; or

    (b) Giving directions or instructions, or failing to give them, if that is the primary cause of the injury or damage; or

(3) Under which the insured, if an architect, engineer or surveyor, assumes liability for an injury or damage arising out of the insured's rendering or failure to render professional services, including those listed in (2) above and supervisory, inspection, architectural or engineering activities.

10. "Leased worker" means a person leased to you by a labor leasing firm under an agreement between you and the labor leasing firm, to perform duties related to the conduct of your business. "Leased worker" does not include a "temporary worker".

11. "Loading or unloading" means the handling of property:

a. After it is moved from the place where it is accepted for movement into or onto an aircraft, watercraft or "auto";

b. While it is in or on an aircraft, watercraft or "auto"; or

c. While it is being moved from an aircraft, watercraft or "auto" to the place where it is finally delivered;

APPENDIX A

---

but "loading or unloading" does not include the movement of property by means of a mechanical device, other than a hand truck, that is not attached to the aircraft, watercraft or "auto".

12. "Mobile equipment" means any of the following types of land vehicles, including any attached machinery or equipment:

a. Bulldozers, farm machinery, forklifts and other vehicles designed for use principally off public roads;

b. Vehicles maintained for use solely on or next to premises you own or rent;

c. Vehicles that travel on crawler treads;

d. Vehicles, whether self-propelled or not, maintained primarily to provide mobility to permanently mounted:

(1) Power cranes, shovels, loaders, diggers or drills; or

(2) Road construction or resurfacing equipment such as graders, scrapers or rollers;

e. Vehicles not described in Paragraph a., b., c. or d. above that are not self-propelled and are maintained primarily to provide mobility to permanently attached equipment of the following types:

(1) Air compressors, pumps and generators, including spraying, welding, building cleaning, geophysical exploration, lighting and well servicing equipment; or

(2) Cherry pickers and similar devices used to raise or lower workers;

f. Vehicles not described in Paragraph a., b., c. or d. above maintained primarily for purposes other than the transportation of persons or cargo.

However, self-propelled vehicles with the following types of permanently attached equipment are not "mobile equipment" but will be considered "autos":

(1) Equipment designed primarily for:

(a) Snow removal;

(b) Road maintenance, but not construction or resurfacing; or

(c) Street cleaning;

(2) Cherry pickers and similar devices mounted on automobile or truck chassis and used to raise or lower workers; and

(3) Air compressors, pumps and generators, including spraying, welding, building cleaning, geophysical exploration, lighting and well servicing equipment.

APPENDIX A

However, "mobile equipment" does not include any land vehicles that are subject to a compulsory or financial responsibility law or other motor vehicle insurance law where it is licensed or principally garaged. Land vehicles subject to a compulsory or financial responsibility law or other motor vehicle insurance law are considered "autos".

13. "Occurrence" means an accident, including continuous or repeated exposure to substantially the same general harmful conditions.

14. "Personal and advertising injury" means injury, including consequential "bodily injury", arising out of one or more of the following offenses:

a. False arrest, detention or imprisonment;

b. Malicious prosecution;

c. The wrongful eviction from, wrongful entry into, or invasion of the right of private occupancy of a room, dwelling or premises that a person occupies, committed by or on behalf of its owner, landlord or lessor;

d. Oral or written publication, in any manner, of material that slanders or libels a person or organization or disparages a person's or organization's goods, products or services;

e. Oral or written publication, in any manner, of material that violates a person's right of privacy;

f. The use of another's advertising idea in your "advertisement"; or

g. Infringing upon another's copyright, trade dress or slogan in your "advertisement".

15. "Pollutants" mean any solid, liquid, gaseous or thermal irritant or contaminant, including smoke, vapor, soot, fumes, acids, alkalis, chemicals and waste. Waste includes materials to be recycled, reconditioned or reclaimed.

16. "Products-completed operations hazard":

a. Includes all "bodily injury" and "property damage" occurring away from premises you own or rent and arising out of "your product" or "your work" except:

(1) Products that are still in your physical possession; or

(2) Work that has not yet been completed or abandoned. However, "your work" will be deemed completed at the earliest of the following times:

(a) When all of the work called for in your contract has been completed.

APPENDIX A

(b) When all of the work to be done at the job site has been completed if your contract calls for work at more than one job site.

(c) When that part of the work done at a job site has been put to its intended use by any person or organization other than another contractor or subcontractor working on the same project.

Work that may need service, maintenance, correction, repair or replacement, but which is otherwise complete, will be treated as completed.

b. Does not include "bodily injury" or "property damage" arising out of:

(1) The transportation of property, unless the injury or damage arises out of a condition in or on a vehicle not owned or operated by you, and that condition was created by the "loading or unloading" of that vehicle by any insured;

(2) The existence of tools, uninstalled equipment or abandoned or unused materials; or

(3) Products or operations for which the classification, listed in the Declarations or in a policy Schedule, states that products-completed operations are subject to the General Aggregate Limit.

17. "Property damage" means:

a. Physical injury to tangible property, including all resulting loss of use of that property. All such loss of use shall be deemed to occur at the time of the physical injury that caused it; or

b. Loss of use of tangible property that is not physically injured. All such loss of use shall be deemed to occur at the time of the "occurrence" that caused it.

For the purposes of this insurance, electronic data is not tangible property.

As used in this definition, electronic data means information, facts or programs stored as or on, created or used on, or transmitted to or from computer software, including systems and applications software, hard or floppy disks, CD-ROMs, tapes, drives, cells, data processing devices or any other media which are used with electronically controlled equipment.

18. "Suit" means a civil proceeding in which damages because of "bodily injury", "property damage" or "personal and advertising injury" to which this insurance applies are alleged. "Suit" includes:

a. An arbitration proceeding in which such damages are claimed and to which the insured must submit or does submit with our consent; or

APPENDIX A

    b. Any other alternative dispute resolution proceeding in which such damages are claimed and to which the insured submits with our consent.

19. "Temporary worker" means a person who is furnished to you to substitute for a permanent "employee" on leave or to meet seasonal or short-term workload conditions.

20. "Volunteer worker" means a person who is not your "employee", and who donates his or her work and acts at the direction of and within the scope of duties determined by you, and is not paid a fee, salary or other compensation by you or anyone else for their work performed for you.

21. "Your product":

    a. Means:

        (1) Any goods or products, other than real property, manufactured, sold, handled, distributed or disposed of by:

            (a) You;

            (b) Others trading under your name; or

            (c) A person or organization whose business or assets you have acquired; and

        (2) Containers (other than vehicles), materials, parts or equipment furnished in connection with such goods or products.

    b. Includes:

        (1) Warranties or representations made at any time with respect to the fitness, quality, durability, performance or use of "your product"; and

        (2) The providing of or failure to provide warnings or instructions.

    c. Does not include vending machines or other property rented to or located for the use of others but not sold.

22. "Your work":

    a. Means:

        (1) Work or operations performed by you or on your behalf; and

        (2) Materials, parts or equipment furnished in connection with such work or operations.

    b. Includes:

        (1) Warranties or representations made at any time with respect to the fitness, quality, durability, performance or use of "your work"; and

        (2) The providing of or failure to provide warnings or instructions.

APPENDIX A

APPENDIX A

Appendix B: Sample Claims Made Form Commercial General Liability Policy Insuring Agreement

COMMERCIAL GENERAL LIABILITY COVERAGE FORM

COVERAGES A AND B PROVIDE CLAIMS-MADE COVERAGE. PLEASE READ THE ENTIRE FORM CAREFULLY.

Various provisions in this policy restrict coverage. Read the entire policy carefully to determine rights, duties and what is and is not covered.

Throughout this policy the words "you" and "your" refer to the Named Insured shown in the Declarations, and any other person or organization qualifying as a Named Insured under this policy. The words "we", "us" and "our" refer to the company providing this insurance.

The word "insured" means any person or organization qualifying as such under Section II – Who Is An Insured.

Other words and phrases that appear in quotation marks have special meaning. Refer to Section VI – Definitions.

SECTION I – COVERAGES

COVERAGE A – BODILY INJURY AND PROPERTY DAMAGE LIABILITY

1. Insuring Agreement

a. We will pay those sums that the insured becomes legally obligated to pay as damages because of "bodily injury" or "property damage" to which this insurance applies. We will have the right and duty to defend the insured against any "suit" seeking those damages. However, we will have no duty to defend the insured against any "suit" seeking damages for "bodily injury" or "property damage" to which this insurance does not apply. We may, at our discretion, investigate any "occurrence" and settle any claim or "suit" that may result. But:

(1) The amount we will pay for damages is limited as described in Section III – Limits Of Insurance; and

(2) Our right and duty to defend ends when we have used up the applicable limit of insurance in the payment of judgments or settlements under Coverages A or B or medical expenses under Coverage C.

APPENDIX B

APPENDIX B

No other obligation or liability to pay sums or perform acts or services is covered unless explicitly provided for under Supplementary Payments – Coverages **A** and **B**.

b. This insurance applies to "bodily injury" and "property damage" only if:

(1) The "bodily injury" or "property damage" is caused by an "occurrence" that takes place in the "coverage territory";

(2) The "bodily injury" or "property damage" did not occur before the Retroactive Date, if any, shown in the Declarations or after the end of the policy period; and

(3) A claim for damages because of the "bodily injury" or "property damage" is first made against any insured, in accordance with Paragraph **c.** below, during the policy period or any Extended Reporting Period we provide under Section **V** – Extended Reporting Periods.

c. A claim by a person or organization seeking damages will be deemed to have been made at the earlier of the following times:

(1) When notice of such claim is received and recorded by any insured or by us, whichever comes first; or

(2) When we make settlement in accordance with Paragraph **a.** above.

All claims for damages because of "bodily injury" to the same person, including damages claimed by any person or organization for care, loss of services, or death resulting at any time from the "bodily injury", will be deemed to have been made at the time the first of those claims is made against any insured.

All claims for damages because of "property damage" causing loss to the same person or organization will be deemed to have been made at the time the first of those claims is made against any insured.

2. Exclusions

This insurance does not apply to:

a. Expected Or Intended Injury

"Bodily injury" or "property damage" expected or intended from the standpoint of the insured. This exclusion does not apply to "bodily injury" resulting from the use of reasonable force to protect persons or property.

b. Contractual Liability

"Bodily injury" or "property damage" for which the insured is obligated to pay damages by reason of the assumption of liability in a contract or agreement. This exclusion does not apply to liability for damages:

(1) That the insured would have in the absence of the contract or agreement; or

(2) Assumed in a contract or agreement that is an "insured contract", provided the "bodily injury" or "property damage" occurs subsequent to the execution of the contract or agreement. Solely for the purposes of liability assumed in an "insured contract", reasonable attorneys' fees and necessary litigation expenses incurred by or for a party other than an insured are deemed to be damages because of "bodily injury" or "property damage", provided:

   (a) Liability to such party for, or for the cost of, that party's defense has also been assumed in the same "insured contract"; and

   (b) Such attorneys' fees and litigation expenses are for defense of that party against a civil or alternative dispute resolution proceeding in which damages to which this insurance applies are alleged.

c. Liquor Liability

"Bodily injury" or "property damage" for which any insured may be held liable by reason of:

(1) Causing or contributing to the intoxication of any person;

(2) The furnishing of alcoholic beverages to a person under the legal drinking age or under the influence of alcohol; or

(3) Any statute, ordinance or regulation relating to the sale, gift, distribution or use of alcoholic beverages.

This exclusion applies even if the claims against any insured allege negligence or other wrongdoing in:

   (a) The supervision, hiring, employment, training or monitoring of others by that insured; or

   (b) Providing or failing to provide transportation with respect to any person that may be under the influence of alcohol;

if the "occurrence" which caused the "bodily injury" or "property damage", involved that which is described in Paragraph **(1)**, **(2)** or **(3)** above.

APPENDIX B

However, this exclusion applies only if you are in the business of manufacturing, distributing, selling, serving or furnishing alcoholic beverages. For the purposes of this exclusion, permitting a person to bring alcoholic beverages on your premises, for consumption on your premises, whether or not a fee is charged or a license is required for such activity, is not by itself considered the business of selling, serving or furnishing alcoholic beverages.

d. Workers' Compensation And Similar Laws

Any obligation of the insured under a workers' compensation, disability benefits or unemployment compensation law or any similar law.

e. Employer's Liability

"Bodily injury" to:

(1) An "employee" of the insured arising out of and in the course of:

(a) Employment by the insured; or

(b) Performing duties related to the conduct of the insured's business; or

(2) The spouse, child, parent, brother or sister of that "employee" as a consequence of Paragraph **(1)** above.

This exclusion applies whether the insured may be liable as an employer or in any other capacity and to any obligation to share damages with or repay someone else who must pay damages because of the injury.

This exclusion does not apply to liability assumed by the insured under an "insured contract".

f. Pollution

(1) "Bodily injury" or "property damage" arising out of the actual, alleged or threatened discharge, dispersal, seepage, migration, release or escape of "pollutants":

(a) At or from any premises, site or location which is or was at any time owned or occupied by, or rented or loaned to, any insured. However, this subparagraph does not apply to:

(i) "Bodily injury" if sustained within a building and caused by smoke, fumes, vapor or soot produced by or originating from equipment that is used to heat, cool or dehumidify the building, or equipment that is used to heat water for personal use by the building's occupants or their guests;

    (ii) "Bodily injury" or "property damage" for which you may be held liable, if you are a contractor and the owner or lessee of such premises, site or location has been added to your policy as an additional insured with respect to your ongoing operations performed for that additional insured at that premises, site or location and such premises, site or location is not and never was owned or occupied by, or rented or loaned to, any insured, other than that additional insured; or

    (iii) "Bodily injury" or "property damage" arising out of heat, smoke or fumes from a "hostile fire";

(b) At or from any premises, site or location which is or was at any time used by or for any insured or others for the handling, storage, disposal, processing or treatment of waste;

(c) Which are or were at any time transported, handled, stored, treated, disposed of, or processed as waste by or for:

    (i) Any insured; or

    (ii) Any person or organization for whom you may be legally responsible; or

(d) At or from any premises, site or location on which any insured or any contractors or subcontractors working directly or indirectly on any insured's behalf are performing operations if the "pollutants" are brought on or to the premises, site or location in connection with such operations by such insured, contractor or subcontractor. However, this subparagraph does not apply to:

    (i) "Bodily injury" or "property damage" arising out of the escape of fuels, lubricants or other operating fluids which are needed to perform the normal electrical, hydraulic or mechanical functions necessary for the operation of "mobile equipment" or its parts, if such fuels, lubricants or other operating fluids escape from a vehicle part designed to hold, store or receive them. This exception does not apply if the "bodily injury" or "property damage" arises out of the intentional discharge, dispersal or release of the fuels, lubricants or other operating fluids, or if such fuels, lubricants or other operating fluids are brought on or to the premises, site or location with the intent that they be discharged, dispersed or released as part of the operations being performed by such insured, contractor or subcontractor;

APPENDIX B

(ii) "Bodily injury" or "property damage" sustained within a building and caused by the release of gases, fumes or vapors from materials brought into that building in connection with operations being performed by you or on your behalf by a contractor or subcontractor; or

(iii) "Bodily injury" or "property damage" arising out of heat, smoke or fumes from a "hostile fire".

(e) At or from any premises, site or location on which any insured or any contractors or subcontractors working directly or indirectly on any insured's behalf are performing operations if the operations are to test for, monitor, clean up, remove, contain, treat, detoxify or neutralize, or in any way respond to, or assess the effects of, "pollutants".

(2) Any loss, cost or expense arising out of any:

(a) Request, demand, order or statutory or regulatory requirement that any insured or others test for, monitor, clean up, remove, contain, treat, detoxify or neutralize, or in any way respond to, or assess the effects of, "pollutants"; or

(b) Claim or suit by or on behalf of a governmental authority for damages because of testing for, monitoring, cleaning up, removing, containing, treating, detoxifying or neutralizing, or in any way responding to, or assessing the effects of, "pollutants".

However, this paragraph does not apply to liability for damages because of "property damage" that the insured would have in the absence of such request, demand, order or statutory or regulatory requirement, or such claim or "suit" by or on behalf of a governmental authority.

g. Aircraft, Auto Or Watercraft

"Bodily injury" or "property damage" arising out of the ownership, maintenance, use or entrustment to others of any aircraft, "auto" or watercraft owned or operated by or rented or loaned to any insured. Use includes operation and "loading or unloading".

This exclusion applies even if the claims against any insured allege negligence or other wrongdoing in the supervision, hiring, employment, training or monitoring of others by that insured, if the "occurrence" which caused the "bodily injury" or "property damage" involved the ownership, maintenance, use or entrustment to others of any aircraft, "auto" or watercraft that is owned or operated by or rented or loaned to any insured.

This exclusion does not apply to:

APPENDIX B

(1) A watercraft while ashore on premises you own or rent;

(2) A watercraft you do not own that is:

  (a) Less than 26 feet long; and

  (b) Not being used to carry persons or property for a charge;

(3) Parking an "auto" on, or on the ways next to, premises you own or rent, provided the "auto" is not owned by or rented or loaned to you or the insured;

(4) Liability assumed under any "insured contract" for the ownership, maintenance or use of aircraft or watercraft; or

(5) "Bodily injury" or "property damage" arising out of:

  (a) The operation of machinery or equipment that is attached to, or part of, a land vehicle that would qualify under the definition of "mobile equipment" if it were not subject to a compulsory or financial responsibility law or other motor vehicle insurance law where it is licensed or principally garaged; or

  (b) The operation of any of the machinery or equipment listed in Paragraph **f.(2)** or **f.(3)** of the definition of "mobile equipment".

h. Mobile Equipment

"Bodily injury" or "property damage" arising out of:

(1) The transportation of "mobile equipment" by an "auto" owned or operated by or rented or loaned to any insured; or

(2) The use of "mobile equipment" in, or while in practice for, or while being prepared for, any prearranged racing, speed, demolition, or stunting activity.

i. War

"Bodily injury" or "property damage", however caused, arising, directly or indirectly, out of:

(1) War, including undeclared or civil war;

(2) Warlike action by a military force, including action in hindering or defending against an actual or expected attack, by any government, sovereign or other authority using military personnel or other agents; or

(3) Insurrection, rebellion, revolution, usurped power, or action taken by governmental authority in hindering or defending against any of these.

j. Damage To Property

"Property damage" to:

APPENDIX B

(1) Property you own, rent, or occupy, including any costs or expenses incurred by you, or any other person, organization or entity, for repair, replacement, enhancement, restoration or maintenance of such property for any reason, including prevention of injury to a person or damage to another's property;

(2) Premises you sell, give away or abandon, if the "property damage" arises out of any part of those premises;

(3) Property loaned to you;

(4) Personal property in the care, custody or control of the insured;

(5) That particular part of real property on which you or any contractors or subcontractors working directly or indirectly on your behalf are performing operations, if the "property damage" arises out of those operations; or

(6) That particular part of any property that must be restored, repaired or replaced because "your work" was incorrectly performed on it.

Paragraphs **(1)**, **(3)** and **(4)** of this exclusion do not apply to "property damage" (other than damage by fire) to premises, including the contents of such premises, rented to you for a period of seven or fewer consecutive days. A separate limit of insurance applies to Damage To Premises Rented To You as described in Section III – Limits Of Insurance.

Paragraph **(2)** of this exclusion does not apply if the premises are "your work" and were never occupied, rented or held for rental by you.

Paragraphs **(3)**, **(4)**, **(5)** and **(6)** of this exclusion do not apply to liability assumed under a sidetrack agreement.

Paragraph **(6)** of this exclusion does not apply to "property damage" included in the "products-completed operations hazard".

k. Damage To Your Product

"Property damage" to "your product" arising out of it or any part of it.

l. Damage To Your Work

"Property damage" to "your work" arising out of it or any part of it and included in the "products-completed operations hazard".

This exclusion does not apply if the damaged work or the work out of which the damage arises was performed on your behalf by a subcontractor.

m. Damage To Impaired Property Or Property Not Physically Injured

"Property damage" to "impaired property" or property that has not been physically injured, arising out of:

APPENDIX B

(1) A defect, deficiency, inadequacy or dangerous condition in "your product" or "your work"; or

(2) A delay or failure by you or anyone acting on your behalf to perform a contract or agreement in accordance with its terms.

This exclusion does not apply to the loss of use of other property arising out of sudden and accidental physical injury to "your product" or "your work" after it has been put to its intended use.

n. Recall Of Products, Work Or Impaired Property

Damages claimed for any loss, cost or expense incurred by you or others for the loss of use, withdrawal, recall, inspection, repair, replacement, adjustment, removal or disposal of:

(1) "Your product";

(2) "Your work"; or

(3) "Impaired property";

if such product, work, or property is withdrawn or recalled from the market or from use by any person or organization because of a known or suspected defect, deficiency, inadequacy or dangerous condition in it.

o. Personal And Advertising Injury

"Bodily injury" arising out of "personal and advertising injury".

p. Electronic Data

Damages arising out of the loss of, loss of use of, damage to, corruption of, inability to access, or inability to manipulate electronic data.

However, this exclusion does not apply to liability for damages because of "bodily injury".

As used in this exclusion, electronic data means information, facts or programs stored as or on, created or used on, or transmitted to or from computer software, including systems and applications software, hard or floppy disks, CD-ROMs, tapes, drives, cells, data processing devices or any other media which are used with electronically controlled equipment.

q. Recording And Distribution Of Material In Violation Of Law

"Bodily injury" or "property damage" arising directly or indirectly out of any action or omission that violates or is alleged to violate:

(1) The Telephone Consumer Protection Act (TCPA), including any amendment of or addition to such law;

APPENDIX B

    (2) The CAN-SPAM Act of 2003, including any amendment of or addition to such law;

    (3) The Fair Credit Reporting Act (FCRA), and any amendment of or addition to such law, including the Fair and Accurate Credit Transactions Act (FACTA); or

    (4) Any federal, state or local statute, ordinance or regulation, other than the TCPA, CAN-SPAM Act of 2003 or FCRA and their amendments and additions, that addresses, prohibits, or limits the printing, dissemination, disposal, collecting, recording, sending, transmitting, communicating or distribution of material or information.

Exclusions **c.** through **n.** do not apply to damage by fire to premises while rented to you or temporarily occupied by you with permission of the owner. A separate limit of insurance applies to this coverage as described in Section **III** – Limits Of Insurance.

COVERAGE B – PERSONAL AND ADVERTISING INJURY LIABILITY

1. Insuring Agreement

  a. We will pay those sums that the insured becomes legally obligated to pay as damages because of "personal and advertising injury" to which this insurance applies. We will have the right and duty to defend the insured against any "suit" seeking those damages. However, we will have no duty to defend the insured against any "suit" seeking damages for "personal and advertising injury" to which this insurance does not apply. We may, at our discretion, investigate any offense and settle any claim or "suit" that may result. But:

    (1) The amount we will pay for damages is limited as described in Section **III** – Limits Of Insurance; and

    (2) Our right and duty to defend end when we have used up the applicable limit of insurance in the payment of judgments or settlements under Coverages **A** or **B** or medical expenses under Coverage **C.**

  No other obligation or liability to pay sums or perform acts or services is covered unless explicitly provided for under Supplementary Payments – Coverages **A** and **B.**

  b. This insurance applies to "personal and advertising injury" caused by an offense arising out of your business, but only if:

    (1) The offense was committed in the "coverage territory";

    (2) The offense was not committed before the Retroactive Date, if any, shown in the Declarations or after the end of the policy period; and

(3) A claim for damages because of the "personal and advertising injury" is first made against any insured, in accordance with Paragraph **c.** below, during the policy period or any Extended Reporting Period we provide under Section **V** – Extended Reporting Periods.

c. A claim made by a person or organization seeking damages will be deemed to have been made at the earlier of the following times:

(1) When notice of such claim is received and recorded by any insured or by us, whichever comes first; or

(2) When we make settlement in accordance with Paragraph **a.** above.

All claims for damages because of "personal and advertising injury" to the same person or organization as a result of an offense will be deemed to have been made at the time the first of those claims is made against any insured.

2. Exclusions

This insurance does not apply to:

a. Knowing Violation Of Rights Of Another

"Personal and advertising injury" caused by or at the direction of the insured with the knowledge that the act would violate the rights of another and would inflict "personal and advertising injury".

b. Material Published With Knowledge Of Falsity

"Personal and advertising injury" arising out of oral or written publication, in any manner, of material, if done by or at the direction of the insured with knowledge of its falsity.

c. Material Published Prior To Policy Period

"Personal and advertising injury" arising out of oral or written publication, in any manner, of material whose first publication took place before the Retroactive Date, if any, shown in the Declarations.

d. Criminal Acts

"Personal and advertising injury" arising out of a criminal act committed by or at the direction of the insured.

e. Contractual Liability

"Personal and advertising injury" for which the insured has assumed liability in a contract or agreement. This exclusion does not apply to liability for damages that the insured would have in the absence of the contract or agreement.

APPENDIX B

f. Breach Of Contract

"Personal and advertising injury" arising out of a breach of contract, except an implied contract to use another's advertising idea in your "advertisement".

g. Quality Or Performance Of Goods – Failure To Conform To Statements

"Personal and advertising injury" arising out of the failure of goods, products or services to conform with any statement of quality or performance made in your "advertisement".

h. Wrong Description Of Prices

"Personal and advertising injury" arising out of the wrong description of the price of goods, products or services stated in your "advertisement".

i. Infringement Of Copyright, Patent, Trademark Or Trade Secret

"Personal and advertising injury" arising out of the infringement of copyright, patent, trademark, trade secret or other intellectual property rights. Under this exclusion, such other intellectual property rights do not include the use of another's advertising idea in your "advertisement".

However, this exclusion does not apply to infringement, in your "advertisement", of copyright, trade dress or slogan.

j. Insureds In Media And Internet Type Businesses

"Personal and advertising injury" committed by an insured whose business is:

(1) Advertising, broadcasting, publishing or telecasting;

(2) Designing or determining content of web sites for others; or

(3) An Internet search, access, content or service provider.

However, this exclusion does not apply to Paragraphs **14.a., b.** and **c.** of "personal and advertising injury" under the Definitions section.

For the purposes of this exclusion, the placing of frames, borders or links, or advertising, for you or others anywhere on the Internet, is not by itself, considered the business of advertising, broadcasting, publishing or telecasting.

k. Electronic Chatrooms Or Bulletin Boards

"Personal and advertising injury" arising out of an electronic chatroom or bulletin board the insured hosts, owns, or over which the insured exercises control.

APPENDIX B

l. Unauthorized Use Of Another's Name Or Product

"Personal and advertising injury" arising out of the unauthorized use of another's name or product in your e-mail address, domain name or metatag, or any other similar tactics to mislead another's potential customers.

m. Pollution

"Personal and advertising injury" arising out of the actual, alleged or threatened discharge, dispersal, seepage, migration, release or escape of "pollutants" at any time.

n. Pollution-related

Any loss, cost or expense arising out of any:

(1) Request, demand, order or statutory or regulatory requirement that any insured or others test for, monitor, clean up, remove, contain, treat, detoxify or neutralize, or in any way respond to, or assess the effects of, "pollutants"; or

(2) Claim or suit by or on behalf of a governmental authority for damages because of testing for, monitoring, cleaning up, removing, containing, treating, detoxifying or neutralizing, or in any way responding to, or assessing the effects of, "pollutants".

o. War

"Personal and advertising injury", however caused, arising, directly or indirectly, out of:

(1) War, including undeclared or civil war;

(2) Warlike action by a military force, including action in hindering or defending against an actual or expected attack, by any government, sovereign or other authority using military personnel or other agents; or

(3) Insurrection, rebellion, revolution, usurped power, or action taken by governmental authority in hindering or defending against any of these.

p. Recording And Distribution Of Material In Violation Of Law

"Personal and advertising injury" arising directly or indirectly out of any action or omission that violates or is alleged to violate:

(1) The Telephone Consumer Protection Act (TCPA), including any amendment of or addition to such law;

(2) The CAN-SPAM Act of 2003, including any amendment of or addition to such law;

APPENDIX B

---

(3) The Fair Credit Reporting Act (FCRA), and any amendment of or addition to such law, including the Fair and Accurate Credit Transactions Act (FACTA); or

(4) Any federal, state or local statute, ordinance or regulation, other than the TCPA, CAN-SPAM Act of 2003 or FCRA and their amendments and additions, that addresses, prohibits, or limits the printing, dissemination, disposal, collecting, recording, sending, transmitting, communicating or distribution of material or information.

COVERAGE C – MEDICAL PAYMENTS

1. Insuring Agreement

a. We will pay medical expenses as described below for "bodily injury" caused by an accident:

(1) On premises you own or rent;

(2) On ways next to premises you own or rent; or

(3) Because of your operations;

provided that:

(a) The accident takes place in the "coverage territory" and during the policy period;

(b) The expenses are incurred and reported to us within one year of the date of the accident; and

(c) The injured person submits to examination, at our expense, by physicians of our choice as often as we reasonably require.

b. We will make these payments regardless of fault. These payments will not exceed the applicable limit of insurance. We will pay reasonable expenses for:

(1) First aid administered at the time of an accident;

(2) Necessary medical, surgical, X-ray and dental services, including prosthetic devices; and

(3) Necessary ambulance, hospital, professional nursing and funeral services.

2. Exclusions

We will not pay expenses for "bodily injury":

a. Any Insured

To any insured, except "volunteer workers".

APPENDIX B

b. Hired Person

To a person hired to do work for or on behalf of any insured or a tenant of any insured.

c. Injury On Normally Occupied Premises

To a person injured on that part of premises you own or rent that the person normally occupies.

d. Workers' Compensation And Similar Laws

To a person, whether or not an "employee" of any insured, if benefits for the "bodily injury" are payable or must be provided under a workers' compensation or disability benefits law or a similar law.

e. Athletics Activities

To a person injured while practicing, instructing or participating in any physical exercises or games, sports, or athletic contests.

f. Products-Completed Operations Hazard

Included within the "products-completed operations hazard".

g. Coverage A Exclusions

Excluded under Coverage **A.**

SUPPLEMENTARY PAYMENTS – COVERAGES A AND B

1. We will pay, with respect to any claim we investigate or settle or any "suit" against an insured we defend:

   a. All expenses we incur.

   b. Up to $250 for cost of bail bonds required because of accidents or traffic law violations arising out of the use of any vehicle to which the Bodily Injury Liability Coverage applies. We do not have to furnish these bonds.

   c. The cost of bonds to release attachments, but only for bond amounts within the applicable limit of insurance. We do not have to furnish these bonds.

   d. All reasonable expenses incurred by the insured at our request to assist us in the investigation or defense of the claim or "suit", including actual loss of earnings up to $250 a day because of time off from work.

   e. All court costs taxed against the insured in the "suit". However, these payments do not include attorneys' fees or attorneys' expenses taxed against the insured.

APPENDIX B

f. Prejudgment interest awarded against the insured on that part of the judgment we pay. If we make an offer to pay the applicable limit of insurance, we will not pay any prejudgment interest based on that period of time after the offer.

g. All interest on the full amount of any judgment that accrues after entry of the judgment and before we have paid, offered to pay, or deposited in court the part of the judgment that is within the applicable limit of insurance.

These payments will not reduce the limits of insurance.

2. If we defend an insured against a "suit" and an indemnitee of the insured is also named as a party to the "suit", we will defend that indemnitee if all of the following conditions are met:

a. The "suit" against the indemnitee seeks damages for which the insured has assumed the liability of the indemnitee in a contract or agreement that is an "insured contract";

b. This insurance applies to such liability assumed by the insured;

c. The obligation to defend, or the cost of the defense of, that indemnitee, has also been assumed by the insured in the same "insured contract";

d. The allegations in the "suit" and the information we know about the "occurrence" are such that no conflict appears to exist between the interests of the insured and the interests of the indemnitee;

e. The indemnitee and the insured ask us to conduct and control the defense of that indemnitee against such "suit" and agree that we can assign the same counsel to defend the insured and the indemnitee; and

f. The indemnitee:

(1) Agrees in writing to:

(a) Cooperate with us in the investigation, settlement or defense of the "suit";

(b) Immediately send us copies of any demands, notices, summonses or legal papers received in connection with the "suit";

(c) Notify any other insurer whose coverage is available to the indemnitee; and

(d) Cooperate with us with respect to coordinating other applicable insurance available to the indemnitee; and

(2) Provides us with written authorization to:

(a) Obtain records and other information related to the "suit"; and

APPENDIX B

(b) Conduct and control the defense of the indemnitee in such "suit".

So long as the above conditions are met, attorneys' fees incurred by us in the defense of that indemnitee, necessary litigation expenses incurred by us and necessary litigation expenses incurred by the indemnitee at our request will be paid as Supplementary Payments. Notwithstanding the provisions of Paragraph **2.b.(2)** of Section **I** – Coverage **A** – Bodily Injury And Property Damage Liability, such payments will not be deemed to be damages for "bodily injury" and "property damage" and will not reduce the limits of insurance.

Our obligation to defend an insured's indemnitee and to pay for attorneys' fees and necessary litigation expenses as Supplementary Payments ends when we have used up the applicable limit of insurance in the payment of judgments or settlements or the conditions set forth above, or the terms of the agreement described in Paragraph **f.** above, are no longer met.

SECTION II – WHO IS AN INSURED

1. If you are designated in the Declarations as:

   a. An individual, you and your spouse are insureds, but only with respect to the conduct of a business of which you are the sole owner.

   b. A partnership or joint venture, you are an insured. Your members, your partners, and their spouses are also insureds, but only with respect to the conduct of your business.

   c. A limited liability company, you are an insured. Your members are also insureds, but only with respect to the conduct of your business. Your managers are insureds, but only with respect to their duties as your managers.

   d. An organization other than a partnership, joint venture or limited liability company, you are an insured. Your "executive officers" and directors are insureds, but only with respect to their duties as your officers or directors. Your stockholders are also insureds, but only with respect to their liability as stockholders.

   e. A trust, you are an insured. Your trustees are also insureds, but only with respect to their duties as trustees.

2. Each of the following is also an insured:

APPENDIX B

---

a. Your "volunteer workers" only while performing duties related to the conduct of your business, or your "employees", other than either your "executive officers" (if you are an organization other than a partnership, joint venture or limited liability company) or your managers (if you are a limited liability company), but only for acts within the scope of their employment by you or while performing duties related to the conduct of your business. However, none of these "employees" or "volunteer workers" are insureds for:

   (1) "Bodily injury" or "personal and advertising injury":

   (a) To you, to your partners or members (if you are a partnership or joint venture), to your members (if you are a limited liability company), to a co-"employee" while in the course of his or her employment or performing duties related to the conduct of your business, or to your other "volunteer workers" while performing duties related to the conduct of your business;

   (b) To the spouse, child, parent, brother or sister of that co-"employee" or "volunteer worker" as a consequence of Paragraph **(a)** above;

   (c) For which there is any obligation to share damages with or repay someone else who must pay damages because of the injury described in Paragraph **(a)** or **(b)** above; or

   (d) Arising out of his or her providing or failing to provide professional health care services.

   (2) "Property damage" to property:

   (a) Owned, occupied or used by;

   (b) Rented to, in the care, custody or control of, or over which physical control is being exercised for any purpose by;

   you, any of your "employees", "volunteer workers", any partner or member (if you are a partnership or joint venture), or any member (if you are a limited liability company).

b. Any person (other than your "employee" or "volunteer worker") or any organization while acting as your real estate manager.

c. Any person or organization having proper temporary custody of your property if you die, but only:

   (1) With respect to liability arising out of the maintenance or use of that property; and

   (2) Until your legal representative has been appointed.

d. Your legal representative if you die, but only with respect to duties as such. That representative will have all your rights and duties under this Coverage Part.

3. Any organization you newly acquire or form, other than a partnership, joint venture or limited liability company, and over which you maintain ownership or majority interest, will qualify as a Named Insured if there is no other similar insurance available to that organization. However:

   a. Coverage under this provision is afforded only until the 90th day after you acquire or form the organization or the end of the policy period, whichever is earlier;

   b. Coverage **A** does not apply to "bodily injury" or "property damage" that occurred before you acquired or formed the organization; and

   c. Coverage **B** does not apply to "personal and advertising injury" arising out of an offense committed before you acquired or formed the organization.

No person or organization is an insured with respect to the conduct of any current or past partnership, joint venture or limited liability company that is not shown as a Named Insured in the Declarations.

SECTION III – LIMITS OF INSURANCE

1. The Limits of Insurance shown in the Declarations and the rules below fix the most we will pay regardless of the number of:

   a. Insureds;

   b. Claims made or "suits" brought; or

   c. Persons or organizations making claims or bringing "suits".

2. The General Aggregate Limit is the most we will pay for the sum of:

   a. Medical expenses under Coverage **C**;

   b. Damages under Coverage **A,** except damages because of "bodily injury" or "property damage" included in the "products-completed operations hazard"; and

   c. Damages under Coverage **B**.

3. The Products-Completed Operations Aggregate Limit is the most we will pay under Coverage **A** for damages because of "bodily injury" and "property damage" included in the "products-completed operations hazard".

4. Subject to Paragraph **2.** above, the Personal And Advertising Injury Limit is the most we will pay under Coverage **B** for the sum of all damages because of all "personal and advertising injury" sustained by any one person or organization.

5. Subject to Paragraph **2.** or **3.** above, whichever applies, the Each Occurrence Limit is the most we will pay for the sum of:

   a. Damages under Coverage **A;** and

APPENDIX B

---

b. Medical expenses under Coverage **C**

because of all "bodily injury" and "property damage" arising out of any one "occurrence".

6. Subject to Paragraph **5.** above, the Damage To Premises Rented To You Limit is the most we will pay under Coverage **A** for damages because of "property damage" to any one premises, while rented to you, or in the case of damage by fire, while rented to you or temporarily occupied by you with permission of the owner.

7. Subject to Paragraph **5.** above, the Medical Expense Limit is the most we will pay under Coverage **C** for all medical expenses because of "bodily injury" sustained by any one person.

The Limits of Insurance of this Coverage Part apply separately to each consecutive annual period and to any remaining period of less than 12 months, starting with the beginning of the policy period shown in the Declarations, unless the policy period is extended after issuance for an additional period of less than 12 months. In that case, the additional period will be deemed part of the last preceding period for purposes of determining the Limits of Insurance.

SECTION IV – COMMERCIAL GENERAL LIABILITY CONDITIONS

1. **Bankruptcy**

   Bankruptcy or insolvency of the insured or of the insured's estate will not relieve us of our obligations under this Coverage Part.

2. **Duties In The Event Of Occurrence, Offense, Claim Or Suit**

   a. You must see to it that we are notified as soon as practicable of an "occurrence" or offense which may result in a claim. To the extent possible, notice should include:

   (1) How, when and where the "occurrence" or offense took place;

   (2) The names and addresses of any injured persons and witnesses; and

   (3) The nature and location of any injury or damage arising out of the "occurrence" or offense.

   Notice of an "occurrence" or offense is not notice of a claim.

   b. If a claim is received by any insured, you must:

   (1) Immediately record the specifics of the claim and the date received; and

   (2) Notify us as soon as practicable.

   You must see to it that we receive written notice of the claim as soon as practicable.

APPENDIX B

c. You and any other involved insured must:

  (1) Immediately send us copies of any demands, notices, summonses or legal papers received in connection with the claim or a "suit";

  (2) Authorize us to obtain records and other information;

  (3) Cooperate with us in the investigation or settlement of the claim or defense against the "suit"; and

  (4) Assist us, upon our request, in the enforcement of any right against any person or organization which may be liable to the insured because of injury or damage to which this insurance may also apply.

d. No insured will, except at that insured's own cost, voluntarily make a payment, assume any obligation, or incur any expense, other than for first aid, without our consent.

3. Legal Action Against Us

No person or organization has a right under this Coverage Part:

a. To join us as a party or otherwise bring us into a "suit" asking for damages from an insured; or

b. To sue us on this Coverage Part unless all of its terms have been fully complied with.

A person or organization may sue us to recover on an agreed settlement or on a final judgment against an insured; but we will not be liable for damages that are not payable under the terms of this Coverage Part or that are in excess of the applicable limit of insurance. An agreed settlement means a settlement and release of liability signed by us, the insured and the claimant or the claimant's legal representative.

4. Other Insurance

If other valid and collectible insurance is available to the insured for a loss we cover under Coverages **A** or **B** of this Coverage Part, our obligations are limited as follows:

a. Primary Insurance

This insurance is primary except when Paragraph **b.** below applies. If this insurance is primary, our obligations are not affected unless any of the other insurance is also primary. Then, we will share with all that other insurance by the method described in Paragraph **c.** below.

b. Excess Insurance

  (1) This insurance is excess over:

    (a) Any of the other insurance, whether primary, excess, contingent or on any other basis:

APPENDIX B

(i) That is effective prior to the beginning of the policy period shown in the Declarations of this insurance and applies to "bodily injury" or "property damage" on other than a claims-made basis, if:

   i. No Retroactive Date is shown in the Declarations of this insurance; or

   ii. The other insurance has a policy period which continues after the Retroactive Date shown in the Declarations of this insurance;

(ii) That is Fire, Extended Coverage, Builders' Risk, Installation Risk or similar coverage for "your work";

(iii) That is Fire insurance for premises rented to you or temporarily occupied by you with permission of the owner;

(iv) That is insurance purchased by you to cover your liability as a tenant for "property damage" to premises rented to you or temporarily occupied by you with permission of the owner; or

(v) If the loss arises out of the maintenance or use of aircraft, "autos" or watercraft to the extent not subject to Exclusion **g.** of Section **I** – Coverage **A** – Bodily Injury And Property Damage Liability.

(b) Any other primary insurance available to you covering liability for damages arising out of the premises or operations, or the products and completed operations, for which you have been added as an additional insured.

(2) When this insurance is excess, we will have no duty under Coverages **A** or **B** to defend the insured against any "suit" if any other insurer has a duty to defend the insured against that "suit". If no other insurer defends, we will undertake to do so, but we will be entitled to the insured's rights against all those other insurers.

(3) When this insurance is excess over other insurance, we will pay only our share of the amount of the loss, if any, that exceeds the sum of:

(a) The total amount that all such other insurance would pay for the loss in the absence of this insurance; and

(b) The total of all deductible and self-insured amounts under all that other insurance.

(4) We will share the remaining loss, if any, with any other insurance that is not described in this Excess Insurance provision and was not bought specifically to apply in excess of the Limits of Insurance shown in the Declarations of this Coverage Part.

APPENDIX B

c. Method Of Sharing

If all of the other insurance permits contribution by equal shares, we will follow this method also. Under this approach each insurer contributes equal amounts until it has paid its applicable limit of insurance or none of the loss remains, whichever comes first.

If any of the other insurance does not permit contribution by equal shares, we will contribute by limits. Under this method, each insurer's share is based on the ratio of its applicable limit of insurance to the total applicable limits of insurance of all insurers.

5. Premium Audit

a. We will compute all premiums for this Coverage Part in accordance with our rules and rates.

b. Premium shown in this Coverage Part as advance premium is a deposit premium only. At the close of each audit period we will compute the earned premium for that period and send notice to the first Named Insured. The due date for audit and retrospective premiums is the date shown as the due date on the bill. If the sum of the advance and audit premiums paid for the policy period is greater than the earned premium, we will return the excess to the first Named Insured.

c. The first Named Insured must keep records of the information we need for premium computation, and send us copies at such times as we may request.

6. Representations

By accepting this policy, you agree:

a. The statements in the Declarations are accurate and complete;

b. Those statements are based upon representations you made to us; and

c. We have issued this policy in reliance upon your representations.

7. Separation Of Insureds

Except with respect to the Limits of Insurance, and any rights or duties specifically assigned in this Coverage Part to the first Named Insured, this insurance applies:

a. As if each Named Insured were the only Named Insured; and

b. Separately to each insured against whom claim is made or "suit" is brought.

APPENDIX B

8. Transfer Of Rights Of Recovery Against Others To Us

If the insured has rights to recover all or part of any payment we have made under this Coverage Part, those rights are transferred to us. The insured must do nothing after loss to impair them. At our request, the insured will bring "suit" or transfer those rights to us and help us enforce them.

9. When We Do Not Renew

If we decide not to renew this Coverage Part, we will mail or deliver to the first Named Insured shown in the Declarations written notice of the nonrenewal not less than 30 days before the expiration date.

If notice is mailed, proof of mailing will be sufficient proof of notice.

10. Your Right To Claim And Occurrence Information

We will provide the first Named Insured shown in the Declarations the following information relating to this and any preceding general liability claims-made Coverage Part we have issued to you during the previous three years:

a. A list or other record of each "occurrence", not previously reported to any other insurer, of which we were notified in accordance with Paragraph **2.a.** of the Section **IV** – Duties In The Event Of Occurrence, Offense, Claim Or Suit Condition. We will include the date and brief description of the "occurrence" if that information was in the notice we received.

b. A summary by policy year, of payments made and amounts reserved, stated separately, under any applicable General Aggregate Limit and Products-Completed Operations Aggregate Limit.

Amounts reserved are based on our judgment. They are subject to change and should not be regarded as ultimate settlement values.

You must not disclose this information to any claimant or any claimant's representative without our consent.

If we cancel or elect not to renew this Coverage Part, we will provide such information no later than 30 days before the date of policy termination. In other circumstances, we will provide this information only if we receive a written request from the first Named Insured within 60 days after the end of the policy period. In this case, we will provide this information within 45 days of receipt of the request.

We compile claim and "occurrence" information for our own business purposes and exercise reasonable care in doing so. In providing this information to the first Named Insured, we make no representations or warranties to insureds, insurers, or others to whom this information is furnished by or on behalf of any insured. Cancellation or nonrenewal will be effective even if we inadvertently provide inaccurate information.

APPENDIX B

SECTION V – EXTENDED REPORTING PERIODS

1. We will provide one or more Extended Reporting Periods, as described below, if:

   a. This Coverage Part is canceled or not renewed; or

   b. We renew or replace this Coverage Part with insurance that:

      (1) Has a Retroactive Date later than the date shown in the Declarations of this Coverage Part; or

      (2) Does not apply to "bodily injury", "property damage" or "personal and advertising injury" on a claims-made basis.

2. Extended Reporting Periods do not extend the policy period or change the scope of coverage provided. They apply only to claims for:

   a. "Bodily injury" or "property damage" that occurs before the end of the policy period but not before the Retroactive Date, if any, shown in the Declarations; or

   b. "Personal and advertising injury" caused by an offense committed before the end of the policy period but not before the Retroactive Date, if any, shown in the Declarations.

   Once in effect, Extended Reporting Periods may not be canceled.

3. A Basic Extended Reporting Period is automatically provided without additional charge. This period starts with the end of the policy period and lasts for:

   a. Five years with respect to claims because of "bodily injury" and "property damage" arising out of an "occurrence" reported to us, not later than 60 days after the end of the policy period, in accordance with Paragraph **2.a.** of the Section **IV** – Duties In The Event Of Occurrence, Offense, Claim Or Suit Condition;

   b. Five years with respect to claims because of "personal and advertising injury" arising out of an offense reported to us, not later than 60 days after the end of the policy period, in accordance with Paragraph **2.a.** of the Section **IV** – Duties In The Event Of Occurrence, Offense, Claim Or Suit Condition; and

   c. Sixty days with respect to claims arising from "occurrences" or offenses not previously reported to us.

   The Basic Extended Reporting Period does not apply to claims that are covered under any subsequent insurance you purchase, or that would be covered but for exhaustion of the amount of insurance applicable to such claims.

4. The Basic Extended Reporting Period does not reinstate or increase the Limits of Insurance.

APPENDIX B

5. A Supplemental Extended Reporting Period of unlimited duration is available, but only by an endorsement and for an extra charge. This supplemental period starts when the Basic Extended Reporting Period, set forth in Paragraph **3.** above, ends.

You must give us a written request for the endorsement within 60 days after the end of the policy period. The Supplemental Extended Reporting Period will not go into effect unless you pay the additional premium promptly when due.

We will determine the additional premium in accordance with our rules and rates. In doing so, we may take into account the following:

a. The exposures insured;

b. Previous types and amounts of insurance;

c. Limits of Insurance available under this Coverage Part for future payment of damages; and

d. Other related factors.

The additional premium will not exceed 200% of the annual premium for this Coverage Part.

This endorsement shall set forth the terms, not inconsistent with this section, applicable to the Supplemental Extended Reporting Period, including a provision to the effect that the insurance afforded for claims first received during such period is excess over any other valid and collectible insurance available under policies in force after the Supplemental Extended Reporting Period starts.

6. If the Supplemental Extended Reporting Period is in effect, we will provide the supplemental aggregate limits of insurance described below, but only for claims first received and recorded during the Supplemental Extended Reporting Period.

The supplemental aggregate limits of insurance will be equal to the dollar amount shown in the Declarations in effect at the end of the policy period for such of the following limits of insurance for which a dollar amount has been entered:

General Aggregate Limit
Products-Completed Operations Aggregate Limit

Paragraphs **2.** and **3.** of Section **III** – Limits Of Insurance will be amended accordingly. The Personal and Advertising Injury Limit, the Each Occurrence Limit and the Damage To Premises Rented To You Limit shown in the Declarations will then continue to apply, as set forth in Paragraphs **4., 5.** and **6.** of that section.

APPENDIX B

SECTION VI – DEFINITIONS

1. "Advertisement" means a notice that is broadcast or published to the general public or specific market segments about your goods, products or services for the purpose of attracting customers or supporters. For the purposes of this definition:

   a. Notices that are published include material placed on the Internet or on similar electronic means of communication; and

   b. Regarding web sites, only that part of a web site that is about your goods, products or services for the purposes of attracting customers or supporters is considered an advertisement.

2. "Auto" means:

   a. A land motor vehicle, trailer or semitrailer designed for travel on public roads, including any attached machinery or equipment; or

   b. Any other land vehicle that is subject to a compulsory or financial responsibility law or other motor vehicle insurance law where it is licensed or principally garaged.

   However, "auto" does not include "mobile equipment".

3. "Bodily injury" means bodily injury, sickness or disease sustained by a person, including death resulting from any of these at any time.

4. "Coverage territory" means:

   a. The United States of America (including its territories and possessions), Puerto Rico and Canada;

   b. International waters or airspace, but only if the injury or damage occurs in the course of travel or transportation between any places included in Paragraph **a.** above; or

   c. All other parts of the world if the injury or damage arises out of:

      (1) Goods or products made or sold by you in the territory described in Paragraph **a.** above;

      (2) The activities of a person whose home is in the territory described in Paragraph **a.** above, but is away for a short time on your business; or

      (3) "Personal and advertising injury" offenses that take place through the Internet or similar electronic means of communication;

   provided the insured's responsibility to pay damages is determined in a "suit" on the merits, in the territory described in Paragraph **a.** above or in a settlement we agree to.

5. "Employee" includes a "leased worker". "Employee" does not include a "temporary worker".

APPENDIX B

---

6. "Executive officer" means a person holding any of the officer positions created by your charter, constitution, bylaws or any other similar governing document.

7. "Hostile fire" means one which becomes uncontrollable or breaks out from where it was intended to be.

8. "Impaired property" means tangible property, other than "your product" or "your work", that cannot be used or is less useful because:

   a. It incorporates "your product" or "your work" that is known or thought to be defective, deficient, inadequate or dangerous; or

   b. You have failed to fulfill the terms of a contract or agreement;

   if such property can be restored to use by the repair, replacement, adjustment or removal of "your product" or "your work" or your fulfilling the terms of the contract or agreement.

9. "Insured contract" means:

   a. A contract for a lease of premises. However, that portion of the contract for a lease of premises that indemnifies any person or organization for damage by fire to premises while rented to you or temporarily occupied by you with permission of the owner is not an "insured contract";

   b. A sidetrack agreement;

   c. Any easement or license agreement, except in connection with construction or demolition operations on or within 50 feet of a railroad;

   d. An obligation, as required by ordinance, to indemnify a municipality, except in connection with work for a municipality;

   e. An elevator maintenance agreement;

   f. That part of any other contract or agreement pertaining to your business (including an indemnification of a municipality in connection with work performed for a municipality) under which you assume the tort liability of another party to pay for "bodily injury" or "property damage" to a third person or organization. Tort liability means a liability that would be imposed by law in the absence of any contract or agreement.

   Paragraph f. does not include that part of any contract or agreement:

   (1) That indemnifies a railroad for "bodily injury" or "property damage" arising out of construction or demolition operations, within 50 feet of any railroad property and affecting any railroad bridge or trestle, tracks, road-beds, tunnel, underpass or crossing;

   (2) That indemnifies an architect, engineer or surveyor for injury or damage arising out of:

    (a) Preparing, approving, or failing to prepare or approve, maps, shop drawings, opinions, reports, surveys, field orders, change orders or drawings and specifications; or

    (b) Giving directions or instructions, or failing to give them, if that is the primary cause of the injury or damage; or

  (3) Under which the insured, if an architect, engineer or surveyor, assumes liability for an injury or damage arising out of the insured's rendering or failure to render professional services, including those listed in Paragraph (2) above and supervisory, inspection, architectural or engineering activities.

10. "Leased worker" means a person leased to you by a labor leasing firm under an agreement between you and the labor leasing firm, to perform duties related to the conduct of your business. "Leased worker" does not include a "temporary worker".

11. "Loading or unloading" means the handling of property:

    a. After it is moved from the place where it is accepted for movement into or onto an aircraft, watercraft or "auto";

    b. While it is in or on an aircraft, watercraft or "auto"; or

    c. While it is being moved from an aircraft, watercraft or "auto" to the place where it is finally delivered;

but "loading or unloading" does not include the movement of property by means of a mechanical device, other than a hand truck, that is not attached to the aircraft, watercraft or "auto".

12. "Mobile equipment" means any of the following types of land vehicles, including any attached machinery or equipment:

    a. Bulldozers, farm machinery, forklifts and other vehicles designed for use principally off public roads;

    b. Vehicles maintained for use solely on or next to premises you own or rent;

    c. Vehicles that travel on crawler treads;

    d. Vehicles, whether self-propelled or not, maintained primarily to provide mobility to permanently mounted:

      (1) Power cranes, shovels, loaders, diggers or drills; or

      (2) Road construction or resurfacing equipment such as graders, scrapers or rollers;

    e. Vehicles not described in Paragraph a., b., c. or d. above that are not self-propelled and are maintained primarily to provide mobility to permanently attached equipment of the following types:

APPENDIX B

    (1) Air compressors, pumps and generators, including spraying, welding, building cleaning, geophysical exploration, lighting and well servicing equipment; or

    (2) Cherry pickers and similar devices used to raise or lower workers;

  f. Vehicles not described in Paragraph **a., b., c.** or **d.** above maintained primarily for purposes other than the transportation of persons or cargo.

  However, self-propelled vehicles with the following types of permanently attached equipment are not "mobile equipment" but will be considered "autos":

    (1) Equipment designed primarily for:

      (a) Snow removal;

      (b) Road maintenance, but not construction or resurfacing; or

      (c) Street cleaning;

    (2) Cherry pickers and similar devices mounted on automobile or truck chassis and used to raise or lower workers; and

    (3) Air compressors, pumps and generators, including spraying, welding, building cleaning, geophysical exploration, lighting and well servicing equipment.

However, "mobile equipment" does not include land vehicles that are subject to a compulsory or financial responsibility law or other motor vehicle insurance law where it is licensed or principally garaged. Land vehicles subject to a compulsory or financial responsibility law or other motor vehicle insurance law are considered "autos".

13. "Occurrence" means an accident, including continuous or repeated exposure to substantially the same general harmful conditions.

14. "Personal and advertising injury" means injury, including consequential "bodily injury", arising out of one or more of the following offenses:

  a. False arrest, detention or imprisonment;

  b. Malicious prosecution;

  c. The wrongful eviction from, wrongful entry into, or invasion of the right of private occupancy of a room, dwelling or premises that a person occupies, committed by or on behalf of its owner, landlord or lessor;

  d. Oral or written publication, in any manner, of material that slanders or libels a person or organization or disparages a person's or organization's goods, products or services;

  e. Oral or written publication, in any manner, of material that violates a person's right of privacy;

APPENDIX B

f. The use of another's advertising idea in your "advertisement"; or

g. Infringing upon another's copyright, trade dress or slogan in your "advertisement".

15. "Pollutants" mean any solid, liquid, gaseous or thermal irritant or contaminant, including smoke, vapor, soot, fumes, acids, alkalis, chemicals and waste. Waste includes materials to be recycled, reconditioned or reclaimed.

16. "Products-completed operations hazard":

a. Includes all "bodily injury" and "property damage" occurring away from premises you own or rent and arising out of "your product" or "your work" except:

(1) Products that are still in your physical possession; or

(2) Work that has not yet been completed or abandoned. However, "your work" will be deemed completed at the earliest of the following times:

(a) When all of the work called for in your contract has been completed.

(b) When all of the work to be done at the job site has been completed if your contract calls for work at more than one job site.

(c) When that part of the work done at a job site has been put to its intended use by any person or organization other than another contractor or subcontractor working on the same project.

Work that may need service, maintenance, correction, repair or replacement, but which is otherwise complete, will be treated as completed.

b. Does not include "bodily injury" or "property damage" arising out of:

(1) The transportation of property, unless the injury or damage arises out of a condition in or on a vehicle not owned or operated by you, and that condition was created by the "loading or unloading" of that vehicle by any insured;

(2) The existence of tools, uninstalled equipment or abandoned or unused materials; or

(3) Products or operations for which the classification, listed in the Declarations or in a policy Schedule, states that products-completed operations are subject to the General Aggregate Limit.

APPENDIX B

---

17. "Property damage" means:

   a. Physical injury to tangible property, including all resulting loss of use of that property. All such loss of use shall be deemed to occur at the time of the physical injury that caused it; or

   b. Loss of use of tangible property that is not physically injured. All such loss of use shall be deemed to occur at the time of the "occurrence" that caused it.

For the purposes of this insurance, electronic data is not tangible property.

As used in this definition, electronic data means information, facts or programs stored as or on, created or used on, or transmitted to or from, computer software, including systems and applications software, hard or floppy disks, CD-ROMs, tapes, drives, cells, data processing devices or any other media which are used with electronically controlled equipment.

18. "Suit" means a civil proceeding in which damages because of "bodily injury", "property damage" or "personal and advertising injury" to which this insurance applies are alleged. "Suit" includes:

   a. An arbitration proceeding in which such damages are claimed and to which the insured must submit or does submit with our consent; or

   b. Any other alternative dispute resolution proceeding in which such damages are claimed and to which the insured submits with our consent.

19. "Temporary worker" means a person who is furnished to you to substitute for a permanent "employee" on leave or to meet seasonal or short-term workload conditions.

20. "Volunteer worker" means a person who is not your "employee", and who donates his or her work and acts at the direction of and within the scope of duties determined by you, and is not paid a fee, salary or other compensation by you or anyone else for their work performed for you.

21. "Your product":

   a. Means:

      (1) Any goods or products, other than real property, manufactured, sold, handled, distributed or disposed of by:

         (a) You;

         (b) Others trading under your name; or

         (c) A person or organization whose business or assets you have acquired; and

APPENDIX B

    (2) Containers (other than vehicles), materials, parts or equipment furnished in connection with such goods or products.

  b. Includes:

    (1) Warranties or representations made at any time with respect to the fitness, quality, durability, performance or use of "your product"; and

    (2) The providing of or failure to provide warnings or instructions.

  c. Does not include vending machines or other property rented to or located for the use of others but not sold.

22. "Your work":

  a. Means:

    (1) Work or operations performed by you or on your behalf; and

    (2) Materials, parts or equipment furnished in connection with such work or operations.

  b. Includes:

    (1) Warranties or representations made at any time with respect to the fitness, quality, durability, performance or use of "your work"; and

    (2) The providing of or failure to provide warnings or instructions.

APPENDIX B